CEREBUS

by

Dave Sim

PRINTED IN CANADA

Contents © 1987 Dave Sim

Aardvark-Vanaheim Inc.
First printing, August 1987
Second printing, January 1990
Third printing, January 1991
Fourth printing, January 1992
Fifth printing, July 1993
Sixth printing, July 1994
Seventh printing, August 1995
Eight printing, February 1998
Ninth printing, November 1999
Tenth printing, May 2001
Eleventh printing, July 2003
Twelfth printing, June 2005
Thirteenth printing, October 2008
Fourteenth printing, January 2010

ISBN 0-919359-08-6

Printed in Windsor, Ontario by
Preney Print & Litho Inc. 1987 to 2008

PRINTED IN CANADA
by IMPRIMERIE LEBONFON
Val-d'Or Québec

Dedication:

to the memory of Gene Day
and to Michael, Karen, Deni, Bob
and Eric because they were there
at the beginning.

CONTENTS

Introduction:

These are the first adventures of Cerebus the Aardvark which I
began in the pages of his comic book in December of 1977. Although
crude, I hope the dedication of a rookie taking his first tentative steps
unburdened by editorial interference still shows through. It was a
wonderful time. And my hair was much longer.

Dave Sim
Kitchener, Ontario
July 29, 1987

HE CAME TO OUR CITY IN THE EARLY DAWN...

THOUGH LATER HE WOULD BE CALLED THE FINEST WARRIOR TO ENTER OUR GATES, AT THE TIME, HE WAS BUT A *CURIOSITY*...

YOU SEE, HE STOOD ONLY FIVE HANDS HIGH, HAD A LENGTHY SNOUT, A LONG TAIL AND WAS COVERED WITH SHORT GREY FUR...

HE WAS, IN SHORT...

CEREBUS
THE AARDVARK

© 1977 DAVE SIM

9

HIS FIRST STOP...

THE TAVERN!

IT WAS TECHOT THAL WHO DE-CIDED TO BEGIN *CEREBUS'* EDUCATION IN MANNERS!

NEEDLESS TO SAY, THE REMAINDER OF THE AARDVARK'S JOURNEY WAS UNEVENTFUL...

I CAN'T SERVE *YOU* HERE...

YOU'RE A...

"...GUEST...AND--EH-- I ALWAYS SERVE MY GUESTS AT THEIR TABLES"

I ADMIRE YOUR *COWARDICE*, OBESE ONE...

AS CEREBUS MAKES HIS WAY TO A VACANT TABLE, A WHISPERED *INVITATION* FROM A SHADOWED ALCOVE CATCHES HIS ATTENTION...

THERE FOLLOWED SEVERAL MOMENTS OF TENSE NEGOTIATION BEFORE THE TRIO ROSE...

"...AND ENTERED THE DARKENED STREETS OF THE CITY! THERE WAS *MUCH* TO DO BEFORE DAWN..."

11

WE ARE FORTUNATE TO GET THIS FAR WITHOUT THE WIZARD BEING AWARE OF OUR PRESENCE

WITH *MOON-RISE* HIS POWER IS *HALVED*...

IT IS THEN WE SHALL *ASSAULT* THE MAIN TOWER, IN SEARCH OF THE *FLAME JEWEL!*

IT IS THE *FLAME JEWEL* YOU SEEK, THEN?

AVE! IT IS SAID TO BE *FLAWLESS* AND WORTH A *KING'S RANSOM*...

WE HIDE OURSELVES HERE ANOTHER HOUR AND...

NAY! LURKING IN THE BUSHES IS NOT FOR AN *EARTH-PIG BORN!* IF *CEREBUS* DIES THIS DAY...

LET HIM DIE WITH SWORD AND TAIL HELD HIGH...

THERE WAS NO CHANCE TO CALL BACK THE IMPETUOUS AARDVARK, SO THE THIEVES DASHED AFTER HIM AS THEY NERVOUSLY WATCHED THE SHIFTING SHADOWS ABOUT THEM...

...AS WELL THEY MIGHT! FOR, NEARBY SEVERAL SHADOWS GROW AND MERGE!

BY CLOVIS' BEARD!

CEREBUS' SWORD SWUNG UP AND ACROSS; SLASHED A LINE OF LIGHT THROUGH THE SHADOW BEAST! STUNNED, IT LUNGED FORWARD...

...AND, AGAIN, THE SWORD CUTS DEEP! EARTH-PIG STEEL SOUGHT SHADOW-BEAST VITALS, AS CEREBUS SIDESTEPPED THE ATTACK

EACH STRIKE WAS MEASURED AND ARTFUL -- AND STILL THE SHADOW-BEAST LUMBERED FORWARD...

THE DEADLY DANCE CONTINUED UNTIL, AT LAST, CEREBUS STUMBLED! THERE WAS TIME FOR A FINAL STROKE BEFORE THE SHADOW-BEAST LUNGED FORWARD...

AND *DIED*, BECOMING, IN THE PROCESS, JUST ANOTHER SHADOW...

WE HAVE CHOSEN OUR WARRIOR WELL, MY BROTHER-- HE SEEMS TOTALLY WITHOUT FEAR OF SORCERY...

...OR ANYTHING ELSE!

ARE YOU *INJURED*, MY FRIEND?...PERHAPS WE SHOULD WAIT UNTIL YOU'RE...

CEREBUS WILL SURVIVE....THE WIZARD AWAITS US, THOUGH, AND OUR ONLY HOPE IS TO ATTACK HIM...

...*BEFORE* HE ATTACKS US!

15

THEY PASSED THROUGH SEEMINGLY ENDLESS STONE CORRIDORS IN SEARCH OF THE WIZARD AND HIS FLAME JEWEL...

I LIKE THIS NOT ONE BIT! I FEAR, *CEREBUS*, THAT THESE SKELETONS ARE A *BAD OMEN*...!

A BAD OMEN? AYE -- BONES FOUND STRIPPED OF FLESH ARE ALWAYS A *BAD OMEN*...

...FOR THEIR *FORMER OWNERS*...!

THEY ARE LONG *DEAD*, AND WE ARE -- AS YET -- *ALIVE!*

DON'T CONCERN YOUR- SELVES WITH OLD *BONES*

16

CEREBUS!

THE SKELETON'S SORCERY-SPAWNED SPEED WAS UNMATCHABLE! THE AARDVARK REALIZED HIS ONLY HOPE WAS TO STAY OUT OF RANGE AND WAIT FOR AN OPENING...

GET OUT.... AS FAST AS YOU CAN!

THE HEAVY BLADE SLICED THE GLOOMY AIR AND CRASHED AGAINST THE AARDVARK'S BLADE AS CEREBUS BACKED UP THE SHADOWED STAIRS...

LIKE A BLINDING FLAME, THE STEEL FLICKERED AND SLASHED IN FRONT OF HIM...

HIS EYES INTENT, CEREBUS WATCHED EACH SUBTLE MOTION OF THE BLADE AND MET IT EACH TIME WITH HIS OWN...

HE MUST ATTACK! WHY DOESN'T HE *ATTACK* LIKE THE OTHERS DID?

INCH BY AGONIZING INCH WAS SURRENDERED AS BEADS OF SWEAT STOOD OUT ON THE EARTH PIG'S FOREHEAD.

BEFORE HIM LOOMED THE UNDEAD FORM! IT'S EYES *BLAZED* COLDLY, LIKE TWIN FIRES IN SOME HELLISH *TOMB*...

18

INEXPLICABLY, THE SKELETON HESITATED FOR A SPLIT SECOND! IN THAT SAME INSTANT **CEREBUS** LEAPT UNDER THE OUTSTRETCHED SWORD...

...AND THREW BOTH HIMSELF AND THE ENSORCELLED SKELETON INTO THE YAWNING BLACKNESS...

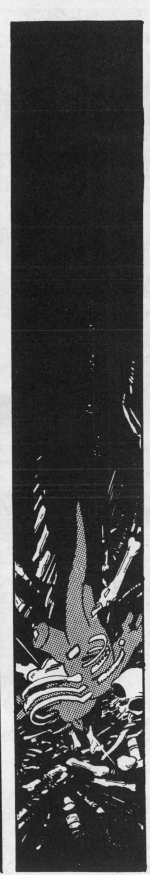

AS CEREBUS REJOINED HIS COMPANIONS, THE WIZARD CONTEMPLATED NEW STRATEGY

TWICE HAS MY SORCERY FAILED ME, DAMMIT!

WITHIN THE ALCOVE, HE SLID HIS HAND ALONG A JUTTING STONE UNTIL HE HEARD A DISTINCTIVE CLICK...

WHERE SORCERY HAS FAILED, MAYHAP BOTANY WILL SUCCEED...

EH?

FLOWERS?

WHAT MADNESS IS THIS? IF HE SEEKS TO STOP CEREBUS WITH FLOWERS HE...

CEREBUS, IGNORANT OF HALUCINOGENS, WAS TAKEN BY SURPRISE BY THE **NAMA LOTUS** BLOSSOMS...

HIS THOUGHTS WERE CONFUSED AS HE STRAINED TO KEEP HIS BALANCE...

IF **CEREBUS** IS TO BE DEFEAT-ED LET IT BE BY SWORD OR *NECROMANCY* ...

THE AARDVARK STRUGGLED UP FROM THE MIRE THAT ENFOLDED HIS MIND...EVERY FIBRE OF HIS BEING WAS APPLIED TO THE TASK...

...NOT ...BY... DAMNED...

...PETUNIAS!

AT LAST, HE HAD FELT THE GROUND GROW SOLID BENEATH HIS FEET...

CEREBUS! LET US LEAVE THIS PLACE OF HORRORS!

AVE!

A SHOVE PROPELLED CEREBUS' COMPANIONS AWAY FROM THE INFLUENCE OF THE LOTUS

...AND, WITHIN MOMENTS, SANITY RETURNS! AND WITH SANITY COMES... REALIZATION...!

NO GEM COULD BE WORTH ALL THIS MADNESS...

...ALL THIS TORTURE!

NAY! YOU HAVE AGREED TO PAY CEREBUS A POUCH OF GOLD FOR THE FLAME JEWEL!...

...AND THE FLAME JEWEL YOU SHALL HAVE!...

THOUGH THE GRIM REAPER HIMSELF BARS MY WAY!...

IT HAS GROWN VERY **QUIET**, MY FRIEND... YOU DON'T SUPPOSE THE WIZARD HAS...

NAY! IT IS BUT THE CALM BEFORE THE STORM...

I HAVE REALIZED ONE THING IN THE LAST FEW MINUTES, **ANYWAY...**

WE'VE BEEN WALKING IN CIRCLES SINCE WE LEFT THE FOYER...

IF **WE** CAN'T FIND THIS WIZARD, WE'LL HAVE TO LET HIM FIND **US**...

...AND IF THAT LIGHT IS ANY **INDICATION**...

I WOULD GUESS HE ALREADY **HAS**...

WELCOME!

THE TENTACLES SNAKED OUT INCREDIBLY FAST, DRAWING THE SWIRLING SMOKE BEHIND IT IN WISPY TRAILS...

CEREBUS! ATTACK THIS THING!

YOUR FRIEND CANNOT HELP YOU-- NONE ESCAPE THE MONSTER FROM TIME'S DAWNING!

HOWEVER, AT THAT MOMENT, HIS EYES CLOSED, THE AARDVARK WAS SEARCHING WITH HAND AND SWORD EXTENDED...

A HORRIBLE FATE AWAITS YOU, MORTALS A THOUSAND DEATHS WILL YOU SUFFER ...

SUBMIT TO ITS EMBRACE! NONE CAN ESCAPE THE DEATH GRASP OF...

EH? THE GREY DWARF WITH THE SWORD-- WHAT'S HE UP TO?

THEN CAME THE REALIZATION-- IF THE "DWARF" COULDN'T SEE THE CONJURED BEAST, IT WOULD BE IMPOSSIBLE TO STOP HIM...

CEREBUS FOCUSED ON THE RUSTLING OF THE WIZARD'S ROBES -- THE DRONE OF HIS VOICE! THERE WAS NO WAY THE WIZARD COULD GET PAST HIM ...

HALT! NONE MAY APPROACH THE DARK MAJESTY'S PERSON...uh...

A MOMENT LATER, HIS FINGER BRUSHED THE WIZARD'S TREMBLING HAND...

DOOM SHALL BE YOURS IF...

HARK TO MY WORDS! FOR MINE IS THE POWER OF ASHEM, SOGGOT RA, MINE IS...

THE SWORD GLITTERED BRIEFLY IN THE SHADOWED GLOOM, AND THEN...

...AW NUTS...

SORCERY UPON SORCERY! ONE MOMENT THE BEAST IS ABOUT TO DEVOUR ME-- AND THE NEXT, IT *VANISHES* LIKE MORNING FROST...

AYE! AND HERE STANDS OUR WARRIOR! BY THE LOOK OF THAT CLOAK, THE *WIZARD* IS ...*uh*...

...*QUITE* DEAD... AND CRUMBLED TO *DUST*...

HE WAS *DOUBTLESS* SEVERAL CENTURIES OLD...

TAURAN'S BLOOD! THAT LIGHT! WE HAVE IT... IT'S *OURS!*

THE FLAME JEWEL!

FIRST, MY FRIENDS-- WE HAVE *BUSINESS* TO *SETTLE*...

27

THE JEWEL WAS WRAPPED CAREFULLY IN A PIECE OF THE WIZARD'S CLOAK AS THEY LEFT THE CENTRAL CHAMBER...

YOU PROMISED ME A POUCH OF GOLD IF I GOT YOU THE JEWEL...

OF COURSE! BUT ONCE WE SELL THE JEWEL YOU SHALL HAVE A THOUSAND-- NAY! TEN TIMES A THOUSAND POUCHES OF GOLD!

A NEARBY STATUE BECAME, SLOWLY, LESS SUBSTANTIAL AS THE WIZARD'S SORCERY SLIPPED AWAY, LIKE SANDS IN AN HOUR-GLASS...

ONE POUCH WILL SUFFICE....

GRADUALLY, THE HALL SHIMMERED AND FADED AROUND THEM LIKE A BAD DREAM...

...AND THEY WERE OUTSIDE IN THE PRE-DAWN AIR...

ALL THAT REMAINED WAS THE SURROUNDING GARDEN AND A FEW ORNAMENTAL GATES AND WALLS...

HOW DID YOU COME TO KNOW SO MUCH OF THE WAYS OF THESE WIZARDS

CEREBUS HAS HIS FEET IN TWO WORLDS ...

THOUGH I WAS BORN TO BE A WARRIOR, THE WAYS OF SORCERY ARE NOT UNKNOWN TO ME...

BUT HOW DID YOU DEFEAT THE WIZARD'S WHERE OTHERS HAVE FAILED...

YOUR WIZARD WAS ORIENTED TO ANIMATION AND ILLUSION SPELLS WHICH ARE DIFFICULT TO MAINTAIN

WITH THE SKELETON AND SHADOW BEAST, IT WAS MOSTLY A MATTER OF STAYING OUT OF REACH...

..UNTIL AN OPENING CAME UP!

BY THE WAY, THAT ISN'T A JEWEL YOU'VE GOT ...IT'S JUST A SIMPLE...

29

...WALNUT.

YOU RISKED YOUR LIFE FOR...

...A POUCH OF GOLD.

THE JEWEL WAS A PRODUCT OF THE WIZARD'S SORCERY, NOT THE SOURCE OF IT... WHEN HE DIED, IT CHANGED TO ITS ORIGINAL FORM...

SO YOU HAVE YOUR "FLAME JEWEL" AND I HAVE MY POUCH OF GOLD...

...WHICH MAY NOT SEEM *EXACTLY* FAIR...

...BUT *CEREBUS* HAS NO CAUSE FOR COMPLAINT.

IT WAS, THE THIEVES WOULD LATER SAY THE FIRST TIME THEY HAD HEARD AN EARTH-PIG *LAUGH*...

"AFTER HIS BRUSH WITH WIZARDRY AND THE FLAME JEWEL, **CEREBUS** VANISHES FOR A TIME, HIS INTEREST IN THE CITIES OF THE SOUTH OBVIOUSLY ON THE WANE. HE IS NEXT SEEN IN THE NORTHERN PROVINCE OF TANSUBAL WHERE, HIS POUCH OF GOLD LONG GONE, HE JOINS A MILITARY EXPEDITION BOUND FOR BOREALA AND THE COUNTRIES NORTH-EAST OF THERE, WHERE IT IS SAID THERE IS A GREAT DEMAND FOR MERCENARIES TO FIGHT IN THE **BLOOD WARS**...."

SOUND CARRIES A LONG DISTANCE IN THIS LAND...

TO SOME, EACH SOUND IS ALIKE, BE IT AVALANCHE OR ECHO...

TO THE EARTH-PIG BORN, EACH SOUND BEARS IT'S OWN TALE! SO IT IS, AS HIS COMPANIONS PANT AND WHEEZE AROUND HIM...

...CEREBUS HOLDS HIS BLADE AT THE READY AND WATCHES EACH DARKENED CREVICE OF THE SURROUNDING WALLS OF ICE AND SNOW...

THEY ARE ON THE EXPEDITION IN A MOMENT! FOUR ARE DEAD BEFORE ANY, SAVE CEREBUS, IS EVEN AWARE OF THE PRESENCE OF DANGER! THEY ARE **BOREALAN MARAUDERS**, MOST FEARED AND HATED OF THE THIEVING AND NOMADIC NORTHERN TRIBES...

THERE ISN'T EVEN TIME FOR A WARNING SHOUT! CEREBUS TURNS, HIS BLADE READY, AND HE, TOO, IS SWEPT UP IN THE FRENZIED **BLOOD-LETTING!**...

EVEN AS THE MARAUDERS' HEAVY SWORDS TAKE THEIR TOLL OF THE EXHAUSTED AND NEARLY FROZEN SOUTHLANDERS...

CAPTIVE in BOREALA

...CEREBUS THE AARDVARK IS AMONG THEM, HIS BLADE, LIKE A WHIRLWIND, DISPATCHING THE RAGGED MARAUDERS WITH EACH THRUST...!

©1978 Dave Sim

SHEER NUMBERS ARE CEREBUS' UNDOING AND, MOMENTS LATER, DISARMED, HE **GLOWERS** AT HIS CAPTORS....

WHATEVER MANNER OF MAN OR BEAST HE MIGHT BE...

...HE IS A GOOD AND FEARLESS WARRIOR, MY **CHIEFTAIN**...!

LET HIM LIVE...

...WE CAN SELL HIM TO A FREAK SHOW IN **GURANN!**

CEREBUS RECOGNIZES THE PARANIAN *LILT* OF THE CHIEFTAIN'S WORDS AND SPITS A CURSE AT THE TOWERING NORTHLANDER...

...COMNE YE TAMA STET FEGRIA!

THE CHIEFTAIN NARROWS HIS GAZE....

...THE REFERENCE IS AN UNSAVORY ONE, ALLUDING TO FREAK SHOWS AND CERTAIN OF THE CHIEFTAIN'S BODILY ORIFICES...!

YOU HAVE MADE A GRAVE ERROR, ANIMAL! THERE IS NO REASON I SHOULDN'T *KILL* YOU FOR THAT...

...SAVE ONE...

...I AM A SWORD FOR HIRE -- AND YOU ARE IN NEED OF ONE...

THE CHIEFTAIN'S BROWS PUCKER AND HE FLASHES A SUDDEN GRIN...

WE HAVE SEEN YOU IN COMBAT AGAINST MANY FOES...

BUT WE KNOW NOTHING OF YOUR PROWESS AGAINST A *SINGLE* ENEMY...

IT IS UNDENIABLY A CHALLENGE AND CEREBUS RETURNS THE CHIEFTAIN'S STARE WITH HIS OWN STEELY GAZE...

PERHAPS YOU WOULD PERMIT ME TO *PRACTICE* ON ONE OF YOUR MEN?!

PERHAPS! YOU'D LIKE TO TEACH OUR "FRIEND" HOW TO *KNIFE-FIGHT*...

...WOULDN'T YOU, *KLOG?*...

unh? KNIFE FIGHT? *JA!*...

KLOG TEACH GOOD! hunh-hunh

KLOG HAS AGREED TO YOUR CHALLENGE -- OUR LAWS STATE THAT YOU MUST FACE HIM IN THE SACRED *DUEL OF THE LONG KNIVES!*

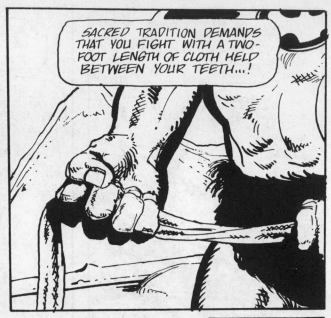

SACRED TRADITION DEMANDS THAT YOU FIGHT WITH A TWO-FOOT LENGTH OF CLOTH HELD BETWEEN YOUR TEETH...!

unnh?

BY CLOVIS' BEARD!

MY CHIEFTAIN -- PERHAPS A *SIX*-FOOT LENGTH OF CLOTH WOULD BE MORE -- uh *SACRED?*

THERE IS WISDOM IN YOUR WORDS -- VERY WELL...

...SO BE IT!

MOMENTS LATER THE TWO ARE JOINED AND THE DEADLY DANCE BEGINS...

ABRUPTLY, KLOG TWISTS AWAY, THROWING CEREBUS FROM HIS FEET -- CEREBUS' KNIFE FLIES SEVERAL FEET AWAY...

THE AARDVARK'S FEET AND TAIL FIND PURCHASE IN THE POWDERY SNOW AS HE PREPARES TO MEET KLOG'S CHARGE...

THE THRUST IS AWKWARD AND CEREBUS EASILY DODGES IT...

unnhh?

...DRAWS KLOG TOWARD HIM WITH THE TWISTED CLOTH...

SMAK!

...AND UNLEASHES THE DREADED EARTH-PIG SNOUT PUNCH!

AS A SOUTHLANDER, YOU DOUBTLESS HAVE A MORAL CODE WHICH PROHIBITS YOUR KILLING AN UNCONSCIOUS FOE...

...THAT BEING THE CASE...

SACRED TRADITION DEMANDS...

...OH.....

OUTFIT THIS MAN ...er.....

AARDVARK.

...AARDVARK FOR THE MARCH...

"THE MARCH".... THOUGH IT IS INTENDED TO BE MUCH LONGER, IT IS FATED TO LAST BUT TWO DAYS FROM THE TIME CEREBUS JOINS THE BOREALAN MARAUDERS...

IT IS ON THE THIRD DAY OF THE MARCH THAT THE MARAUDERS FIND THEMSELVES FACING AN ATTACK BETWEEN THE WALLS OF A SNOWY VALLEY! THE AARDVARK IS APPREHENSIVE -- THOUGH THE ATTACKERS ARE ON FOOT THEY ARE ADVANCING INCREDIBLY FAST...

THEY NUMBER ABOUT FIFTY... THE ONLY SOUND THAT REACHES CEREBUS' EARS IS THE LOW RUMBLE OF SHIFTING SNOW! THERE IS NO CHALLENGING WAR CRY OR SONG....

AS THEY DRAW NEARER, CEREBUS CAN SEE THEIR BLADES -- HEAVY AND COMPOSED OF SOME FORM OF BLACK METAL...

"WHAT MANNER OF ARMY IS THIS?" HISSES CEREBUS, AS HE NOTICES THEIR GLOWING WHITE EYES....

THERE IS TIME FOR ONE STRAY THOUGHT IN THE INSTANT BEFORE THE TWO ARMIES CLASH!...

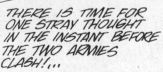

...SORCERY!

A DECISION MUST BE MADE, CEREBUS REALIZES, EVEN AS A LOOMING FIGURE CUTS HIM OFF FROM THE **BOREALANS!**

ENSORCELLED THE BEINGS ARE... BUT THEIR MOVEMENTS ARE SWIFT ...**TOO** SWIFT FOR AN ANIMATION SPELL...TOO SUBSTANTIAL FOR **CONJURE**...

HE AVOIDS THE ATTACKER AS HIS EXPERIENCE DICTATES! THE SWORD-WIELDER LEAVES OPENINGS...SHOULD HE MATCH BLADES OR CONTINUE STAYING OUT OF REACH?...

AS THE SLOPE BENEATH HIS FEET INCREASES...

HE RECOGNIZES THE NEED TO DECIDE...

...AND **SOON!**

PERHAPS HE IS BEING HERDED TOWARD THIS PRECIPICE-- TOWARD DANGER UNKNOWN AND INFINITELY GREATER?

...THE UNKNOWN!

HIS DESCENT BEGINS WITH *GRACE*...

...AND BECOMES CLUMSY AS CEREBUS BRACES...

PERHAPS! BUT HE IS UNABLE TO FATHOM THE MAGIC RACING TOWARD HIM!

...FOR IMPACT IN THE POWDER-SOFT DRIFTS AT THE BASE OF THE CLIFF!

AND, ALWAYS, GIVEN THE CHOICE BETWEEN UNFATHOMABLE SORCERY AND UNKNOWN DANGER-- THE EARTH-PIG BORN WILL OPT FOR...

...DISCOVERING, IN THE PROCESS, THAT APPEARANCES CAN BE *DECEIVING*...

41

CEREBUS BLINKS IN THE **MURKY** DARKNESS, DISORIENTED MOMENTARILY BY HIS SITUATION -- IN A FEW SECONDS, HE RECOVERS...

THERE IS NO HOPE OF CLIMBING FREE HE CONCLUDES, NOTING FOOTPRINTS IN THE DUST AROUND HIM. THE PRINTS ARE ABOUT A WEEK OLD...

NEARBY, WRITINGS ON THE WALL ATTRACT HIS ATTENTION -- SOMETHING ABOUT TIME AND THE IMMORTALITY OF ALL BEINGS...

THERE IS NO CLUE AS TO ESCAPE ROUTES, AND HE READS NO FURTHER...

IF ANOTHER EXIT IS TO BE FOUND, IT IS BY INVESTIGATION! CEREBUS SETS OFF INTO THE **SHADOWS** ...

HIS EARS TWITCH AND SWIVEL AS HE WALKS...

THOUGH NO SOUND BETRAYS THEIR PRESENCE THE AARDVARK IS CERTAIN OTHERS LURK IN THIS GLOOMY HALL...

"THEY WILL SHOW THEM-SELVES IN GOOD TIME," HE DECIDES, SLAPPING THE SWORD LIGHTLY AGAINST HIS THIGH...

THE GLOOMY HALLWAY GIVES WAY TO EERILY LIT CAVERNS! CRUDE AND WATER SCOURED CARVINGS GAZE DOWN ON THE **AARDVARK**...

THE FLOOR IS UNEVEN...

...BUT CEREBUS HAS THE IMPRESSION OF GRADUAL DESCENT...

THERE IS THE SOUND OF DRIPPING WATER -- OF HIS OWN ECHOING **FOOTSTEPS**...

...AND **ANOTHER** SOUND...

A SOUND MUFFLED BY TONS OF ROCK! BUT A SOUND WHICH DOES NOT ESCAPE THE SENSITIVE EARS OF THE EARTH-PIG...

IT IS THE SOUND OF DEEP, SARDONIC **LAUGHTER**...

IN MID-STRIDE, THE AARDVARK STOPS, STUNNED!

CLOVIS' BEADS! "WITHIN THE EARTH IN DARK BOREALA LIES..." IMPOSSIBLE!

IT'S A LEGEND-- A CHILD'S FAIRY TALE

HIS SWORD CLATTERS TO THE STONE FLOOR AS CEREBUS SAGS AGAINST A STONE, HIS MOUTH AGAPE! "THE EYE OF TERIM, GOLD AND SHINING PRIZE-- NO MORTAL SHALL WREST THE GEM..."

HE RECALLS THE ANCIENT TOME-- WORDS OBLITERATED, PASSAGES DELETED BY THE JEALOUS PRIESTS OF TERIM!

"FROM CRIMSON CLAW OF THE DEMON KHEM!"

UNBIDDEN FEARS CLUTCH AT THE EARTH PIG'S SPINE...

KHEM! THE DARK DEMON!

I MUST FIND AN EXIT--HE'S HERE SOMEW--※

THEN COMES ANOTHER THOUGHT!

THE EYE OF TERIM!

...IT'S HERE!

THOUGH FEAR CLAWS AT HIS SPINE, IT IS GREED THAT TAKES POSSESSION OF IT!

THE PATH THAT HE TRAVELS IS WELL WORN...

...BUT NO LESS TREACHEROUS FOR ITS AGE! HIS HANDS PASS OVER **CARVINGS** REPRESENTATIVE OF THE MANY FACES OF **KHEM**...

WINKING LIGHTS FOLLOW HIM, AS HE GOES, LIKE SMALL **INSECTS**...

THEY POSE NO THREAT, SO THE AARDVARK IGNORES THEM...

THE LIGHT GROWS IN INTENSITY AS HE NEARS THE BOTTOM...

CEREBUS NEARLY LOSES HIS FOOTING AS HE GETS HIS FIRST SIGHT OF IT...

THE LEGENDS HAVE NOT LIED...

IT IS THE **EVE OF TERIM,** THE MOST PRECIOUS OF THE FIVE **SPHERES OF THE GODS!**...

HIS EYES ARE RIVETED ON THE BALL OF GOLD FIRE! IT IS LIKE A SMALL SUN, BLAZING IN THE SHADOWS BELOW HIM...

HE TRIES TO PICTURE THE PRICE THAT IT WOULD FETCH IN THE GURRANIAN MARKET-PLACE...

...AND A SMILE CROSSES HIS LIPS...

TARIM! WHAT A PRIZE! I'LL BUY A **KINGDOM** WITH THE...

EH?

PERHAPS A WIZARD WOULD PAY MORE DEARLY FOR THE KNOWLEDGE CONTAINED IN ONE OF THE FIVE S...

CLOVIS' BLOOD!

CEREBUS' MIND IS PLAYING TRICKS ON HIM -- *BUT NO* TRICKS WILL KEEP ME FROM THE GOLDEN EYE!

IT IS ONLY WHEN HE'S PAST THE ORB THAT THE AARDVARK NOTICES A DISTANT EXIT...

"KHEM SHALL HAVE TO FIND A NEW TREASURE TO GUARD," HE MUSES...

"FOR CEREBUS LAYS CLAIM TO THE EYE OF TERIM!"

THE AARDVARK SOON LEARNS THAT THE EYE OF A NORTHERN GOD IS WEIGHTY, INDEED...

CLOVIS' BEARD! HOW CAN SOMETHING SO SMALL WEIGH SO MUCH?

THE GLOW BLINDS HIM AND HE REELS DRUNKENLY ON THE STONES OF THE *PATHWAY*...

THE GLOWING MOTES HUM AROUND HIM LIKE THE INSECTS THEY RESEMBLE, INCREASING IN NUMBERS WITH EACH STEP THE EARTH-PIG TAKES...

THE PATH SUDDENLY DROPS AND THE AARDVARK STUMBLES ...

...HIS FEET, FOR THE MOMENT, FINDING ONLY CRUMBLING STONES AND AIR!

THE PATH HE HAD SEEN WAS STRAIGHT.' CEREBUS IS SUDDENLY HESITANT AS HE RECOVERS HIS BALANCE...

WHAT TRICKERY IS *AFOOT* HERE?

AS IF IN ANSWER, HE'S SUDDENLY AWARE AGAIN OF SARDONIC LAUGHTER...

...AND SOMETHING ELSE!

ENERGY! ENERGY LIKE A DARKLING LATICEWORK WOVEN ABOUT HIS HEAD...

ENERGY--LIKE FINGERS WHICH PROBE HIS MIND; **RENDING-- SEARCHING**...

...CEREBUS WHIRLS

GONE IS THE BLINDING GLOW IN HIS HANDS-- GONE, TOO, IS THE ILLUSION OF PURITY AND BEAUTY! IN IT'S PLACE ALL THAT REMAINS IS MIND-NUMBING, **SPINE-CHILLING**...

...REALITY!

BY CLOVIS' TEETH!

A *SUCCUBUS!* EVEN AS IT REACHES, CEREBUS CURSES HIMSELF FOR A FOOL FOR NOT REALIZING IT EARLIER...

THE TENTACLES REACH OUT -- REACH TO STEAL THE AARDVARK'S VERY SOUL....

FOR THE FIRST TIME IN CENTURIES A PREY HAS BROKEN THE SUCCUBUS' SPELL -- HAS **SEEN** IT IN ITS ORIGINAL FORM...

DEFENSELESS, IT SEEKS TO ATTACK CEREBUS, SHREDDING THE TISSUES OF THE AARDVARK'S MIND...DESPERATION MARKS THE SUCCUBUS' MOVEMENTS....!

THE NATURE OF THIS BEAST IS DIFFERENT FROM ITS OTHER VICTIMS -- THE SOUL **MUST** BE FOUND BEFORE...BEFORE...

THE EARTH-PIG STUMBLES AND PLUNGES HEAD-LONG INTO THE UNKNOWN ONCE MORE...

STILL, THE TENTACLES FLIP AND DART ABOUT THE TUMBLING FORM SEEKING...**SEEKING**...

CEREBUS TWISTS, DISORIENTED...AWARE ONLY OF A PULLING, TEARING SENSATION...

WHERE IS ITS **SOUL?**

THE AARDVARK BOUNCES, SHRINKING BACK FROM THE TENTACLES! HE SEES THEM TWIST HELPLESSLY...

WHERE?

HE SEES THE WINKING LIGHTS RETURN, SURROUNDING HIM, AS HE DROPS INTO SPACE...

A MOMENT LATER, ALL GOES **BLACK!**...

NO! NO! NO!

AN INSTANT--OR AN HOUR--LATER, CEREBUS AWAKENS TO THE SOUND OF WHINING SCREAMS AND A RUSH OF WIND LIKE BIRDS IN FLIGHT...

HIS EYES SLOWLY FOCUS ON THE TARNISHED IRON SPHERE BEFORE HIM, HALF-BURIED IN THE SNOW

ABOVE HIM, WINKING LIGHTS SWIRL UPWARD, MINGLING WITH THE EVENING STARS...

THE SOUND IS UNMISTAKABLE!

IT IS THE SOUND OF SUDDEN FREEDOM AFTER CENTURIES OF CAPTIVITY...

IT IS NOT A SOUND FOR THE EARS OF A MORTAL EARTH-PIG, THOUGH, AND CEREBUS TURNS...

WONDERING FOR THE MOMENT, WHERE HE IS...

BUT ONLY FOR A MOMENT ...

IT IS THE SITE OF THE DAY'S BATTLE! CORPSES ARE GRADUALLY BEING COVERED BY DRIFTING SNOW -- INCONGRUOUS SKELETONS VISIBLE AMID THE BOREALAN DEAD...

"WHICH WHITE-EYED WARRIOR WERE YOU?" MUTTERS CEREBUS...

HE THINKS OF ALL THE SOULS THAT HAVE BEEN FREED THIS NIGHT...

HOW MANY HAD FALLEN PREY TO THE SUCCUBUS' DECEPTION?

HOW MANY OTHER SOUL-LESS WARRIORS HAVE CRUMBLED TO SKELETONS? HOW MANY OTHERS ARE AT LAST **RESTING** IN THE NEW FALLEN SNOW? -- NO LONGER IN MINDLESS FLIGHT -- NO LONGER DESTROYING ALL IN THEIR PATH?...

THE MOON RISES AS CEREBUS EXITS THE BOREALAN VALLEY...

HE·BREATHES DEEPLY... AND CONSIDERS HIS FATE; SAVED BY VIRTUE OF HIS UNUSUAL NATURE...

...ELSE HE MIGHT BE LANGUISHING NOW, IN THAT GLOOMY CAVERN WITH THE OTHER TRAPPED SOULS...

...AWAITING A SAVIOUR TO BREAK THE SUCCUBUS' CONTROL!

EVEN NOW, THE SUCCUBUS MUST BE ATTRACTING NEW VICTIMS, HE MUSES...

...AND THEN TURNS HIS ATTENTION TO MORE **URGENT** CONCERNS!

...FOR HIS BELLY AND PURSE ARE EMPTY...

THE NEAREST COAST IS TWELVE MILES...

THE NEAREST PORT AT LEAST TWICE THAT DISTANCE!

...AND THE EARTH-PIG INTENDS TO QUAFF A DOZEN ALES AND START AS MANY BRAWLS BEFORE ANOTHER MOON HAS RISEN!

FIN

TO COME TO THE POINT, **MY FRIEND**, I AM NEED OF AN ASSASSIN...!

BOREALA IS FILLED WITH WARRIORS -- WHY DO YOU CHOOSE **CEREBUS**?

I NEED SOMEONE WITH STRENGTH, BUT I AM ALSO PAYING FOR SOMEONE WITH KNOWLEDGE IN THE WAYS OF TORTURE...

THE INTENDED VICTIM MUST **SUFFER** BEFORE HIS DEATH...

AND WHAT MAKES YOU THINK CEREBUS IS THIS "SOME-ONE"?

MY HERBS, MY CRYSTAL-- ALL INDICATE YOU ARE A MAN-- ER-- AARDVARK OF YOUR WORD...

IF YOU PROMISE TO MAKE HIM SUFFER, YOUR PAYMENT WILL BE A SACK OF BOREALAN GOLD...

"ASSASSIN" THE WORD IS AN UGLY ONE TO THE **EARTH-PIG**! BUT A QUICK ESCAPE FROM BOREALA IS IMPERATIVE!

VERY WELL...I'LL **DO** IT...!

LOOKS LIKE YOU HAVE *EVERYTHING!* THERE'S ONE MORE THING I FORGOT TO MENTION...

...MY DAUGHTER *RED SOPHIA!* SHE MUST SEE THE MAN DIE SLOWLY-- YOU SEE HE HAS BE-SMIRCHED HER HONOUR AND MUST SUFFER THE PENALTY...

YOU WILL *DOUBTLESS* APPRECIATE MY COMPANY, SHORT GREY ONE!

A NUMBER OF CHOICE ANSWERS OCCUR TO THE EARTH-PIG. VISIONS OF BOREALAN GOLD SERVE, HOWEVER TO STILL HIS TONGUE...

YOU NEEDN'T WORRY ABOUT HER ...SHE'S *QUITE* HANDY WITH THAT *SWORD*...

GOODBYE, *FATHER!*

GOODBYE, *SOPHIA!* TARIM BE WITH YOU, *CEREBUS*...

GRUMBLE-GRUMBLE-NA *GININ*...

SO, AFTER I GOT OUT OF SCHOOL, I STARTED WORKING WITH DAD, BUT THAT WAS A *DRAG!* SO I STARTED PLAYING AROUND WITH SWORDS-- NOW I CAN BEAT ANY *FIVE* OF THE TOWN BOYS...

BUM BA DA BA DA DA

I ALSO TOOK A FEW DANCE COURSES--YOU *DANCE?* I GUESS NOT! I'M ONE OF THE BEST OF COURSE-- I FIND IT LOOSENS ME UP, Y'KNOW? HELPS ME TO EXPRESS MYSELF...

DA DUM DA-DA DUM DA

I WOULDN'T WANT TO DO IT FOR A LIVING, BUT I ALWAYS SAY "YOU ONLY GO AROUND ONCE, SO YOU SHOULD GRAB ALL TH...

OOPS!

SMACK

IDIOTIC BRAT! I HAVE *ENDURED* ENOUGH OF...

SO! YOU CHALLENGE *RED SOPHIA* AND BESMIRCH HER *HONOUR*...

BESMIRCH YOUR...?

HA!

SOPHIA'S SINGLE BLADE BECOMES TWO EVEN AS CEREBUS LEADS!

"THIS," THINKS CEREBUS, "IS WHAT COMES OF SEEKING YOUR FORTUNE IN THESE *INSANE* NORTHLANDS..."

"STANDARD PANROVIAN DUEL ASSAULT! DOUBTLESS TAUGHT THE WENCH BY ONE OF THE LIQUOR SODDEN BARONS IN EXILE..."

THE LAGGING DAGGER BEGINS ITS SWEEP "PANROVIAN BEYOND A DOUBT."

"SHE WILL DISCOVER THAT CEREBUS IS NO TOWN BUMPKIN TO FALL FOR SUCH DATED TECHNIQUES" A TEMPTING AND ROTUND TARGET PRESENTS ITSELF!

THUD

"...AS THE FLAT OF CEREBUS' BROADSWORD PAINFULLY INTRODUCES *RED SOPHIA* TO PROFESSIONAL SWORDPLAY..."

CEREBUS WHIRLS AND BRACES FOR A RENEWED ATTACK; HE MUST DEFEAT THE WENCH WITHOUT HARMING HER...

WITH LUCK, THEY WILL BE ON THEIR WAY ONCE MORE WITHIN THE HOUR...

THERE IS A RUSTLING IN THE BUSHES AND, GRADUALLY, HER PLENTIFUL FORM RISES UP-- BUT HER EXPRESSION BETRAYS NO BATTLE-LUST! ONLY....**WHAT?**

OHHHH! MY LORD CEREBUS!

I HAVE SWORN A VOW THAT ANY MAN WHO DEFEATS ME IN BATTLE SHALL POSSESS ME...

I AM **YOURS** TO COMMAND.!

LET ME DO YOUR **BIDDING**, OH SHORT GREY MASTER...

MY BODY IS YOURS!

DO MY **BIDDING** EH?

CEREBUS IS **MOST** PLEASED!

YOU CAN CARRY THE SUPPLIES!

IT IS JUST BEFORE SUNSET THAT CEREBUS AND SOPHIA REACH THE TOP OF A GRASSY HILL -- A WELCOME SIGHT!

PERHAPS WE WON'T *NEED* YOUR FATHER'S SUPPLIES...

TARIM! I COULD USE AN ALE!

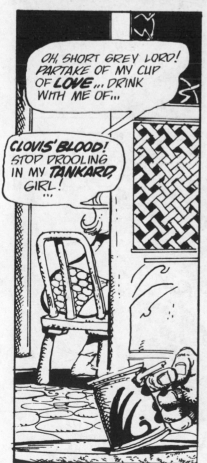

OH, SHORT GREY LORD! PARTAKE OF MY CUP OF *LOVE*...DRINK WITH ME OF...

CLOVIS' BLOOD! STOP DROOLING IN MY *TANKARD,* GIRL!...

SOPHIA'S AMPLE DIMENSIONS COME UNDER CAREFUL SCRUTINY IN THE DINGY TAVERN...

ASHTOTH TAKE ME! A COMELY WENCH REDUCED TO BEGGING FOR A BED-MATE!...

...METHINKS THUGG THE UNSEEMLY WILL TAKE A HAND, HERE

FORGET THE GREY BEAST, RED HAIR -- JOIN *THUGG* FOR A TANKARD AT *HIS* TABLE...

NAY! CEREBUS IS MY LORD AND MASTER AND MY FAVOURS ARE FOR HIM ALONE!

EH?

TARIM! THIS ALE IS...... POTENT!

YOU PREFER *HIM* OVER THUGG THE UNSEEMLY-- A *REAL* MAN?

I AM HIS BY RIGHT OF CONQUEST

THEN THUGG HAS NO CHOICE ...

I CHALLENGE THEE, SHORT GREY PERVERT ... ...SO!

TWAK

CEREBUS HITS THE FLOOR WITH A RESOUNDING THUMP AND IRON RESOLVE TO PAY CLOSER ATTENTION TO *SOPHIA'S* CONVERSATIONS....

MY LORD CEREBUS WILL BEST YOU WITH *EASE*, YOU OVERBLOWN AND BRAINLESS LOUT!

I SHOULD HAVE HAD THE WENCH FITTED WITH A *MUZZLE* ...

MY HONOUR HAS BEEN *BE-SMIRCHED* AND CEREBUS WILL AVENGE ME...

TARIM'S TEETH! DOES NO ONE GO TO TAVERNS FOR A QUIET DRINK *ANYMORE?*

PRAY NOW TO YOUR WORTHLESS SNOW GODS, SCUM ...YOUR TIME IS NIGH!

TARIM! I HAVE NO INTENTION OF KILLING ANY-ONE IN THE WENCH'S NAME!

MY SLOW-WITTED FRIEND STRIKES ME AS UNLIKELY TO LISTEN TO REASON...

MAYHAP IT IS TIME FOR CEREBUS TO DEMONSTRATE THERE'S MORE THAN ONE WAY TO FELL A BEARDED TREE

FORTUNATELY, THUGG'S SIZE MAKES HIM EXTREMELY PONDEROUS AND SLOW-MOVING! AS WELL, HIS CONTEMPT FOR THOSE SHORTER THAN HIMSELF MAKES HIM AN IDEAL FOE FOR THE EARTH PIG!

CEREBUS SPOTS AN OPENING, AND...

THOK

WAIT! WE CAN'T LEAVE YET....! MY HONOUR HAS BEEN BESMIRCHED! YOU HAVE TO...

ANOTHER DAY'S TRAVEL TO BRANDUR-- THANK TARIM-- CEREBUS HAS ALMOST FORGOTTEN WHAT SILENCE SOUNDS LIKE...

SO ANYWAY-- IT'S MY OWN RECIPE... I LIKE COOKING TOO! I'M REALLY GOOD AT IT...

CLOVIS' MOLARS! I'M NOT LOOKING FORWARD TO THIS TASK... *TORTURE!* BAH!

THERE'S NO SANITY IN THIS WORLD... WIZARDS BUYING WARRIORS...

OVER-ENDOWED FEMALES TAKING UP MY TIME IN USELESS REVENGE...

WHY CEREBUS HAS TO BE THE ONE TO... BE THE... ONE T...*

WHAT IN TARIM'S NAME *IS* THIS STUFF?

IT'S GRANOLA, FOR SET'S SAKE! YOU KNOW-- NUTS, OATS, MOLASSES?

HORSE FEED?!

YOU WOULD PREPARE *HORSE FEED* FOR AN *EARTH-PIG BORN?*

A SHORT HUNT TURNS UP A MORE SUITABLE MEAL FOR THE AARDVARK...

HOW CAN YOU STAND TO EAT THAT? IT WAS *ALIVE* JUST A MINUTE AGO...

ALIVE OR DEAD, MEAT IS MEAT ...*CEREBUS* ALWAYS EATS MEAT...

BUT IF YOU THINK THAT WAY-- THAT "MEAT IS MEAT" YOU'D HAVE TO INCLUDE HUMAN BEINGS AS *FOOD,* TOO!

ONLY IF GAME IS *SCARCE.*

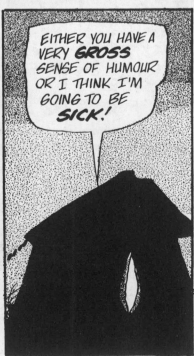

EITHER YOU HAVE A VERY *GROSS* SENSE OF HUMOUR OR I THINK I'M GOING TO BE *SICK!*

NO LONGER ENCUMBERED BY THE SUPPLIES FOR WHICH THEY INTEND TO RETURN SOPHIA AND CEREBUS MAKE BETTER TIME TOWARDS **BRANDUR**

I CAN'T UNDERSTAND IT! YOU BEAT ME IN BATTLE AND YET YOU WON'T LET ME **SERVE** YOU...!

ON MY FATHER'S LIFE, I VOW TO DO **ANYTHING** THAT WILL PLEASE YOU, EARTH-PIG MASTER...

HOW ABOUT A TAIL MASSAGE ...OR MAYBE I COULD SEW SEQUINS ON YOUR HELMET?

MAYBE YOU'D LIKE A MON-OGRAMMED HANDKERCHIEF SET?

CRAK

THERE APPEARS TO BE METHOD TO **HENROT'S** MAD-NESS -- A SACK OF GOLD IS A SMALL PRICE TO PAY FOR A FEW DAYS OF QUIET AND SAFETY...

NOT SO VERY LONG AGO IN SOME WAYS ...BUT DECADES AGO IN OTHERS!...

LOOKS LIKE DIRT ON YOUR *SNOUT*-- YOU-- EH-- WANT ME TO LICK IT OFF?

NEARBY, A WELL-DRESSED YOUNG MAN RECOGNIZES A FAMILIAR VOICE...

...AND AN EVEN MORE FAMILIAR LEWD PRO-POSAL...

SOPHIA!

TANES, FERAS!...

...*YOU!*

CLOVIS' EARS!

SOPHIA! WHAT DO YOU,... *AAAAAK!*

YOU HAVE BESMIRCHED MY HONOUR, *FERAS*...

TARIM! IF CEREBUS WAITS MUCH LONGER THERE WILL BE NAUGHT BUT *HAMBURGER* LEFT TO TORTURE...

67

FAINTED! TARIM -- IT WILL TAKE FOREVER FOR THE IRON TO HEAT UP ENOUGH IN *THIS* FIRE...

HE WOULD RISK HIS LIFE TO LOOK UPON THE WENCH

THE WAYS OF MEN ARE STRANGE, INDEED TO ONE WHO IS AN EARTH-PIG BORN...

OH MY BELOVED MUMBLE... IF ONLY YOU WOULD

MUMBLE MUMBLE ANYTHING YO WANT--MUMBLE--I'LL DO ANYTHING MY LORD CEREBUS...

AND I'LL HAVE TO LISTEN TO SUCH DRIVEL ALL THE WAY BACK TO *TANSUBAL!*

HEAVEN HE CALLS IT! BEING AT THE WENCH'S SIDE IS MORE SUFFERING THAN CEREBUS...

MAYHAP CEREBUS HAS JUST FOUND *ONE* SOLUTION FOR *TWO* PROBLEMS!

73

I TOLD HER SHE WOULD MAKE CEREBUS VERY HAPPY IF SHE MARRIED FERAS...

SHE DID *THAT?*...

...FOR *YOU?*

RED SOPHIA WILL DO ANYTHING FOR *CEREBUS!*

BUT...WHO... WHAT...

I HAVE NO DOUBT THAT THE MARRIAGE OF YOUR DAUGHTER AND FERAS WILL LAST *MANY* YEARS...

...AND IF YOU CAN THINK OF GREATER SUFFERING THAN THAT, YOU ARE WELCOME TO TRY THEM ON YOUR NEW SON-IN-LAW, *HENROT*...

FIN

THE PRIZE IS HIS, AND HE RUNS, CLUTCHING IT TO HIM....

HE LOOKS OVER HIS SHOULDER CONSTANTLY.... JUST A LITTLE BIT FURTHER...

SUDDENLY, THE ROOFTOPS SPREAD BEFORE HIM... A SINGLE LEAP AND HE WAS SAFE..... **SAFE!**

TOO LATE HE REALIZED HIS MISTAKE....

TOO LATE COMES HIS AWARENESS OF A DARK PRESENCE IN- SIDE HIM....

A SHARP SPASM IN HIS CHEST...

....THEN BLACKNESS!

AND AS HE FALLS, AS THE BAUBLE BOUNCES AWAY..... THERE IS

TIME FOR ONE THOUGHT,

MAY TARIM BE MER- CIFUL WITH WHOEVER FINDS IT!

DEATH'S DARK TREAD

USING HENROT'S GOLD, CEREBUS BRIBES HIS WAY ONTO A MERCHANT VESSEL ON THE SOFIM RIVER. A WEEK LATER, HE IS WITHIN THE SEPRAN EMPIRE'S BOUNDARIES, POSING AS A TRADER IN TEXTILES! AT SERREA, THE INFORMAL CAPITAL OF THE LOOSELY-KNIT AND MILITANT EMPIRE, THE EARTH-PIG SEES HIS CHANCE FOR A MUCH-NEEDED VACATION! HE LOSES HIMSELF AMID THE BUSTLING CROWDS AND, WITH THE LAST OF HIS BOREALAN GOLD, SETS ABOUT THE SERIOUS BUSINESS OF DRINKING, EATING AND GAMBLING...

THE EYE, BY ITS NATURE, IS ATTRACTED TO BRIGHT **OBJECTS.**

THIS EFFECT, AIDED BY THE BETTER HALF OF A PINT BOTTLE OF **APRICOT BRANDY...**

... TENDS TO BE SOMEWHAT.... **ENHANCED!**

76

EH? SOME KIND OF GEM-- TARIM! IT SHINES LIKE FIVE SUNS!

SLIPPERY, TOO! DOUBTLESS LOST BY SOME IDIOT *NOBLEMAN!*

AH WELL *NOBILITY'S* LOSS IS AN EARTH-PIG'S GAIN...

MAYHAP I CAN USE IT AS A STAKE IN *DIAMONDBACK* THIS NIGHT...

AND AS CEREBUS' THOUGHTS TURN TO GAMBLING...

...AND AS HE CONSIDERS VARIOUS PLOYS AND WAGERS...

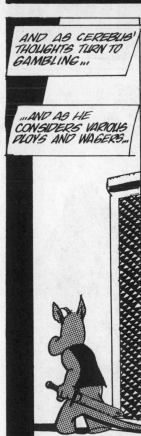

"HE FAILS TO SEE...

...THAT THE VERY ACT OF PICKING UP THE GEM...

...IS PROBABLY THE BIGGEST GAMBLE HE WILL TAKE THIS NIGHT...

THE EARTH-PIG TURNS A CORNER, COMING **ABRUPTLY** FACE-TO-FACE WITH A WITH ONE OF COUNTLESS **DEAD ENDS** IN THIS SOUTHERN METROPOLIS...

UNH?

FROM NOW ON, *CEREBUS* WILL SLAKE HIS THIRST WITH *ALES* AND *MEADS!*

THESE CITY WINES MAY TASTE LIKE FRUIT JUICE, BUT THEY WREAK HAVOC WITH MY...*!*

CLOVIS' TEETH AND TANKARD!

THE SHORT BLADE GLITTERS DULLY IN THE HALF-LIGHT...

THOUGH THERE IS A MERCILESS THROBBING BEHIND THE EARTH-PIG'S WINE-BLURRED EYES...

...INGRAINED SKILLS INSTANTLY DICTATE HIS ACTIONS...!

"SOON" MURMURS **DEATH**," SOON THE GEM WILL BE **MINE!**"

"ONCE THE CRAWLER HERDS THIS PREY TO-WARD ME, IT WILL BE CHILD'S PLAY TO GET THE GEM IN MY HANDS..."

CEREBUS SENSES YOU WISH HIM TO RUN, DEVILSPAWN!

...BUT WHAT IF I CHOOSE TO FIGHT INSTEAD?

"A MOST 'VALIANT' WORM," CHUCKLES DEATH, "IF HE RE-FUSES TO RUN, THEN THE CRAWLER WILL REMOVE THE GEM AND LEAVE IT FOR ANOTHER TO FIND!"

I AM NO CITY-BRED MORSEL-FOR-THE-TAKING! ..., YOU FACE AN EARTH PIG BORN, DEMON!

"AMAZING! BUT IT IS IMPOSSIBLE FOR HIM TO DEFEAT THE CRAWLER! NO MATTER HOW..."

WOUNDED, EH, MONSTER? YOUR MAW GAPES TO DEVOUR ME...

MAYHAP, INSTEAD...

"BY THE FIVE SPHERES," DEATH HISSES, ONE BROW ARCHING SLIGHTLY...

...YOU SHALL FEED ON THIS! ...,

"A CREATURE FROM THE DAWN OF TIME, A CREATURE OF SORCERY ...BREATHING ITS LAST..."

"DEFEATED BY MERE FLESH AND BLOOD AND IRON...

"...AND STILL, I DO NOT POSSESS THE GEM...!"

AND TO THINK THAT *CEREBUS* CAME SOUTH TO SEEK *SANITY*...!

THE BEAST IS ENORMOUS-- BUT FROM *WHERE* DID IT....

"MY FOE SEEMS MORE CEREBRAL THAN THE *AVERAGE* BARBARIAN," MUSES DEATH.

THE BARBARIAN SIDE OF THE EARTH-PIG REACTS INSTANTLY, THE SWORD BITING INTO *PULPY* FLESH....

...EVEN AS HIS BRAIN REGISTERS THE MOTION FOR WHAT IT IS -- THE BEAST'S DEATH THROES ....

KNOWLEDGEABLE IN SORCERERS' WAYS, HE IS MOVED TO WONDERMENT AT THE POWER OF THE BEAST'S *MASTER*....

"THE BARBARIAN IS TOO HEADSTRONG -- TOO **INTELLIGENT** TO CONTROL! THE GEM MUST BE BROUGHT WILLINGLY TO ME -- I NEED A MORE MALLEABLE PERSONALITY TO BRING THE GEM TO ME...."

THE EARTH-PIG HEAVES A SIGH AND TURNS BACK ONTO THE MAIN AVENUE...

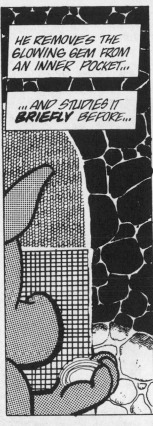

HE REMOVES THE GLOWING GEM FROM AN INNER POCKET...

...AND STUDIES IT **BRIEFLY** BEFORE...

...HOOKING IT ONTO HIS **NECK CHAIN**...

HE CONSIDERS, AGAIN, HIS CHANCES AT **DIAMONDBACK**...

"SOMEONE NEARBY--A PERSONALITY CAPABLE OF WRESTING THE GEM FROM THE **BARBARIAN**..."

"A PERSONALITY WITH NO SUBTLETY --AN **EASY** VICTIM OF....."

A SATISFIED CHUCKLE ISSUES FROM DEEP IN **DEATH'S** THROAT...

CEREBUS REFLECTS THAT THERE ARE DRAWBACKS TO POSING AS A MERCHANT--ONE HAS TO ASSOCIATE WITH HIS KIND UNDER THE **CITY GUARD'S** WATCHFUL GAZE!

THE MERCHANTS AND TRADERS IN SERREA ARE CONSERVATIVE GAMBLERS AND FAVOUR SIPPING WINE TO GULPING ALE....

NEARLY DAWN! NO **MERCHANT** WILL BE THINKING OF ALE OR **DIAMONDBACK** 'TIL SUNSET...

TARIM!

MAYHAP I SHOULD RISK CONSORTING WITH SOME OF THE **DEHRSION** MERCENARIES...

THEY ARE GAMBLERS AND **DRINKERS** WHO HAVE NO DOUBT OF...

AAAK!

STAND--I SAY--STAND ASIDE!!

MAKE **WAY**, BOY!

82

MAKE WAY FOR-- **ELROD** *THE ALBINO!*

WHY, HELLO THERE SHORT, GREY AND FUZZY-- YOU HAVE A THING FOR CRUSHED **VELVET?**

SPEAK WHEN YOU'RE SPOKEN TO, SON-- YOU'RE MAKING A BAD FIRST *IMPRESSION!*

AND STAND UP! YOU'LL NEVER LEAVE YOUR MARK ON THE WORLD HIDING BEHIND BOLTS OF CLOTH ALL DAY...

SOONER OR LATER YOU'LL HAVE TO TAKE OFF THE **BUNNY SUIT,** KID-- THEN, I SAY *THEN* WHERE WILL YOU BE?

OH--I GET IT-- YOU'RE OVER-COME BY MY PRESENCE-- **AWED** BY THE SIGHT OF A *TRUE KING!* BY THE REALITY OF THE RULER OF MELVIN-BONE-- LAST LORD OF A DYING RACE --A **WANDERER** THAT IS....

YOU GETTING ALL THIS **DOWN** BOY? OR AM I GOING TOO FAST FOR YA?

WHERE WAS I?

OH-- YEAH! SORCERER AND SLAYER OF MY KIN, DESPOILER OF MY HOMELAND...

WOULD THAT CEREBUS WAS NOT PASSING FOR A MERCHANT...

PAY ATTENTION, SON-- EARS THAT LONG MUST BE GOOD FOR SOMETHING!

I'M FEARED IN BATTLE -- I'M AN OUTCAST FROM MY RACE -- MY SWORD IS BLACK!

RUNE-CARVED, THAT IS...!

CEREBUS WOULD LIKE YOU TO REMOVE SOME OF YOUR WEIGHT FROM HIS FOOT!

MIND YOUR MANNERS, SON! I'VE GOT A TALL POINTY HAT! STATUS, BOY! YOU CAN ARGUE WITH ME, BUT YOU CAN'T ARGUE WITH STATUS!

DON'T WALK AWAY WHEN I'M TALKING TO YOU, BOY! IT'S *BAD MANNERS!*

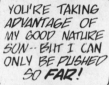

YOU'RE TAKING ADVANTAGE OF MY GOOD NATURE SON-- BUT I CAN ONLY BE PUSHED *SO FAR!*

ALL RIGHT! YOU *ASKED* FOR IT, NOW YOU MUST FACE MY SWORD...

...SEERSUCKER!

THAT'S A JOKE, SON-- BUT NO ONE'S GOING TO GET IT FOR, AT *LEAST* FIVE THOUSAND YEARS...

TARIM!

WHO WOULD *BELIEVE* A SWORD COULD GET RUSTY ENOUGH TO TURN *BLACK*?

DEATH ABSENTLY CARESSES ONE OF THE HOVERING GEMS. "AN EVEN DOZEN," HE MUSES, "A SOURCE OF GREAT POWER, YES! *BUT*, CONSIDER THE THIRTEENTH GEM-- NOW SO CLOSE AT HAND." WITH THAT GEM WOULD COME A NEW GOLDEN AGE FOR *DEATH* ,.... DISEASES, FAMINE -- WHOLE POPULATIONS WIPED OUT IN MERE DAYS! THE THOUGHT, AS ALWAYS, REINFORCES HIS GRIM DETERMINATION!

EVEN NOW, HIS NEW "ALLY" PREPARES TO DRIVE THE BARBARIAN HERE -- UNAWARE THAT THE IDEA IS NOT HIS OWN.....

AFTER UNTOLD CENTURIES, THE GEM IS ON ITS WAY. *THE CHAOS GEM.* THE BARBARIAN WILL BE MADE TO COOPERATE ONCE HE DRAWS NEAR!

DEATH SETTLES BACK TO WATCH THE DRAMA UNFOLD!

86

uh

YOU'RE RIGHT, BOY! WHY SHOULD WE FIGHT? WHY, WE'RE PROBABLY THE TWO BEST FIGHTERS IN THESE SOUTHLANDS!

WE'LL TEAM UP! OH--I KNOW WHAT YOU'RE GOING TO SAY! YOU'RE GOING TO SAY-- YOU'RE NOT GOOD ENOUGH!

YOU'RE PROBABLY RIGHT!

BUT THAT'S OKAY, SON! WHAT YOU LACK IN SKILL YOU MAKE UP FOR IN SHORTNESS...

LOOK AT ME, BOY! HOW DO YOU EXPECT TO IMPROVE WHEN YOU DON'T PAY ATTENTION?

TELL YOU WHAT-- WHY DON'T YOU GRUNT IF ANY OF THIS IS SINKING IN...

NO LOITERING ON THE AVENUES, **MERCHANT**...

MOVE ALONG AND TEND YOUR **WARES** OR...

AVE!

TENDING HIS WARES IS THE BEST IDEA **CEREBUS** HAS HEARD YET THIS...

HANG ON A CHICKEN-PLUCKING **MINUTE!** WHO ARE YOU CALLING MERCHANT, DUNG FACE?

WE'RE **WARRIORS!** THE MIGHTIEST SWORDS IN THE **SOUTHLANDS...**

GUARDS! ALIEN WARRIORS HERE!

CLOVIS' BEADS!

YOU CAN'T LET THESE TIN-PLATED TURKEYS PUSH YOU **AROUND,** SON...

UNH!

OHO! **REINFORCEMENTS!** BUT THESE HALF-WITS DON'T FRIGHTEN ELROD THE ALBINO...

WE'LL LET THEM KNOW THEY CAN'T MESS AROUND WITH US...!

ER -- I'LL HANDLE THE ONE ON THE LEFT AND LEAVE THE REST FOR YOU...

WHAT?!

WATCH *THIS*, SON! WITH BUT A SINGLE BLOW, *ELROD* DEFEATS THE =UMPH=

WITH ONLY TWO =UMPH= OR =UMPH= THREE PUNCHES *ELROD* DEF....

WITH BARELY =UMPH= =UMPH= A HALF DOZEN PUNCHES, ELR....

OH HELL! WHERE'S A BIG ROCK I CAN HIT HIM WITH?

HEY *CEREBUS!* -- YOU GOT ANY BIG ROCKS OVER...

...THERE?

NOT MUCH OF A *SCRAPPER*, ARE YOU, BOYZ?

WE'LL LET THEM ROT IN THE *SOUTHGATE* PRISON....

USE YOUR **HEAD,** BOY! ALL YOU'RE GOING TO DO IS BREAK A BONE! *INJURE* AN APPENDAGE! *CONTUSE* YOUR ULNA AND *LIKEWISE* DO GRIEVOUS HARM TO THE *REST* OF YOUR SHORT, GREY BODY!

SNAP

THAT'S JUST *TERRIFIC* SON -- NOW, YOU CAN PICK YOUR NOSE IF YOU WANT TO...

OH, COME **ON** NOW, BOY! JUST BECAUSE YOU FOUND A WEAK LINK IN ONE *CHAIN,* DOESN'T MEAN YOU CAN *POSSIBLY...*

SNAP

CRAK

* *CEREBUS* **DID** *HAVE SOME DIALOGUE ON THIS PAGE...IT'S JUST THAT NONE OF IT WAS PRINTABLE —* **DAVE**

YOU *DID* IT, SON-- I KNEW YOU HAD IT IN YOU! NOW-- GRAB THAT IRON BAR AND...

NO, NO! BOY-- USE IT TO *DIG* -- DIG, SON--LIKE A SHOVEL....

YOU CAN'T DIG THROUGH A WOODEN DOOR, BOY!...

ANY *MORON* KNOWS THAT-- THE *INERTIA'S* ALL WRONG!

WE'RE *ONLY* A FEW THOUSAND METRES *UNDERGROUND,* SON....

WITH A LITTLE *ELBOW* GREASE YOU COULD BE BLINKING IN THE SUNLIGHT BY NEXT SHROVE TUESDAY...

SAY! LOOKS LIKE YOU'RE ONTO SOMETHING THERE, KID! JUST GET YOUR BACK INTO IT!

NOW WE'RE IN BUSINESS, SON! YOU SET ME LOOSE AND WE CAN MAKE A RUN FOR IT...!

SNAPK

94

IF ELROD IS TO BE KILLED, METHINKS THEY'LL FIRST HAVE TO BEAT HIS TONGUE TO DEATH WITH A STICK!

TARIM! CEREBUS MUST HAVE CRAWLED MILES THROUGH THIS VENTILATION TUNNEL!

CLOVIS' ORBS! SUNLIGHT! A WELCOME SIGHT FOR AN EARTH-PIG BORN...

NORMALLY, CEREBUS IS NOT ONE TO BELIEVE IN BAD OMENS ....

...BUT, ALL MY TROUBLE BEGAN WHEN I FOUND THIS SHINING ABOMINATION!

SO, MY FIRST TWO ORDERS OF BUSINESS ARE...

...TO DIVEST MYSELF OF THIS TROUBLEMAKER ...

...AND TO FIND A BLACKSMITH TO REMOVE THESE SHACKLES...

"SOME DAYS..."

"SOME DAYS..." DEATH THOUGHT TO HIMSELF...

"IT JUST DOESN'T PAY TO GET OUT OF BED."

CEREBUS the AARDVARK

AFTER LEAVING SERREA, CEREBUS DRIFTS WEST INTO THE RED MARCHES WHERE HE ENTERS THE EMPLOY OF **TURAN GENN**, A MERCENARY CAPTAIN! THE SUMMER RAINS ARE AT THEIR PEAK AND THE EARTH-PIG EXECUTES HIS TASKS AMID MUCH GRUMBLING ABOUT SUB-TROPICAL RAINFALL...

TARIM'S BLOOD! THREE WEEKS OF NON-STOP RAIN! DAMN THESE BORDER PATROLS!

I'D BETTER FIND SHELTER BEFORE TOO LONG...

IT DOESN'T LOOK LIKE I'LL MAKE IT TO THE OUTPOST TONIGHT...

TARIM! NOT VERY LARGE -- BUT IT IS THE FIRST DRY SPOT I'VE SEEN IN THE LAST TWENTY MILES!

GRIMLY, CEREBUS SQUEEZES INTO THE TINY HOLLOW. ALMOST INSTANTLY THE ENCLOSURE FILLS WITH THE ODOR OF WET AARDVARK FUR...

THE SMELL DOESN'T SERVE TO BRIGHTEN THE EARTH PIG'S DISPOSITION...

SOME MANNER OF CREATURE...QUIETLY PARTHA QUA NON

YOU WORRY LIKE AN OLD WOMAN, CROMAG MACS MILC, THE CREATURE IS **ASLEEP!**

ONE CUT AND....

UNH?

IMPOSSIBLE.

ISHTAR TAKE US ALL!

NO ONE WILL BELIEVE US! NO ONE!

WE MUST TAKE HIM TO BRAN MAC MUFIN!

ALTHOUGH THE EARTH-PIG IS WELL USED TO THE REACTIONS OF MEN TO HIS APPEARANCE...

...THERE IS SOMETHING **DISTURBING** IN THE SAVAGES' ASTONISHMENT!

CEREBUS GOES WITH NO ONE UNTIL THEY EXPLAIN THEIR INTEREST IN HIM...

YOU *MUST* COME WITH US.... YOU'RE THE...

uh -- YOU'RE *OBVIOUSLY* IN NEED OF A WARM SHELTER...

THE OTHERS SOON JOIN IN, URGING CEREBUS TO TAKE ADVANTAGE OF THEIR HOSPITALITY...

THE EARTH-PIG AGREES, RESOLVING, HOWEVER, TO KEEP AN EYE ON HIS TOO-EAGER HOSTS...

ESPECIALLY THOSE WHO STAND BEHIND HIM...

THE CAMP IS ABOUT A HALF HOUR FROM HERE...

WE SHOULD BE THERE BY SUNSET...

CEREBUS SAYS NOTHING, BUT CONTINUES TO ASSESS HIS COMPANIONS! WITH THE EXCEPTION OF THE SIMPLE KNIFE, THEY ARE WEAPONLESS...

PERHAPS THEY ARE SIMPLE FARMERS OR NOMADS AS THEIR SPEECH SUGGESTS...

ABRUPTLY, THE LEADER CHANGES DIRECTION, HEADING FOR A PATCH OF TALLER GRASS

A PITY WE CAN'T ALWAYS TRAVEL WITHOUT OUR WEAPONS...

...BUT THE MARCHES GROW DANGEROUS AS NIGHT APPROACHES...

AND A GOOD SWORD CAN SPELL THE DIFFERENCE BETWEEN LIFE AND DEATH...

THE WEAPONS ARE HAND-MADE AND, EVEN WITH A GLANCE, THE EARTH-PIG APPRAISES THEM AS FORMIDABLE...AND DEADLY...

HAVE YOU NOTICED THAT **SMELL**, CROMAG?

AYE--THE PLAINS DWELLERS MUST BE BURNING THEIR CEREMONIAL SKUNKS AGAIN...

NAY-- THE SMELL IS RICHER THAN THAT...

...THE SMELL OF A THOUSAND **DUNG WORMS** MATING IN THE NOON SUN...

WE SHOULD TRY AND FIND THE SOURCE OF THE ODOUR...

IT MAY BE **SORCERY** ... OR A NEW PLAGUE!

DAMNED INSECTS!

MAKES ME LONG FOR THE WINTERS IN THE NORTH...!

UNWITTINGLY (AND TO HIS INSTANT REGRET) ONE OF THE MEN PASSES WITHIN RANGE OF THE EARTH-PIG'S SWEEPING GESTURE...

COUGH!

ASHTOTH PRESERVE ME....

EH -- IF YOU'LL FORGIVE US, **FRIEND**, YOUR FUR SEEMS TO ..... THAT IS, THE SMELL IS......UH....

CEREBUS REALIZES THE PROBLEM AND IS SYMPATHIC ... HE CAN BARELY STAND THE SMELL HIMSELF.....

PERHAPS A LITTLE DISTANCE WILL HELP..

HOW'S THIS?

EXCELLANT! THE STINGING IN MY **NOSTRILS** IS BARELY NOTICEABLE!

WHO IS THIS **BRAN MAK MUFIN...?**

BRAN MAK MUFIN IS THE FINEST LEADER OF MEN ON THE FACE OF THE EARTH...

HE IS A TACTICIAN WITHOUT PEER... AN ARTIST WHEN IT COMES TO DEFENDING OR ATTACKING...

...ALSO, HE IS THE PENULTIMATE *SWORDSMAN!* HE HAS BEEN KNOWN TO EMASCULATE FLIES IN MID-AIR...

...A SLAYER OF KINGS AND THE KING OF KINGS *HIMSELF!*

HE CAN REPAIR A BROKEN LIMB WITH BUT A GLANCE ...HE MAKES THE BLIND SIGHTED--THE WEAK, *STRONG...*

ALL HAIL BRAN MAK MUFIN!!

...HE ALSO MAKES THE FINEST BOREALAN COLE SLAW WEST OF THE SOFIM...

WE LIVE UNDER THE EARTH! THE TUNNELS ARE ANCIENT... THIS SECTION IS MORE RECENT...

...MOST OF THE TUNNELS WIND FOR MILES WITH NUMEROUS EXITS LIKE THIS ONE!

WE ARE A PRIVATE PEOPLE AND FIND THE PRIVACY COMFORTING...

WE'LL TAKE YOU TO BRAN MAK MUFIN DIRECTLY...

AYE! HE'LL BE ANXIOUS TO SEE YOU...

STRANGELY ENOUGH I FIND THIS DEMI-GOD'S CONCERN FOR CEREBUS SOMETHING LESS THAN TOUCHING!

107

YOU ARE NO DOUBT **CURIOUS** ABOUT THIS SET-UP....

A DRINK FIRST, AND THEN I'LL ANSWER ALL YOUR QUESTIONS!

PHHIFST

FERMENTED GOAT'S BLOOD! IT TAKES A WHILE TO GET USED TO THE AFTER-TASTE...

CEREBUS WOULD SOONER GET USED TO RAT POISON!...

THOUGH YOU SPEAK A FLUENT CONNIPTIN DIALECT, I DON'T RECOGNIZE YOUR...

WE ARE THE **PIGTS**...

...AN ANCIENT AND FEARED RACE

WE ARE AVENGERS OF THE MEEK, THE RECALCITRANT, THE SCARED, THE DUBIOUS AND THE **OPPRESSED**. WE EXIST ONLY TO **TOPPLE** THE EMPIRE....

WHICH EMPIRE?

ANY EMPIRE-- YOU NAME IT AND WE'VE TOPPLED IT... THE REDEEMER DYNASTY, THE EASTERN MONOLITHS, THE BLACK TOWER EMPIRE....

RIGHT NOW WE'RE WORKING ON A TIGHT SCHEDULE OF TOPPLING THE *DEHRSION* MONARCHY ...BUT I HOPE TO GET TO THE *BOREALANS* WITHIN A DECADE...

YOU MUST HAVE ORGANIZED A TRULY *FORMIDABLE* FIGHTING FORCE...

HOW MANY MEN DO YOU HAVE UNDER YOUR COMMAND?

I COMMAND AN ELITE GROUP OF *FIFTY* ARMED WARRIORS

A LOT OF THEM ARE ARMED WITH *SWORDS*, TOO...

THE PHRASE "PARANOID SCHIZOPHRENIC WITH DELUSIONS OF GRANDEUR" IS NOT IN THE AARDVARK'S VOCABULARY, SO, IN HIS MIND, HE SUBSTITUTES "CRAZY AS A PANROVIAN MONK..."

NOW *I* HAVE A QUESTION FOR *YOU*...

WHAT... ARE YOU?

CEREBUS DOES NOT TURN. HE REALIZES BRAN MAK MUFIN IS INTERESTED IN THE ANSWER. FOR WHAT REASON? HE IS UNABLE TO GUESS...

I AM *CEREBUS*, AN EARTH-PIG BORN...

HOW *OLD* ARE YOU?

GUESS.

YOU'RE TWENTY-SIX....

...AREN'T YOU?

YOU LOOK *TIRED.* COME WITH ME AND I'LL SHOW YOU YOUR BED. WE CAN TALK AGAIN TOMORROW ....

THOUGH THE BED IS SOFTER THAN *ANY* HE HAS SEEN IN COUNTLESS MONTHS....

HE IS DIS-TURBED BY HIS BRIEF MEETING WITH....

THE AVERAGE PERSON WOULD HAVE DISMISSED THE SOUND AS A "BUMP IN THE NIGHT"!.

HOWEVER, WHEN YOUR LIFE HAS OFTEN HINGED ON A RANDOM SOUND....

CEREBUS IS UNABLE TO SLEEP....

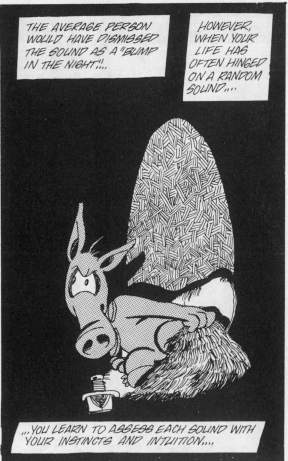

...YOU LEARN TO ASSESS EACH SOUND WITH YOUR INSTINCTS AND INTUITION....

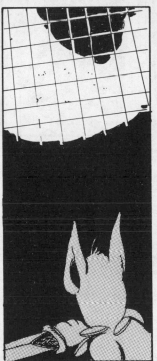

HMMM! SMELLS LIKE SOMEONE BROUGHT A DEAD GOAT WITH THEM...

THE CHANTING IS LOUDER NOW! THE ANCIENT AND CRUMBLING THEATRE SEEMS TO HUM WITH UNSEEN ENERGY....

BRAN MAK MUFIN! WHY WOULD HE CALL A MEETING AT NIGHT?

.....TIME WE HAVE AWAITED IS AT HAND...

OUR REDEEMER WALKS AMONG US..."IN HIS TWENTY-SIXTH YEAR HE SHALL COME TO US..."

unh?

FOR A THOUSAND YEARS, THE PICTS HAVE BEEN WITHOUT THEIR GOD-KING ....

NOW, HE HAS BEEN RESTORED *NOW*, EMPIRES WILL BE TRAMPLED BENEATH OUR FEET...

NOW WE NEED NO LONGER CONTENT OURSELVES WITH AN IDOL IN HIS IMAGE!

ALL HAIL!

ALL HAIL!! ALL HAIL!! ALL HAIL!!

TARIM!

112

IT WAS PERHAPS FIFTEEN FEET TALL, MADE OF SOME KIND OF SOFT GREY STONE! BRAN MAK MUFIN'S INTEREST IN HIM WAS NOW EASILY UNDERSTOOD-- THE RESEMBLANCE WAS **ASTOUNDING**!

SOME KIND OF PREDICTION HAD BEEN FULFILLED BY THE EARTH-PIG'S ARRIVAL IN THE RED MARCHES, CEREBUS REALIZED...

BRAN MAK MUFIN SAW HIM AS THE REINCARNATION OF SOME GOD-KING FROM THE DISTANT PAST.....

" AND THE PIGS OF MANY LANDS WILL FOLLOW AND DEVASTATION WILL BE THE LOT OF THE UNBELIEVERS....

" FOLLOW HIM, O SONS OF THE PIG, FOR VENGEANCE WILL BE YOURS!"

THE PIGT LEADER'S WORDS FADE TO A DISTANT HUM IN **CEREBUS'** EARS-- UNABLE TO TEAR HIS EYES AWAY FROM THE IDOL, HE LOSES HIMSELF IN HIS OWN MUSINGS...

"AM I THE REDEEMER?" HE DECIDES HE IS NOT. THE IDOL'S EYES REMAIN IMPASSIVE...

HE IS BROUGHT BACK TO REALITY BY THE SHOUTS OF THE PIGTS WHO HAVE BEGUN EXITING THE GREAT HALL...

EVIDENTLY THEIR MEETING IS AT AN END!

IN A FEW MOMENTS, THE CAVERNOUS ROOM IS EMPTY, HYSTERICAL SHOUTS AND LAUGHTER VANISHING ALONG THE ANCIENT CORRIDORS...

IN A FEW MOMENTS, THE GLOW OF THEIR TORCHES IS ALL THAT REMAINS...

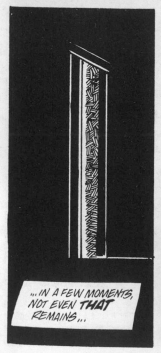

...IN A FEW MOMENTS, NOT EVEN **THAT** REMAINS...

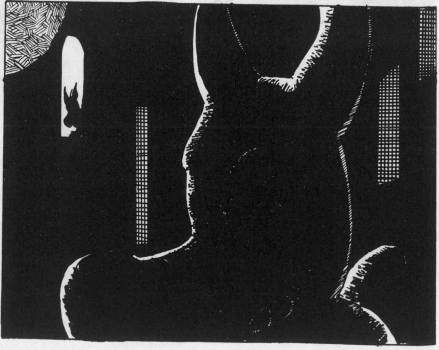

CEREBUS DESCENDED THE NOW-DARKENED STAIRWAY....

IT LOOMED IN THE HALF-LIGHT...

HIS FOOTSTEPS, LIGHT THOUGH THEY ARE, ECHO IN THE TOMB-LIKE HALL....

THE STONE IS EVEN SOFTER THAN IT HAD APPEARED FROM A DISTANCE. CLAY PERHAPS?

A GOD OF CLAY-- CEREBUS SHAKES HIS HEAD IN DISGUST...

THERE WAS NO FATHOMING THE HUMAN MIND -- NO WAY TO UNDERSTAND HOW THESE CREATURES THINK...

HE STANDS BEFORE THE IDOL. IT SEEMS DIMINISHED AT CLOSE QUARTERS -- A DECORATION, PERHAPS...

...BUT A GOD?

TARIM, ASHTOTH, THESE WERE GODS....THEY BROUGHT WAR, PAIN, THEY KILLED WITHOUT REASON OR APOLOGY...

HE COULD PORTRAY THE REDEEMER! HE COULD LEAD THE PIGTS EAST .... HE HAD SEEN ARMIES DRIVEN BY RELIGIOUS ZEAL....

WITH TWO DOZEN OF THOSE HAND-CRAFTED WEAPONS ...

WE COULD LAY WASTE TO THE PRIMITIVE LANDS EAST OF THE FELD...

THERE WOULD BE MORE LOOT THAN A KING COULD IMAGINE

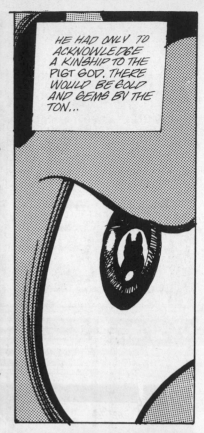

HE HAD ONLY TO ACKNOWLEDGE A KINSHIP TO THE PIGT GOD. THERE WOULD BE GOLD AND GEMS BY THE TON...

MAYHAP THERE *IS* A KINSHIP! MAYHAP CEREBUS *IS* JUST ONE OF THE PIGT RACE ...MAYHAP HE IS ONLY ONE OF ...ONLY A ...

NO.

FOR A THOUSAND YEARS, THE PIG HAS BEEN TENDED, EACH LEADER FORBIDDING EVEN THE MOST CASUAL TOUCH-- ALL FOR BUT ONE REASON:

THE PIG IS COMPOSED OF THE FLIMSIEST MATERIAL-- MATERIAL THAT IS NO MATCH FOR THE PUNCHES OF AN ENRAGED EARTH-PIG!

117

CEREBUS LIFTS HIMSELF FROM THE RUBBLE.... THERE IS NO SOUND FROM THE CORRIDORS BEYOND...

HIS ABSENCE WILL BE NOTICED IN A VERY FEW MINUTES....

...HE HURRIES TOWARD A FAR EXIT...

HE HAS SEEN ENOUGH OF RELIGIOUS FANATICISM... TO KNOW THAT THE **PIGTS** WILL NOT BE UNDERSTANDING ABOUT THE DESTRUCTION OF A CENTURIES-OLD **GOD KING**...

EXITS, AS HE WAS TOLD, PROLIFERATE IN THE UNDER-GROUND CHAMBERS

THE RAINS HAVE STOPPED...

HE EMERGES INTO THE DAWN AND FACES EAST

IEST IS A DAY'S MARCH AWAY AND THE EARTH-PIG FEELS, ONCE MORE, DRAWN TO THE BUSTLE AND CLAMOUR OF THE CITY...

THE SECRET!

TURG THE UNDULY-TALL BELIEVES WE HAVE LOST THE CURLY-HAIR, E'LAGS! ...

NO! -- LOOK!

HE'S DYING -- BUT THERE'S SOMEONE WITH HIM

YOU WANT TURG SHOULD ...

NO! WE HAVEN'T SEEN THE STRANGER YET! WE HAVE TO MAKE SURE HE'S NOT...

... BIGGER THAN YOU ARE :-

RIGHT, TURG -- ASK THE LITTLE FELLOW IF THE CURLY-HAIR TOLD HIM ANYTHING...

CAREFUL, THOUGH! HE LOOKS KIND OF FRAGILE...

WE'LL NEED TWO PACK HORSES FOR THE GOLD... FOOD FOR TWO WEEKS uh ...

THUMP CRAK WHUMP

SHOVELS, PICKS...

HUH?

TARIM! IT NEVER FAILS -- TWO HOURS IN ANY OF THESE ACCURSED CITIES

AND SOME FARMER WITH MORE MUSCLE THAN BRAINS COMES FLYING AT ME...

MOTHER?...

EH... EXCUSE ME?

DOES THIS OXEN-BREATHED SLOB BELONG TO YOU, WIMP?

IN A MANNER OF SPEAKING -- I... EH TOLD HIM TO ASK YOU TO JOIN US FOR A DRINK...!

I'LL DEAL WITH YOU LATER, IDIOT!

IT WOULD APPEAR HE GOT TOO CARRIED AWAY OR...SOMETHING.

IF YOU WILL GRAB A LEG, THOUGH...

CEREBUS' SUSPICIONS ARE AROUSED ...

BUT ARE VERY QUICKLY REPRESSED BY HIS ENORMOUS THIRST....

121

THIS IS ONE OF THE *BEST* TAVERNS IN IEST!

TURG STILL DOES NOT *UNDERSTAND* WHY WE ARE *DRINKING* WITH THE *KILLER-WHO-LOOKS-LIKE-A-BUNNY*

OF COURSE THE MAIN ATTRACTION IS *JAKA*...

CEREBUS HAS NO INTEREST IN SUCH FOOLISHNESS.

EXCELLANT!

AH! OUR ALES HAVE ARRIVED!

NOW MY LITTLE GRAY FRIEND-- LET'S SEE IF YOUR MIND CAN BE CHANGED ABOUT *JAKA!*

THREE OF THOSE PILLS SHOULD MAKE YOU A LITTLE MORE *SUGGESTABLE!*

AND JAKA SHOULD MAKE AS GOOD A TEST AS ANY!

MOMENTS LATER...

CEREBUS CAN'T REMEMBER WHEN HE HAS ENJOYED AN *ALE* SO MUCH!

I *REALLY* THINK YOU SHOULD WATCH THE SHOW... JAKA IS SAID TO BE THE MOST *BEAUTIFUL* WOMAN EAST OF THE SOFIM....

HER HAIR IS LIKE WHITE SILK ... HER MOVEMENTS ARE CAT-LIKE

SHE IS ... SHE ...IS...

CEREBUS?

SIGH

TURG! IT WORKED -- IT WORKED! HE'S IN MY COMMAND! --

DUH! HAHAHA

HE'LL TELL US WHERE THE GOLD IS, TURG! HAHAHAHA

COME ALONG, CEREBUS -- WE'RE GOING OUT FOR A LITTLE ...

...CHAT?

HE'S *GONE!*

TURG! HE'S *GONE!* OUR ONE-WAY TICKET TO A KING'S RANSOM IN GOLD IS *GONE!* WHERE, TURG? WHERE COULD HE HAVE...

unh?

OH TARIM, NO!...

CEREBUS! COME ON! WE HAVE TO TALK ABOUT SOMETHING!

YOU CAN *STOP* WATCHING THE SHOW! WE HAVE TO...

UMPH!

MY... GOD

ARE YOU OKAY, *E'LASS?*

NEVER MIND-- WE NEED *SOMEONE* TO TALK TO CEREBUS-- GET HIM TO COME WITH US

DUH-- YES! WE NEED SOMEONE ...TO... TALK... T....⋇

AWW -- NO, E'LASS -- *PLEASE!* TURG IS STILL SORE FROM HIS LAST TALK WITH THE KILLER-WHO-LOOKS-LIKE-A-BUNNY...

STOP *SNIVELLING!* HE JUST CAUGHT YOU *OFF-GUARD* LAST TIME...

MEANWHILE...

ehm.

YOU WISH SOMETHING, *SHORT GREY ONE?*

uhn.... uh uh--uh uhhn....

YOU WILL *HAVE* TO SPEAK *LOUDER* -- JAKA CANNOT HEAR YOU

IF YOU WISHED, *CEREBUS* WOULD KILL YOU A YAK FOR YOUR SUPPER

JAKA THINKS YOU ARE *CUTE!*...

SMAK#

126

JAKA DANCES AGAIN IN ONE HOUR -- YOU WILL STAY, NO?

BUT, E'LASS HE WON'T WANT...

E'LASS LOOK!

TARIM'S TEETH AND TOOTHPICKS!

TCHENS, TREBU AND LOHI OR I'M A BOREALAN!

W- WHAT DOES IT MEAN, E'LASS?

IT MEANS THE BROTHERS OF THE BLACK SUN ARE BETTER AT TRACKING THAN I THOUGHT!

THEY'LL KILL US IF THEY GET HALF A CHANCE, TURG!

I HAVE TO GET CEREBUS TO *LEAVE* WITH US...

AND THIS TIME I WON'T TAKE NO FOR AN ANSWER

LOOK-- YOU'RE ONLY THREE-FEET-TALL! I'M FIVE-FOOT-EIGHT! *REASON* WILL TELL YOU THAT IT WILL DO YOU NO GOOD TO RESIST ME --SO LET ME JUST TAKE YOUR ARM LIKE THIS AND WE CAN GET OUT OF...

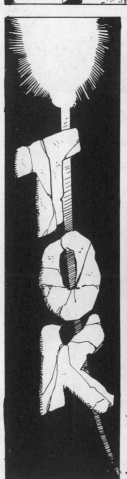

I AM MOVED TO ASK, FRIEND JUST PRIOR TO REARRANGING YOUR FACE...

WHY DID YOU *SMASH* MY ALE MUG?

HELP -ME- TURG!

YOU CAN PRAY TO ALL THE STRANGE GODS YOU WANT, BLIT...

WHUMPF!

WHEN A FIGHT STARTS, YOU SHOULD HIT PEOPLE WITH CHAIRS FIRST...

AND ASK QUESTIONS LATER!

TURG IS NO STRANGE GOD!

JAKA?

PEOPLE WHO ARE HIT WITH CHAIRS SHOULD HAVE THE GOOD MANNERS TO FALL DOWN!

STRIKE A BLOW FOR BOREALA, BROTHER!

DONE, BROTHER!

EXCUSE ME-- DO YOU KNOW WHERE I COULD FIND JAKA?

JAKA? THAT *WHORE*?! WHAT DO YOU WANT WITH *HER*, EH, *MIDGET*?

SAY-- WHAT'S GOING ON OVER THERE?

LOOKS LIKE A HERD OF GREY TEDDY-BEARS ARE BEATING UP ON THAT *BOREALAN* MERCENARY.

THUMP
THUMP
THUMP
THUMP
THUMP

THUMP
THUMP
THUMP
THUMP
THUMP

LIKE I SAID-- I THINK YOU'LL MAKE A CUTE COUPLE*

THAT MUST HURT.

AYE-- I DON'T THINK I'VE EVER SEEN ANYONE SWALLOW HIS OWN ARM UP TO THE ELBOW

TIME IS RUNNING OUT, TURG...

BUT WE HAVE ONE MORE WAY TO GET TO CEREBUS

GOOD DAY, DEAR JAKA--WE MEET AGAIN!

WE KNOW HE TOLD CEREBUS WHERE THE TREASURE IS HIDDEN IN THE TEMPLE.....WE NEED YOU TO FIND THAT OUT!

WE WILL PAY YOU TEN GOLD PIECES, NOW...

... AND CUT YOU IN FOR A PERCENTAGE OF THE TREASURE

AND IF JAKA SHOULD DECLINE YOUR "OFFER", E'LASS?

THEN, JAKA I WILL HAVE TO PREVAIL UPON TURG TO MAKE SURE YOU NEVER DANCE AGAIN!

JAKA ASKED YOU TO STAY BEHIND SO WE COULD... TALK.

CEREBUS LOVES THE LITTLE FRECKLE ON YOUR ELBOW.

I WANT-- I WANT YOU TO TELL ME WHERE... THE MAN YOU--

I'D LOVE TO LICK APRICOT BRANDY OUT OF YOUR NAVEL...

LOOK, CEREBUS-- JAKA HAS TO TELL YOU..... SOMETHING

IF CEREBUS HAD A NAVEL WOULD YOU LICK APRICOT BRANDY OUT OF IT?

OOOOOOOH

YOU DON'T LIKE APRICOT BRANDY?

THEY SAID THEY WOULD KILL JAKA IF....IF SHE DIDN'T= sniff= HELP THEM,

WHO- SAID- THEY- WOULD- KILL- JAKA?

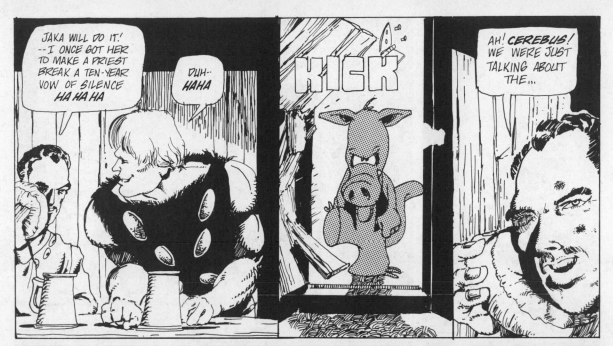

"...AND THEY HAD SAID THE GOLD WAS IN THE "TEMPLE OF THE BLACK SUN.""

TEMPLE OF THE BLACK SUN-- THAT'S NOT FAR FROM HERE

WITH THE MESSAGE I GOT FROM THE DYING MAN...

I NOW KNOW WHERE THE GOLD IS...!

CEREBUS HAS JUST HAD AN IDEA!

WE CAN GET THE GOLD! YOU AND I, JAKA -- IF IT'S THE REAL BLACK SUN TREASURE, YOU AND I CAN BE RICH! RICH BEYOND OUR WILDEST DREAMS!

WE CAN SEE THE WALL OF TSI, SMINA -- THE TCAPMIN KINGDOMS

BUT, IT MEANS YOU'LL HAVE TO STOP DANCING...

NO -- YOU CAN DANCE FOR ME!

I'LL BUY YOU A HOUSE!

AND JEWELS! I'LL BUY YOU A TON!

NO! TWO TONS!!

ALL THIS -- MORE -- WILL BE YOURS, JAKA... YOU JUST HAVE TO AGREE TO COME WITH ME... GOLD, JEWELS, TRAVEL...

YOU DON'T HAVE TO BRIBE JAKA, CEREBUS -- JAKA WANTS TO GO WITH YOU...

CEREBUS HASN'T BEEN THIS HAPPY SINCE HE BEHEADED HIS FIRST BOREALAN...

WE HAVE TO GET TO HIM, TURG. THOSE PILLS WILL BE WEARING OFF VERY SOON.

HE THINKS HE'S BEATEN US, TURG! *HAHAHA!*

DUH-- HAHAHA

LITTLE DOES HE SUSPECT THAT, EVEN *NOW* I'M WORKING ON AN INFALLIBLE MASTER PLAN! HE'LL FIND E'LASS CAN TAKE A PUNCH AND BOUNCE RIGHT....

TURG THINKS YOU SHOULD REST.

NONSENSE. WE HAVE BUSINESS TO DO.

WE'LL TRY BLUFFING HIM!

YOU WILL DELIVER THOSE SUPPLIES TO THE TAVERN IN AN HOUR, **AGREED?**

YES, SIR.

MAYHAP **CEREBUS** SHOULD TAKE A SMALL TRINKET TO JAKA...

...OR PERHAPS SOME FINE SILK TO CLOTHE HER...!

JAKA WILL BE SO **PLEASED.**

HMMM. MAGENTA OR AZURE BLUE I WONDER... I... I...uh...

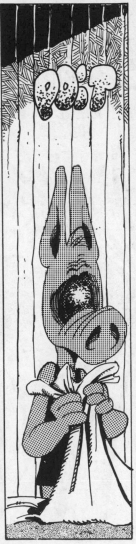

I WONDER WHAT **CEREBUS** WAS DOING LOOKING AT FOPPISH CLOTH WHEN HE HAS MONEY FOR ALE...

PERHAPS YOU SHOULD WAIT UNTIL YOUR NECK IS STRONG ENOUGH TO SUPPORT YOUR HEAD, E'LASS!

I'LL BE FINE TURG! I JUST NEED YOU TO GUIDE ME...

JAKA HAS MOVED TO ONE OF THESE ROOMS! CEREBUS IS PROBABLY WITH HER!

I'LL TRY THE FIRST ONE...

GOOD LUCK, E'LASS.

I KNOW YOU'RE IN THERE! '''

I FINALLY TRACKED YOU TO THIS...

OH.

BEAT ME UP CAREFULLY, WOULD YOU?

I HAVEN'T BEEN WELL LATELY.

TARIM! I MUST HAVE BEEN DRUNK-- I REMEMBER COMING HERE,...

BUT I DON'T REMEMBER *LEAVING*...

DOUBTLESS THE ALE WAS SOUR! CEREBUS WILL SAVE HIS GOLD FOR *ANOTHER* TAVERN!

DAMN THESE CITIES--- *CEREBUS* NEVER KNOWS WHAT AWAITS HIM AROUND ANY CORNER

CEREBUS! YOU'RE *BACK*!

JAKA WAS GETTING WORRIED!

CEREBUS KNOWS NO *JAKA*-- STAND ASIDE, *WENCH*!

CEREBUS! WHAT OF THE WALL OF TSI, SMINA -- THE TCAPMIN KINGDOMS?

WELL? WHAT OF THEM?

YOU REALLY DON'T... REMEMBER! I CAN *TELL*...

SOMETHING HAS....... HAPPENED ...TO YOU!

I'D LIKE YOU TO HAVE THIS.

EH? A BOTTLE OF *APRICOT BRANDY?* WHY WOULD....

SOME DAY -- SOME DAY, SWEET CEREBUS, YOU *WILL* REMEMBER WHY... AND YOU WILL *RETURN*.

AND JAKA WILL WAIT FOR THAT DAY, *BELOVED*. ...

EVEN IF IT TAKES THE *REST* OF HER LIFE!

140

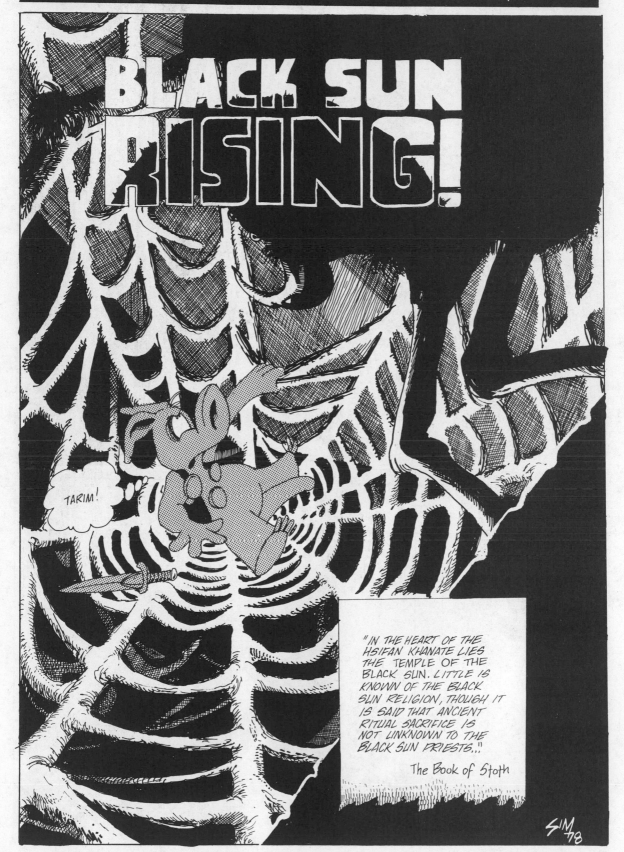

IT WOULD HAVE BEEN EASIER TO FOLLOW THE LOWLANDS TO THE SOUTH AND SWING BACK UP NORTH...

BUT CEREBUS IS A FOLLOWER OF THE "OLD WAYS", SO HE HAS TAKEN THE DIRECT ROUTE THROUGH A DOZEN MOUNTAIN PASSES AND ACROSS TREACHEROUS TERRAIN....

NOW, HE IS WITHIN SIGHT OF HIS GOAL

THE TEMPLE OF THE BLACK SUN!

AND THE BLACK SUN TREASURE CONTAINED THEREIN!

THE EARLY WINTER WINDS STING HIS EYES AS HE DISMOUNTS! THE AIR IS RICH WITH THE SMELL OF SORCERY, SO THE EARTH-PIG PAUSES TO TRY AND CATCH ANY RANDOM SOUNDS

I JUST— I SAY— I JUST *HAPPENED* TO HEAR ABOUT THIS HERE *"FESTIVAL OF THE BLACK SUN"*

AND IF THERE'S ANYTHING OLD ELROD IS A *PUSHOVER* FOR, IT'S A *BLACK SUN COCKTAIL*... SO I BOUGHT SOME DARK ALE, APRICOT BRANDY AND BOREALAN WHISKEY...

TELL YOU WHAT, SON— WHAT SAY YOU AND I WHIP UP A PITCHER OF *BLACK SUNS* AND GET A JUMP ON THE LOCAL YOKELS? WHAT SAY?

WHAT SAY, BOY? HUH? WHAT SAY?

LISTEN TO ME, YOU WHITE-SKINNED, RED-EYED *MORON!* THE *BLACK SUN* IS A CULT OF DEATH WORSHIPERS...

THE CELEBRATION OF THEIR RITES IS A *SECRET!* IF THEY FIND OUT WE'RE HERE THEY WILL *KILL* US! THEY ARE COMPLETELY RUTHLESS—DO YOU *UNDERSTAND? RUTHLESS!*

HEH-HEH-HEH!

HEH-HEH-HEH?

RUTHLESS? YOU GOT -- I SAY -- YOU GOT TAKEN IN -- DUPED, SON! THESE BOYS ARE NO MORE RUTHLESS THAN....

AAAA

W-WHAT -- I SAY -- W-WHAT IS THAT?!

ONE OF THEIR VICTIMS...

...IT'S A WARNING FOR TRESPASSERS...!

WARNING, EH? I TELL YOU WHAT -- YOU CAN FINISH OFF YOUR BUSINESS HERE AND I'LL MEET Y'ALL IN BOREALA WITH TWO ALES ABOUT A WEEK FROM....

AAK

CEREBUS HAS NEED OF YOU HERE -- IF YOU'RE FOUND WANDERING AROUND IT WILL LEAD THEM TO CEREBUS...

YOU'RE BARKING UP THE WRONG ALBINO, SON -- I'M NOBODY'S FLUNKY! --MORON, THAT IS! MY MOTHER DIDN'T RAISE ME TO BE A SECOND FIDDLE BLINK TWICE IF ANY OF THIS IS SINKING IN, SON... I COULD USE THE ENCOURAGEMENT!

SO WHICH ENTRANCE YOU THINK WE OUGHTA TRY?

HOW GO PREPARATIONS FOR THE RITES OF THE THIRD PHASE THIS EVENING.....?

ALL IS IN READINESS --THE FIVE SACRIFICES HAVE BEEN CHOSEN, DARK MAJESTY!

IS THERE NEWS OF THE PIT?

SOME GURGLING NOISES, BUT, AS YET, NO PHYSICAL MANIFESTATIONS OF THE BLACK SUN'S WILL....

THE FAITHFUL GROW RESTLESS, DARK MAJESTY!

AYE. THIS YEAR, THOUGH, WE SHALL SEE THE FORCE OF THE BLACK SUN...

...I KNOW WE SHALL!

I KNEW IT-- RUNNING AROUND ALL DAY IN THAT BUNNY SUIT HAS FINALLY FRIED THE BOY'S *FRONTAL LOBES*...

COMPULSIVE BEHAVIOUR IS ONE THING, BUT ONLY A REAL NUT WOULD BREAK INTO A PLACE LIKE THIS TO COUNT BRICKS--*STONE* THAT IS...

SURE HOPE HE FINDS IT WHATEVER IT IS-- BOY HIS AGE NEEDS TO FEEL *USEFUL*!

DON'T MEAN TO RAIN ON YOUR PARADE, SON, BUT MAYBE IF YOU TOLD ME WHAT YOU'RE LOOKING FOR, I COULD BUY YOU ONE-- DAY ATTENTION, BOY-- YOU'RE LETTING YOUR MIND WANDER...

CEREBUS DOESN'T WANT YOU TO MAKE *ANY* NOISE-- WHETHER YOU ARE QUIET AND *ALIVE* OR QUIET AND *DEAD* MAKES NO DIFFERENCE TO *CEREBUS*

THINK I'LL SCOUT AROUND FOR SOME LOOT OF MY OWN-- PLACE THIS OLD IS BOUND TO HAVE A SILVER TEA SERVICE *SOMEWHERE*!

WITHIN THE PIT, IT WATCHES AND WAITS, WITH A PATIENCE BORN OF *CENTURIES* THE TIME IS AT HAND AND ALREADY ITS VERY MOLECULES HUM WITH *ANTICIPATION...*

...OF THE COMING *SACRIFICES.* THOUGH MISSHAPEN, IT IS *SENTIENT...*

...AND SO, COMMENCES TO TRILL AN ANCIENT SONG OF *TRIUMPH!*

I'VE NEVER--I SAY NEVER SEEN SUCH POOR RELIGIOUS FANATICS....

I MUST HAVE WALKED HALFWAY TO THE *RED MARCHES* AND I STILL HAVEN'T FOUND SO MUCH AS A MISPLACED GOLD FILLING!

HE HAD READ COUNTLESS ANCIENT "TOMES OF THE BLACK SUN." FINALLY HE HAD FOUND THE OBSCURE DEITY HE NEEDED...

A FIGURE FROM HIS RELIGION'S DISTANT PAST-- ONE OF THE REVERED **NAMELESS ONES**...

THE COSTUME HE MADE WAS FAITHFUL TO ALL KNOWN DESCRIPTIONS OF THE DEITY...

WHEN HE APPEARED THIS EVENING BEFORE THE ASSEMBLED BROTHERS QUOTING ANCIENT PROPHECIES, HE WOULD BE HAILED AS A NEW GOD...

THEN HE WOULD NO LONGER BE MIT, THE FOUR FOOT PRIEST-- MIT THE FEEBLE! NO -- THEN HE WOULD BE...

THE NAMELESS GOD OF THE BLACK SUN...!

THIS IS -- I SAY -- THIS IS *DEPRESSING!* IT'S GETTING SO YOU CAN'T COUNT ON PRIESTS TO KEEP STOLEN GOLD AROUND SO'S A BODY CAN *STEAL* IT!

UNH?

THEY WERE SEEN TUNNELING UNDER THE EAST WALL...

IT WILL TAKE US FIFTEEN MINUTES TO SEAL THE TEMPLE...

THEN WE'LL GET THEM...

REMIND ME TO TALK TO THE *DARK MAJESTY* ABOUT BUYING A DECENT-LOOKING STATUE FOR THIS HALLWAY...

I DISCOVERED THIS CONCEALED ENTRYWAY A FEW MONTHS AGO...

THE REAR OF *THE PIT* -- I CAN WATCH THE CEREMONY

AND AT THE *APPROPRIATE* MOMENT, A COUPLE OF SMOKE BOMBS WILL AID MY *"RESURRECTION"*

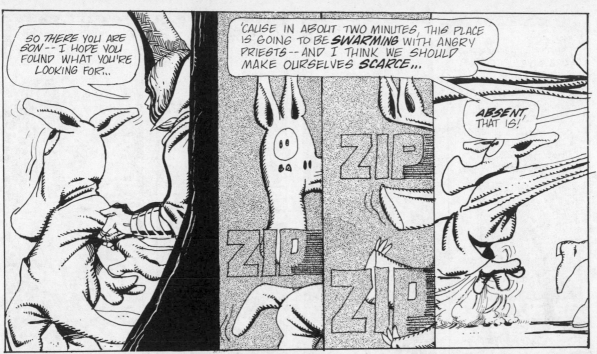

SO THERE YOU ARE SON -- I HOPE YOU FOUND WHAT YOU'RE LOOKING FOR...

'CAUSE IN ABOUT TWO MINUTES, THIS PLACE IS GOING TO BE *SWARMING* WITH ANGRY PRIESTS -- AND I THINK WE SHOULD MAKE OURSELVES *SCARCE*...

ABSENT, THAT IS!

ZIP ZIP ZIP

CEREBUS HAS FOUND HIS TREASURE, ALBINO! IN A FEW MINUTES WE'LL BE...

....Elrod?

WHY, THAT MORONIC HALF-WIT! THAT IDIOT IN ALBINO'S CLOTHING *I'LL...*

BUMP

CEREBUS WOULD LEAVE HIM TO THE PRIESTS IF CEREBUS' WASN'T AFRAID THEY WOULD ONLY *TORTURE* AND *KILL* HIM...

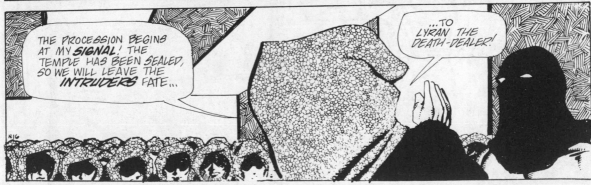

THE PROCESSION BEGINS AT MY *SIGNAL!* THE TEMPLE HAS BEEN SEALED, SO WE WILL LEAVE THE *INTRUDERS* FATE...

...TO *LYRAN THE DEATH-DEALER!*

YOU ARE, WITHOUT DOUBT, THE *STRANGEST* KID I'VE EVER MET, SON!

I LEAVE YOU ALONE FOR TEN -- *I SAY* TEN MINUTES AND Y'ALL GET WASTED AWAY TO SKIN AND BONES...

NOT TO MENTION THAT YOU FOUND TIME TO DYE YOUR BUNNY SUIT *WHITE!*

SPEAK UP SON -- YOU SOUND LIKE YOU'RE TALKING THROUGH AN INCH-THICK PIECE OF BURLAP!

AGITATE YOUR LEGS, BOY -- IF THOSE *PRIESTS* CATCH US, WE HAVEN'T GOT A PRAYER!

THAT'S A *JOKE* SON! GET IT? PRIESTS? PRAYER?

OH, NEVER MIND!

I KEEP THROWIN' 'EM SON AND YOU KEEP MISSIN' 'EM!

NICE BOY, BUT HE'S ABOUT AS MUCH FUN AS A *TOOTHACHE!*

HOLD ON, SON -- WE'VE -- *I SAY* -- WE'VE RUN ACROSS ENOUGH BLACK ROBES TO MAKE A SHROUD FOR *BOREALA*...

NOW JUST KEEP QUIET AND WE ....

AS ONE OF THE ANCIENT *NAMELESS ONES*, I COMMAND YOU TO SEIZE THIS *INFIDEL!*

152

LISTEN TO ME! I'M ELROD THE ALBINO AND AS THE ONLY RULER OF A DYING RACE IN THIS TEMPLE, I DEMAND THAT YOU ARREST THIS KID IN THE BUNNY SUIT!

I WISH HE HADN'T DONE THAT.

ENRAGED BY THE INTERRUPTION, THE BROTHERS OF THE BLACK SUN SURGE FORWARD...

THE SHORT ONE ...IT'S..... MIT?!

ELROD AND MIT, REALIZING THAT NEITHER COMMAND WOULD BE FOLLOWED, SEEK SEPARATE ESCAPE ROUTES...

I'LL GRAB MIT FIRST OF ALL...

AND THEN I'LL GO AFTER THE SKINNY TALL ONE

DAMNED ALBINO! IF I DON'T FIND HIM SOON THE FACT THAT I'M CARRYING TWENTY POUNDS OF UNCUT DIAMONDS IS GOING TO MAKE ME TOO CONTENT TO ENJOY DISMEMBERING HIM...

STOP IN THE NAME OF OUR DARK MAJESTY, TRAITOR!!

SINCE I CAN'T FIND AN IDIOT ALBINO, I'LL JUST HAVE TO SETTLE FOR A HOODED MORON!

IT'S VERY IMPORTANT WHEN YOU'RE A *DEATH-DEALER* TO KNOW WHEN YOUR OPPONENT HAS GOTTEN *LUCKY!*

YOU SHOULD ALWAYS GET RIGHT BACK UP AND TRY AGAIN...

HE WAS RIGHT BEHIND ME--I *KNOW* HE WAS RIGHT BEHIND ME--WHAT COULD HAVE *HAPPENED* TO HIM? MAYBE HE'S SETTING A TRAP FOR ME! THAT'S *PROBABLY* IT.

YOU SURE GOT A LUCKY PUNCH IN THERE, MIT-- YES! A REAL GOOD ONE! BUT THE FUN AND GAMES ARE *OVER!*

DON'T EXPECT ME TO GO EASY ON YOU BECAUSE YOU'RE SO SHORT-- INVOKING THE NAMELESS ONES WITH NO AUTHORIZATION FROM...

EVEN FOR A *PRIEST* YOU TALK TOO MUCH

UGH

FASCINATING THE *GIBBERISH* THESE HUMANS COME UP WITH...

CEREBUS WONDERS WHO THESE *NAMELESS ONES* ARE...OR WHO MIT IS FOR THAT MATTER!

154

THAT'S IT -- WHEN MIT CAN BEAT *LYRAN* UP, IT'S TIME TO RETIRE, GIVE UP RESIGN!

UNH! I CAN BARELY WALK!

I'LL TELL YOU, MY FRIEND, IT'S A *PRIEST-EAT-PRIEST* WORLD IN HERE! THERE'S ALWAYS *SOMEONE* WHO...

OH TARIM! IT'S HIM!

AAAAAAA

I DON'T -- I SAY-- I DON'T BELIEVE IT! A CORRIDOR THAT ISN'T DECORATED IN WALL-TO-WALL *PRIESTS!*

AHA!

THERE YOU ARE SON...!

ELROD! I'VE WANTED TO HAVE A WORD WITH YOU FOR THE LAST...

DON'T TRY TO APOLOGIZE, YOU TURNCOAT! ONCE I GET YOU OUT OF THIS BUNNY SUIT I'M GONNA TEACH Y'ALL A LESSON, SON!

ARE YOU COMING OR NOT, *ALBINO?* CEREBUS PLANS TO LEAVE BEFORE THE *PRIESTS...*

...*PRIESTS?*

OH NO! YOU ALL GOT ME WITH THAT ONE LAST TIME! NOT AGAIN! *NOSIREE!* I'D TRUST YOU ABOUT AS FAR AS I COULD THROW YOU...!

DAMNED ALBINO CONFUSED CEREBUS SO BADLY I FORGOT TO *DISMEMBER* HIM!

SOUNDS TO CEREBUS LIKE COMPANY IS COMING...

THE TEMPLE IS COMPOSED OF A SEEMINGLY ENDLESS SUCCESSION OF DOOR-WAYS, STAIRCASES AND CORRIDORS...

THE EARTH-PIG'S THEORY IS SOUND! KEEP AHEAD OF THE PRIESTS AND TRY TO PROCEED IN ONE GENERAL DIRECTION...

BUT WHAT HAPPENS WHEN YOU REACH THE BOTTOM OF ONE THOSE STAIRCASES, PASS THROUGH ONE OF THOSE DOORWAYS AND FIND YOURSELF FACED WITH A GAPING PIT?

A GAPING PIT FROM WHICH ISSUES AN ODDLY *DISTURBING* TRILLING SOUND...

156

MAYHAP *CEREBUS* CAN CLIMB DOWN A FEW FEET AND ESCAPE WHEN THE PRIESTS HAVE....

HE PLUMMETS INTO THE YAWNING BLACKNESS, THE SMELL OF SORCERY RICHER THAN EVER...

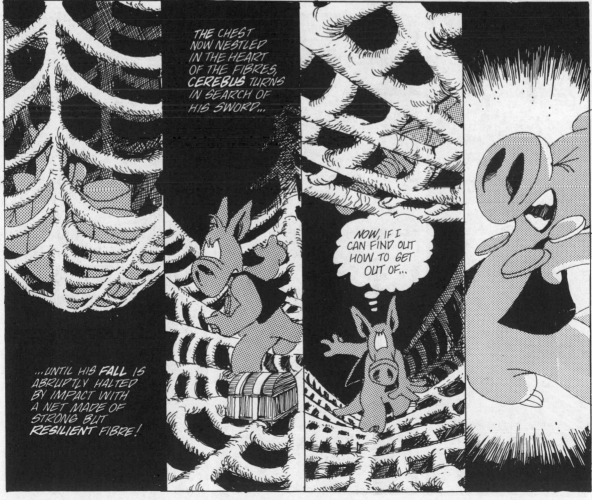

THE CHEST NOW NESTLED IN THE HEART OF THE FIBRES, *CEREBUS* TURNS IN SEARCH OF HIS SWORD...

...UNTIL HIS *FALL* IS ABRUPTLY HALTED BY IMPACT WITH A NET MADE OF STRONG BUT *RESILIENT* FIBRE!

NOW, IF I CAN FIND OUT HOW TO GET OUT OF...

EVEN AS THE **EXPLOSION** OF PAIN IN HIS BACK REGISTERS, CEREBUS **LEAPS** FOR A SAFER PERCH...

UPPERMOST IN HIS MIND IS THE **SWORD**! WITHOUT IT, HE HASN'T A CHANCE OF BEATING A BEAST OF SUCH **IMMENSE** SIZE AND...

...AND HE **CLUTCHES** AT THE ONLY STRAND VISIBLE!

INSTINCTS TAKE OVER AS THE **EARTH-PIG** FALLS THROUGH THE BLACKNESS

CEREBUS REALIZES HE HAS FALLEN SEVERAL HUNDRED METRES! CRISS-CROSSED WITH WEBS, THE PIT ENTRANCE IS VISIBLE ABOVE HIM...

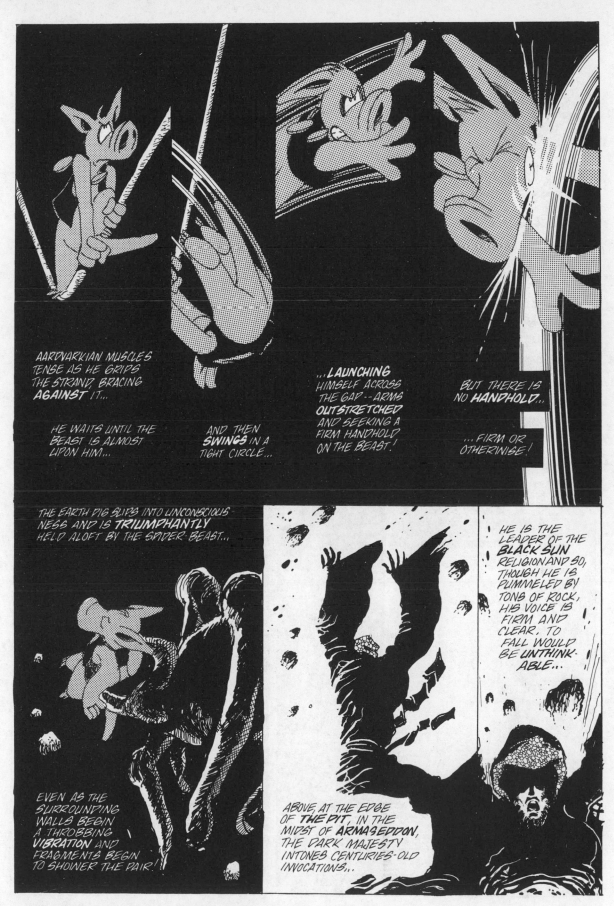

AARDVARKIAN MUSCLES TENSE AS HE GRIPS THE STRAND, BRACING **AGAINST** IT...

HE WAITS UNTIL THE BEAST IS ALMOST UPON HIM...

AND THEN **SWINGS** IN A TIGHT CIRCLE...

...**LAUNCHING** HIMSELF ACROSS THE GAP--ARMS **OUTSTRETCHED** AND SEEKING A FIRM HANDHOLD ON THE BEAST!

BUT THERE IS NO **HANDHOLD**...

...FIRM OR OTHERWISE!

THE EARTH-PIG SLIPS INTO UNCONSCIOUSNESS AND IS **TRIUMPHANTLY** HELD ALOFT BY THE SPIDER-BEAST...

EVEN AS THE SURROUNDING WALLS BEGIN A THROBBING **VIBRATION** AND FRAGMENTS BEGIN TO SHOWER THE PAIR!

HE IS THE LEADER OF THE **BLACK SUN** RELIGION AND SO, THOUGH HE IS PUMMELED BY TONS OF ROCK, HIS VOICE IS FIRM AND CLEAR. TO FALL WOULD BE **UNTHINKABLE**...

ABOVE, AT THE EDGE OF **THE PIT**, IN THE MIDST OF **ARMAGEDDON**, THE DARK MAJESTY INTONES CENTURIES-OLD INVOCATIONS...

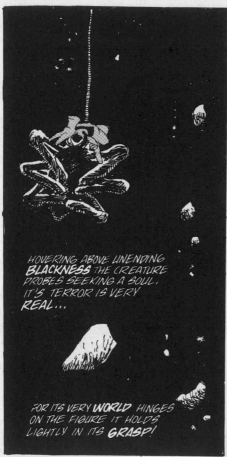

HOVERING ABOVE UNENDING **BLACKNESS** THE CREATURE PROBES SEEKING A SOUL. IT'S TERROR IS VERY **REAL**...

FOR ITS VERY **WORLD** HINGES ON THE FIGURE IT HOLDS LIGHTLY IN ITS **GRASP!**

ITS HIGH-PITCHED **TRILLING** ENDS...

AND IS **REPLACED** BY A LOW AND MOURNFUL **DIRGE!**

AT THE SURFACE, THE TUMULT ENDS AS ABRUPTLY AS IT BEGAN...

AND IS REPLACED BY A DISTANT AND OMINOUS **ROARING**...

OUTSIDE, STONE GRINDS AGAINST STONE! THE AIR SEEMS TO GLOW LIKE **LIQUID FIRE**...THE GROUND HEAVES AND BUCKLES.

CEREBUS FEELS A CURIOUS SENSATION OF **FALLING**....

AND NOTICES AN EIGHT LEGGED **MONSTROSITY** SPIRALLING INTO OBLIVION BELOW HIM...

EVEN AS EVERYTHING **EXPLODES** IN A BLINDING FLASH OF WHITE LIGHT!

MY PEOPLE --GONE!

I WAS ONLY SAVED BE-CAUSE I WAS FORCED TO ESCAPE!

BUT WHAT IS TO BECOME OF MIT NOW THAT ....

CEREBUS, MY BOY! YOU ALL MADE IT! YOU'RE ALIVE -- FUNCTIONAL THAT IS!

Y'EVEN FOUND TIME TO DYE YOUR BUNNY SUIT WHITE AGAIN...!

I KNOW WHAT YOU'RE GOING TO SAY, SON -- YOU'RE GOING TO SAY THAT THIS IS ALL YOUR FAULT... DON'T WORRY ABOUT IT, BOY...

IF A KID IN A BUNNY SUIT CAN'T DESTROY A CENTURIES-OLD DEATH CULT FROM TIME-TO-TIME, LIFE WOULDN'T BE WORTH LIVING!

JUST TO SHOW YOU OLD ELROD'S HEART IS IN THE RIGHT PLACE, I'M GOING TO LET YOU BE MY PERSONAL VALET FOR THE TRIP SOUTH -- SIDEKICK THAT IS!

WE'LL START BY TEACHING Y'ALL HOW TO MIX A BLACK SUN!

IT IS AN HOUR BEFORE THE **EARTH-PIG** RISES. WAS HE HURLED CLEAR BY THE BLAST? RESCUED BY A PRIEST?

HE NEITHER KNOWS NOR **CARES!**

HE HAS JUST **LOST** A KING'S RANSOM IN DIAMONDS....AND ALMOST HIS **LIFE** AS WELL...

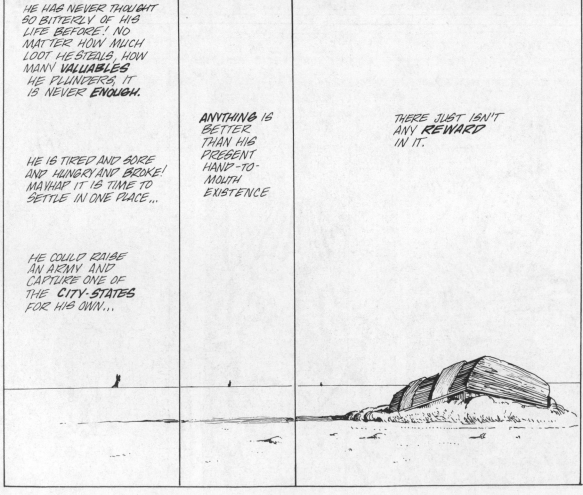

HE HAS NEVER THOUGHT SO BITTERLY OF HIS LIFE BEFORE! NO MATTER HOW MUCH LOOT HE STEALS, HOW MANY **VALUABLES** HE PLUNDERS, IT IS NEVER **ENOUGH.**

HE IS TIRED AND SORE AND HUNGRY AND BROKE! MAYHAP IT IS TIME TO SETTLE IN ONE PLACE...

HE COULD RAISE AN ARMY AND CAPTURE ONE OF THE **CITY-STATES** FOR HIS OWN...

ANYTHING IS BETTER THAN HIS PRESENT HAND-TO-MOUTH EXISTENCE

THERE JUST ISN'T ANY **REWARD** IN IT.

THE SURROUNDINGS ARE FAMILIAR, THOUGH SUBTLY **DIFFERENT**

THE WEB IS LESS SUBSTANTIAL, SO CEREBUS IS NOT SURPRISED AS IT SHREDS IN HIS HANDS

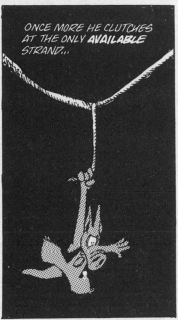

ONCE MORE HE CLUTCHES AT THE ONLY **AVAILABLE** STRAND...

day OF the EARTH-PIG!

THIS TIME, **HOWEVER**, IT SNAPS!

THIS TIME...

...THERE IS NO **FURTHER** STRAND TO GRAB HOLD OF...

IN SHORT...

THIS TIME IS...

...A COMPLETELY DIFFERENT STORY!

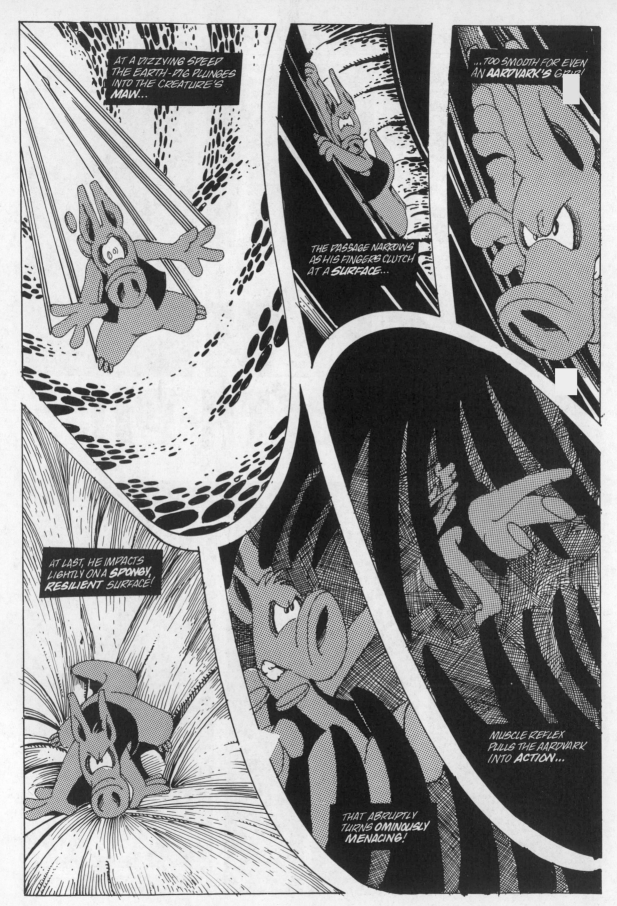

STILL, THE AARDVARK STRAINS UNTIL HIS BREATH COMES IN RAGGED GASPS AND HIS HEART BEATS A STACCATO IN HIS EARS...

EVEN AS THE MADDENINGLY TENACIOUS **FORCE** MAKES FURTHER ACTION **FUTILE!**

CAREFUL THERE! THAT WOUND ON ITS LITTLE BACK LOOKS **SERIOUS!**

CAN'T YOU JUST SORT OF HOLD HIM **DOWN?**

I'D BE GLAD TO STEP ASIDE AND GIVE YOU A CRACK, **YOUR LORDSHIP...**

IT ISN'T TALL ENOUGH TO BE A **BOREALAN!**

THOUGH IT **IS** UGLY ENOUGH TO BE ONE!

WHAT DO YOU INTEND TO DO WITH HIM, **LORD?...**

WATCH OUT FOR THE...

UMPH

...TAIL.

OH **I** DON'T KNOW... IF THE FUR ISN'T TOO **COARSE,** I MIGHT HAVE IT MADE INTO A **BATH ROBE** ...

OTHERWISE, I'LL HAVE IT **STUFFED** AND SENT HOME TO **FATHER...**

THE BEAST FIGHTS LIKE OUR **BEST** MEN...

HE DESERVES THE HONOUR HE IS **DUE...**

OH VERY WELL—I'LL HAVE IT DECORATED WITH FULL MILITARY HONOURS...

...THEN I'LL HAVE IT MADE INTO A BATH ROBE.

TAKE HIM TO MY TENT...

THE SITUATION WORSENS, YOUR LORDSHIP. WITH GREAT HUMILITY, I WOULD SUGGEST WE NEED A NEW COURSE OF ACTION...

WE SHOULD ATTACK THE HGIFAN OUTPOST NOW

IF WE WAIT THEY WILL HAVE TIME TO FORTIFY...

I'M THE KING'S SON AND IT IS MY DECREE THAT WE MUST WAIT FOR A SNOWSTORM!...

AT LEAST THEN WE WON'T HAVE TO LOOK AT ALL THE ICKY BLOOD ON THE SNOW!

THE MEN, SIR-- THEY -- A SOLDIER IS A PROUD PERSON. HE WANTS STRONG LEADERSHIP! AS A CONNIPTIN...

THE MEN! WHAT DO THEY KNOW OF MY BURDEN...

I AM THE SON OF A GOD IN-CAR-NATE! MY PERSONAL MYSTIC DECLARED ME A GOD AS WELL...

SNORT

...AND GAVE ME A LARGE BAG OF WHITE 'POWDER OF THE GODS' TO AID ME...

THANK YOU FOR THIS LITTLE TALK CAPTAIN...IT WAS SO BORING IT WAS PROBABLY GOOD FOR ME...

NOW BE A GOOD FELLOW AND RUN ALONG...

YES, SIR!..

HE FEELS THE ENERGY IN HIS BODY DIMINISH AS HIS LIMBS BEGIN TO SHAKE INVOLUNTARILY

HIS BONDS GRIP MORE FIRMLY THAN BEFORE, ROOTING THE EARTH-PIG TO THE SPOT...

YOU LEFT WORD THAT YOU WISHED TO SEE ME, *COMMANDER?*

AYE *CAPTAIN*-- DO COME IN...

EVEN SO, HIS RAGE BUILDS AND, THOUGH LESS *FREQUENTLY* THAN BEFORE...

AARDVARK MUSCLES CONTINUE TO TEST THEIR RESTRAINTS.

IT'S AN INFECTION IN THE WOUND··EVEN SO, HE'S MAKING AN *EXTRAORDINARY* RECOVERY! IN AN HOUR HE'LL SNAP HIS BONDS LIKE WOVEN GRASS...

I HAVE NO *INTEREST* IN HIS LORDSHIP'S PETS. IF YOU'LL *EXCUSE* ME...

IF YOU DON'T WISH TO DISCUSS HIS *PET'S* FUTURE...

WHAT ABOUT HIS *LORDSHIP'S* FUTURE?

UNABLE TO RUN, HE CEASES HIS STRUGGLES, BUILDING HIS STRENGTH FOR THE INEVITABLE **CONFRONTATION**...

HE HEARS VOICES, NOW, ODDLY MUFFLED AND **INCOHERENT.** "ENEMIES" IS HIS ONLY CONCLUSION...

THE PLAN IS **RISKY**... I KNOW--

IT'S **FOOLHARDY!**... I'M A SOLDIER AND I CAN TELL YOU THAT AN ARMY IS A DELICATE THING! A FEW BAD WORDS FROM A HANDFUL OF MEN WITH **INFLUENCE** WOULD BRING THIS WHOLE MESS DOWN AROUND OUR...

CAPTAIN TURL! OHH, CAP-TAIN! COME OUT COME OUT WHEREVER YOU ARE! I'D LIKE A CUP OF GOAT'S MILK ...

...YOU **KNOW** HOW CRANKY I GET WITHOUT MY GOAT'S MILK!

WE'LL START TOMORROW MORNING...

...RISKY?

168

TOMORROW?! THE BEAST'S WOUND IS TOO SERIOUS FOR WITHSTANDING *STRESS* ...I'M A *DOCTOR*-- NOT A *MAGICIAN!*

WE'RE IN DANGER OF LOSING THIS TERRITORY! WE'LL NEED TO BE *SECURE* IF OUR PLAN IS TO WORK...

I'M A *DOCTOR* NOT A *GENERAL* THE WELFARE OF MY...

WE CAN'T *AFFORD* TO WAIT! IF WE FALTER NOW, WE MAY NEVER HAVE ANOTHER CHANCE! *THE TIME IS RIGHT!*

I'M A *DOCTOR* NOT A *TIME-KEEPER!*

EITHER-THE-PLAN-GOES-INTO-EFFECT TOMORROW-MORNING ...

...OR-I'LL-HAVE-YOUR-TONGUE-CUT-OUT!

I'M A *DOCTOR* NOT A *MARTYR!* ...

...WE'LL BE READY AT *DAWN!*

170

MOMENTS LATER, FOOTSTEPS **CRUNCH** THROUGH THE LATE NOVEMBER SNOWS...

HE IGNORES THE FOUR BODIES SPRAWLED IN THE SNOW AND THE REDDISH POOLS AROUND THEM...

INSTEAD, HE FOLLOWS THE SOUND OF IRREGULAR BREATHING TO ITS SHORT, GREY AND FURRY SOURCE...

HMMM! RESPIRATION AND PULSE *RAPID* BUT STRONG! THE WOUND IS OPEN AGAIN...

...BUT THE INFECTION HAS ALMOST STOPPED SPREADING...

EXCELLENT!

LITTLE GREY FRIEND...

...YOU'RE IN FOR QUITE A *SURPRISE* WHEN YOU WAKE UP!

IF NOTHING *ELSE,* YOU'RE AN *ENTHUSIASTIC* WORKER.

ARE YOU **SURE** HE'S MANACLED TIGHTLY? HEALED, HE HAS ENOUGH STRENGTH TO . . .

AH, HE'S COMING **AROUND** . . .

GOOD MORROW, **YOUR MAJESTY**

MAJESTY? WHAT MANNER OF SORCERY IS **THIS?**

HOW DID **CEREBUS** COME HERE?

THE STORY IS RELATED OF HOW HE WAS DISCOVERED WANDERING THE SNOW FIELDS -- OF HIS DEFEAT OF THE HSIFAN BORDER RAIDERS! **CEREBUS** RECALLS HIS BATTLE WITH THE SPIDER BEAST IN THE TEMPLE OF THE **BLACK SUN!** THE PAIN IN HIS BACK REMINDS HIM OF THE DAYS OF CONFUSION FOLLOWING THE BATTLE;' HIS MIND IN A **WHIRL,** HE HAD BEEN UNABLE TO FIND HIS WAY TO THE COAST AS HE HAD PLANNED. THOUGH THE COMMANDER TRIES TO EXPLAIN "DOCTOR", "INFECTION" AND "FEVER", CEREBUS ATTRIBUTES THEM TO ONE OF THE NEW DEGENERATIVE SORCERY DISCIPLINES AND LISTENS NO FURTHER . . .

THE MEN ARE QUITE TAKEN WITH YOUR ONE MAN **SLAUGHTER** OF THOSE TWENTY-FIVE BORDER RAIDERS . . .

I'D OFFER YOU SOME WINE, BUT I CAN SEE YOU'RE ALL TIED UP . . .

I THOUGHT YOU SAID **CEREBUS** HAD KILLED **FOUR** MEN . . . .

OH, **THAT.**

WE THOUGHT TWENTY-FIVE WOULD BE MORE IMPRESSIVE, SO WE GOT TWENTY-ONE OF OUR OWN ADVANCE TROOPS, DRESSED THEM IN HSIFAN GARB AND **DECAPITATED** THEM.

WHAT YOU LACK IN HEROISM YOU MAKE UP IN **BRUTALITY?**

EXACTLY.

THAT **STILL** LEAVES "WHY?"

WE CONNIPTINS HAVE BEEN DRIVEN NORTH FOR TWO CENTURIES BY THE **HSIFAN**...

OUR MEN REFUSE TO FIGHT FOR LEADERS MORE CONCERNED WITH PLEASURE THAN THEIR **HERITAGE**...

WHEN YOU TURNED UP I SAW YOUR **LEADERSHIP** POTENTIAL, AND FELT YOU WERE THE PERFECT CHOICE TO LEAD THE **CONNIPTIN**...

I CAN SEE A DAY ALL CONNIPTINS WILL UNITE ...A DAY WHEN WE WILL AGAIN LIVE IN OUR SACRED **HOMELAND**!

I CAN SEE A DAY WHEN IEST WILL AGAIN BE OURS! I CAN SEE A DAY WHEN GOLDEN STATUES WILL BE RAISED IN OUR HONOUR...

A-HUNH! A-HUNH! A-HUNH!

I CAN SEE A DAY WHEN YOU'RE PUT AWAY IN A RUBBER **ROOM**!

THESE SOUTHLANDS --THEY'RE **WEALTHY** THEN?

NO, **IMPOVERISHED**. THE GOLD RESERVES ARE DEPLETED... EACH SPRING PRODUCES A SMALLER CROP THAN THE ONE BEFORE...

DISEASE IS **RAVAGING** THE PEOPLE...

THEN WHY **RECAPTURE** THEM?

FOR THE CONNIPTIN **IDEALS**...

MIGHT MAKES **RIGHT**...

MIGHT FOR **RIGHT**!

MIGHT FOR **MIGHT**!

RIGHT FOR **MIGHT**!

FIGHT! FIGHT! FIGHT!

I DON'T KNOW ABOUT **WARRIORS**...

...BUT THE CONNIPTINS SEEM TO MAKE GOOD **CHEERLEADERS**.

IF YOU'LL **AGREE** TO LEAD US, I CAN PROMISE THAT CONNIPTINS ALL ACROSS THE SOUTHLANDS WILL FLOCK TO FOLLOW US...

YOU WILL BE **REVERED** AS A GOD-- WAITED ON HAND AND FOOT! YOUR VERY WORDS WILL BE LAW AS YOU SPEAK THEM! THE PEOPLE WILL SING OF...

COMMANDER -- HIS LORDSHIP IS HEADED THIS WAY!

QUICKLY, MAN!

GIVE ME A HAND WITH THE BOX!

WHAT IN **TARIM'S** NAME ARE YOU GOING TO DO WITH A ....

HEY!

WHY -- YOUR **LORDSHIP**!!

WHAT A **PLEASANT** SURPRISE!

6X!#&6 X!!#8!6

AACK!

176

I DECIDED THAT BEING AMONG MORTALS MIGHT AMUSE MY *OMNIPOTENT* SELF FOR A WHILE...

WHAT IS IN THE BOX, *COMMANDER*?

IT'S A *WOLF*, YOUR LORDSHIP! WE'RE TRAINING IT AS A *WATCH-WOLF*!

I SEE. AND MY *GREYBEAST*... HAVE YOU HAD IT MADE INTO A BATH ROBE AS I ≶*SNORT*≶ ...COMMANDED?

WATCH-WOLF?

YES, YOUR *LORDSHIP*!

I THINK YOU'LL BE *PLEASED* WITH THE QUALITY...

AH!

VERY *NICE*...

VERY NICE *INDEED*!

DANG

I AM *MOST* PLEASED...TELL THE MEN I'M AUTHORIZING DOUBLE RATIONS OF CHOCOLATE GRUEL FOR THE EVENING MEAL...

YOU ARE TOO KIND YOUR *LORDSHIP*...

I *KNOW*. IT'S MY ONLY FLAW.

TARIM!

YOUR LORDSHIP?

NOT *NOW*, IDIOT-- TARIM AND THE OTHER GODS ARE IN NEED OF MY AID IN A GREAT *GOD WAR!!*

I'M COMING, TARIM! HOLD ONTO YOUR THUNDERBOLTS!

WHEW! FOR A MINUTE I THOUGHT THAT WE...

HI THERE...

...REMEMBER ME?

WHO IN *TARIM'S* NAME WAS...

OUR *GLORIOUS* LEADER.

HE IS THE SON OF *HEZZRETH*... WE HAVE LED HIM TO BELIEVE THAT YOU WERE MADE INTO THAT *BATH-ROBE*...

IT WAS *IMPOSSIBLE* FOR US TO KILL *HIS LORDSHIP* AND HAVE YOU FORMALLY INSTALLED AS OUR NEW LEADER...

HEZZRETH'S FORCES WOULD HAVE CLOSED IN AND HOUNDED US TO THE GATES OF *IEST* ITSELF...

SO YOU WISH **CEREBUS** TO TAKE OVER FROM THIS **MORON?**

WE'LL CONTINUE SENDING REPORTS TO KING HEZZRETH OF OUR PROGRESS -- CREDITING IT TO HIS SON'S **LEADERSHIP**...

THE CHANGE FROM FOPPISH VEGETABLE TO DARING GENERAL SHOULD PLEASE OLD HEZZRETH **IMMENSELY**...

UNTIL WE TAKE BACK IEST, HIS LORDSHIP'S THUMBPRINT WILL BE REQUIRED ON THOSE REPORTS. AFTER THAT HE WILL BE **KILLED** ....

AND YOU WILL BE CROWNED **CEREBUS THE FIRST** -- RULER OF THE **NEW CONNIPTIN EMPIRE!**

AND IF CEREBUS SHOULD **REFUSE?**

THAT COULD PROVE **DIFFICULT** ...

THE MEN HAVE THIS ...uh... **QUIRK.**

QUIRK?

BY CONNIPTIN LAW, ANYONE CHOSEN AS LEADER WHO REFUSES THE HONOUR IS ... **DISEMBOWELLED.**

IS CEREBUS *READY*?

YES! WE HAD A LITTLE TROUBLE GETTING THE ARMOUR TO FIT ...

..., BUT HE'S READY. HIS *LORDSHIP*...?

..., SHOULD BE COMMUNING WITH THE GODS FOR SOME *TIME*. I LEFT HIM WITH A GRAM OF WHITE POWDER IN EACH NOSTRIL!

RIGHT.

MEN OF CONNIPTIN!

I GIVE YOU YOUR NEW LEADER ...

AND FUTURE MONARCH OF THE NEW CONNIPTIN EMPIRE ....

A WAVE OF SOUND, RISING IN VOLUME, A SUSTAINED ROAR VIOLENT ENOUGH TO CHALLENGE THE GODS, GREETS THE NEW CONNIPTIN GOD KING

THE ROAR PERSISTS, GRADUALLY, DEAFENINGLY BECOMING A WAR CHANT THAT SHAKES THE MOUNTAINS THEMSELVES; "*CEREBUS! CER-EBUS!*"

MEN OF CONNIPTIN! TOMORROW, WE MARCH TO THE SOFIM RIVER! BOATS BEING PREPARED NOW WILL BEAR US *SOUTHWARD* ...

THERE WE WILL CONQUER THE PORT CITY OF *IMESH* TAKING WHAT LOOT THERE IS TO BE HAD...

ALL WHO PLEDGE LOYALTY TO *CEREBUS* WILL BE MADE MEMBERS OF OUR ARMY,...

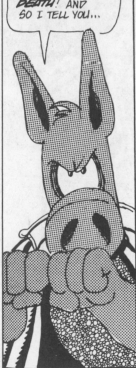

ALL WHO REMAIN LOYAL TO THE *HSIFAN KHANATE* WILL BE PUT TO *DEATH!* AND SO I TELL YOU...

IF YOUR MAJESTY PLEASES, PERHAPS YOU HAVE SOME WORDS OF *INSPIRATION* FOR THE MEN...?

EH? OH -- OF COURSE

DON'T SCREW IT UP OR CEREBUS WILL HAVE YOU ALL FLAYED ALIVE!

MAKE A NOTE TO START DIPLOMACY LESSONS FOR *HIS MAJESTY* TOMORROW...

CEREBUS KNOWS THE WAYS OF MEN TOO WELL! THE COMMANDER BETRAYS HIS AMBITION WITH EVERY WORD! HE WISHES THE **AARDVARK** TO BE A SWORD-WIELDING PUPPET RULER...

ESCAPE SHOULD BE EASY, BUT MUCH DEPENDS ON WHETHER **CEREBUS** CAN REACH THE SOFIM! BEFORE THE MOON RISES...

SMAK

LINH?

YOUR HIGHNESS? IS THERE...

CRAK

SECONDS LATER, CEREBUS HAS SNATCHED UP A HEAVY CLOAK AND PLUNGES OFF INTO THE NIGHT...

HE HAS BARELY GONE FIFTY YARDS, WHEN **CEREBUS** STOPS IN HIS TRACKS...

THE MEN HAD PLEDGED LOYALTY TO **CEREBUS** --NOT THE COMMANDER...

THEY WOULD FOLLOW THE **EARTH-PIG**...

BUT IF HE **LEFT** THEY WOULD BE AFTER HIS BLOOD BY MORNING...

THE PARADOX SINKS IN SLOWLY AS **INSTINCT** AND **REASON** JOCKEY FOR POSITION IN THE AARDVARK'S BRAIN...

INSTINCT DEMANDS THAT HE ESCAPE FROM ANY PRISON--"CEREBUS CALLS NO MAN 'MASTER'"...

REASON DEMANDS THAT HE NOT TURN HIS BACK ON WARM FOOD, GOOD WINE, A SOFT BED AND A CHANCE FOR BATTLE...

A LOW GROWL RUMBLES IN HIS THROAT! SELF-EXAMINATION APPEALS TO CEREBUS ABOUT AS MUCH AS DEBATING THEOLOGY WITH A PANROVIAN MONK...

HE CONCLUDES THAT THE NIGHT IS TOO COLD FOR SUCH IDIOCY... HE WILL PUT OFF DECIDING ON A COURSE OF ACTION FOR A WHILE...

UNBIDDEN, THE THOUGHT COMES: "NO DECISION IS A DECISION"...

IN ANSWER, CEREBUS DECIDES TO **LOBOTOMIZE** HIMSELF IF HIS BRAIN DOESN'T LEARN TO MIND ITS OWN BUSINESS!

BRIEFLY, CEREBUS THINKS THERE MIGHT BE MORE TO LIFE THAN WINE, FOOD, A WARM BED AND A SACK OF GOLD...

MAYHAP TWO SACKS OF GOLDZ

THAT ANSWER IS SO OBVIOUS, CEREBUS IS WILLING TO BET IT ISN'T THE RIGHT ONE...

YOUR HIGHNESS -- AS A CONNIPTIN WARRIOR I WANT TO KNOW WHY YOU JUST NOW ATTACKED ME AND FLED ACROSS THE SNOW...

THE IDEALS OF THE CONNIPTIN DEMAND THAT...

MIGHT MAKES RIGHT!

MIGHT FOR RIGHT!

MIGHT FOR MIGHT!

RIGHT FOR MIGHT!

FIGHT, FIGHT, FIGHT!

IF CEREBUS IS SUPPOSED TO LEAD THESE LOONIES ....

SOMEONE IS GOING TO HAVE TO EXPLAIN ALL THAT GIBBERISH TO HIM....

FIN

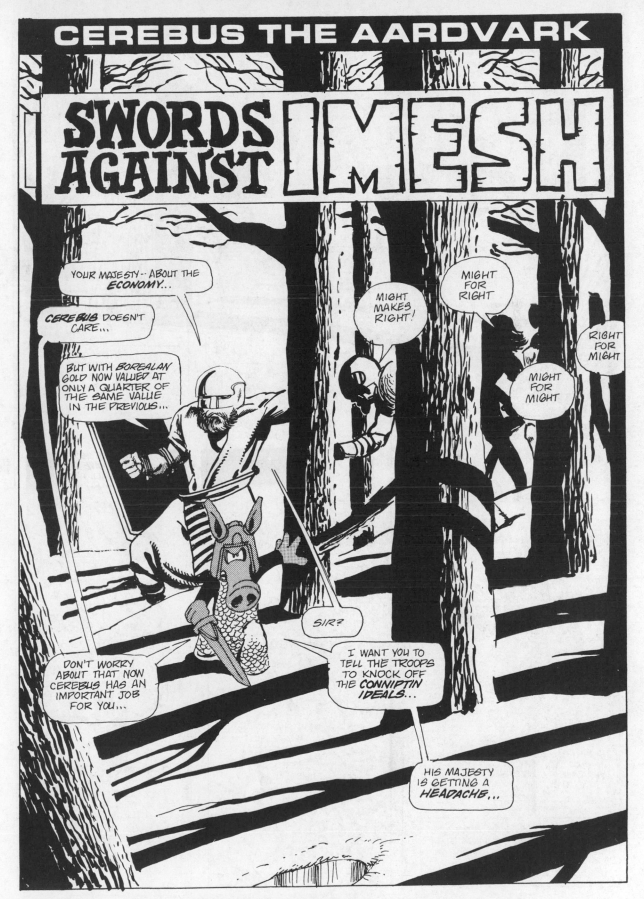

SO MANY YEARS SINCE HE HAD SEEN *IMESH*... THOUGH NONE HAD EVER TAKEN THE CITY FROM THE REAR, CEREBUS BELIEVED IT *POSSIBLE*...

THE HSIFAN HAVEN'T POSTED SENTRIES ON THE SOUTH WALL IN YEARS...

WE'LL MAKE OUR WAY AROUND TO THE GATE! STAY *CLOSE* TO THE WALL AND THEY SHOULDN'T SEE US.

AND IF THEY DO?

IF THEY DO, YOU CAN STOP WORRYING ABOUT THE VALUE OF *BOREALAN* GOLD AND START WORRYING ABOUT YOUR NECK...

THE GATE IS THE SOFT UNDER-BELLY OF *IMESH*! IF WE CAN SURPRISE THE GUARDS AND GET *INSIDE*...

NAUGHT WILL STAND IN OUR WAY, SAVE *UNARMED* CITIZENS OF THE CITY...

EVEN AS HE SPEAKS, CEREBUS WONDERS IF IT *IS* POSSIBLE! WITH HAND-PICKED TROOPS *PERHAPS*...

BUT THE CONNIPTINS LACK WAR MACHINES, BOWMEN, PIKEMEN -- TO LAY SIEGE TO EVEN A *RAVAGED* CITY LIKE IMESH WITH CUT-AND-THRUST SWORDS SEEMS THE *HEIGHT* OF FOLLY...

JUST WHAT CEREBUS ALWAYS WANTED -- TO DIE AS REIGNING KING OF THE *CHEERLEADERS*

MIGHT FOR MIGHT

RIGHT FOR MIGHT

RIGHT FOR RIGHT

FIGHT FIGHT FIGHT

TIGHT AGAINST THE EAST WALL, THE CONNIPTIN FORCES SURGE FORWARD

RIGHT FOR MIGHT

MIGHT FOR MIGHT

HEY-- WATCH WHO YOU'RE SHOVING

SHHH

CEREBUS SHOULD HAVE CHOSEN A SCHOOL FOR THE DEAF AS THE FIRST CONQUEST!

WAP

HERE!-- *YOU* WEAR THAT CAST-IRON NIGHT-SHIRT FOR A FEW HOURS...

BUT, YOUR MAJESTY-- *SURELY...*

AAAG!

OUT OF MY WAY, BISON BREATH!

THE WHOLE LOT OF YOU CAN *FORAGE* FOR GAME AND WATER -- OR *UNICORNS* AND FAIRY DUST IF YOU WISH...

MEANWHILE, CEREBUS WILL SHOW YOU HOW A *TRUE* WARRIOR TAKES A CITY...

YOUR MAJESTY!

THE CONNIPTINS *ALWAYS FOLLOW* THEIR KING!

STOP!

IF THERE ARE ANY CAPABLE OF FOLLOWING *CEREBUS...*

...THEY ARE WELCOME TO *DO* SO!

CEREBUS WONDERS IF THAT OLD TOAD, *GARSK*, IS STILL CAPTAIN OF THE GUARDS

TARIM! I'VE A FEW OLD SCORES TO SETTLE WITH HIM...

HMM! NO GUARDS ON THE *WALL* ANYWAY! FIRST, CEREBUS WILL HAVE TO FIND SOME TALKATIVE CITIZEN TO WAYLAY...

ONCE I HAVE AN IDEA OF THE TROOP STRENGTH, CEREBUS CAN DECIDE HOW BEST TO TAKE...

unh?

"TARIM" MUTTERS THE EARTH PIG "FIRST THE GATE IS MISSING AND NOW IT'S THE WHOLE DAMN *CITY!"* GONE ARE THE WINDING STREETS AND ANCIENT BUILDINGS OF THE AARDVARK'S YOUTH! THE PERIMETER OF THE CITY IS COMPOSED OF CRUDE STONE BUILDINGS WHILE THE CORE IS DOMINATED BY A HUGE ALTAR SWARMING WITH WORKERS AND MASONS! IN POINT OF FACT, THE WHOLE CITY'S ENERGIES SEEM DIRECTED TOWARD THE ALTAR AND THE STRANGE STONE CONSTRUCTION UPON IT...

THEY MUST ALL BE *INSANE!*

NONE BUT *MADMEN* WOULD TEAR DOWN THE RAM AND PEACOCK TAVERN...

WELL- CEREBUS IS HERE TO CONQUER *IMESH*-- NOT TO MOURN THE PASSING OF ITS HISTORIC *LANDMARKS*...

EVEN SO...

CEREBUS WOULD HAVE GIVEN MUCH TO SEE WHAT SURFACED WHEN THEY DEMOLISHED THE RED CRESCENT QUARTER

CLOVIS' INSTEP! THEY'RE ALL CARRYING STONES! EVERYONE IN THE WHOLE CITY IS BUILDING THAT.... THAT...

TO HELL WITH TROOP STRENGTH -- THE FIRST THING *CEREBUS* HAS TO FIND OUT IS WHAT THESE IDIOTS ARE *BUILDING!*

AHA! A LIKELY-LOOKING STRAGGLER FOR CEREBUS TO *BROW-BEAT*...

THESE *IMESHITES* ARE SCRAWNY, BUT SEEM TO MAKE UP FOR IT WITH THEIR SPEED...

I AM *CEREBUS* THE AARDVARK -- I WOULD HAVE INFORMATION FROM...

I'M LATE!

NO TIME! NO TIME!

IF CEREBUS BELIEVED THAT *ACTUALLY* HAPPENED HE'D GRAB THAT SKINNY FOOL AND BREAK HIS...

=PSSST=

SEDRA HAS THE INFORMATION YOU *SEEK*, CUTE GREY ONE...

BUT *FIRST* YOU HAVE TO CATCH HER...

CEREBUS *WILL* CATCH YOU WENCH...

HE'S WILLING TO BET HE'LL *REGRET* IT...

BUT CEREBUS *WILL* CATCH YOU...

AHA! A DOORWAY! NARROW AND CONCEALED ENOUGH THAT CEREBUS WOULD HAVE MISSED IT...

...HAD HE NOT SEEN THE WENCH ENTER...

:TAP TAP:

A STAIRWAY! DOUBTLESS THE WENCH IS COWERING IN THE DARKNESS.

TUMP
TUMP
TUMP
TUMP
TUMP
TUMP

:KLANK:

WELL...

CEREBUS KNEW HE WAS GOING TO REGRET IT...

ABRUPTLY, A SERIES OF TORCHES FLARE TO LIFE, REVEALING A MASSIVE FIGURE...

I AM K'COR... KING OF IMESH!...

SEDRA TELLS ME SHE SAW YOU TALKING TO ONE OF MY SLAVES...

CEREBUS WAS...

WELL? SPEAK UP-- YOU MUST HAVE QUESTIONS ABOUT MY CHANGES...

YES, WHY DID YOU SEAL THE CITY LIKE...

NOT THE CITY, FOOL -- MY CITY! I OWN THE PEOPLE, THE BUILDINGS --EVERYTHING! ALL WITHIN THESE WALLS ARE MY SLAVES...

WE NEED NO GATES! MY SLAVES HAVE NO INTEREST IN THE OUTSIDE WORLD-- SO LONG AS THEY GET THEIR BUZ THEY ARE CONTENT TO SERVE ME...

BUZ?

THIS IS *BUZ* -- A COMPOUND OF MY OWN *INVENTION*

IT IS COMPOSED OF GRAIN, PROTEIN, THREE VITAMINS, STARCHES, SUGARS, AN OPIUM DERIVATIVE, AND ARTIFICIAL COLOURING...

IT IS ONE HUNDRED PER-CENT *ADDICTIVE* AND PROVIDES ALL THE FOOD VALUE NEEDED BY AN ADULT FOR ONE DAY...

EACH OF MY SLAVES WHO FILLS HIS QUOTA OF *ROCKS* GETS ONE EACH DAY -- THEY ARE, AS A RESULT, ETERNALLY *STUPEFIED* AND WELL FED...

NEEDLESS TO ADD, THEIR ADDICTION ALSO MAKES THEM *DILIGENT* WORKERS...

WHEN *IMESH'S* ECONOMY COLLAPSED I GAVE ONE TO EACH MEMBER OF THE COUNCIL OF ELDERS TO GET THEM 'HOOKED' -- THEY GAVE ME THE CITY IN EXCHANGE FOR A YEAR'S SUPPLY...

NOW THAT THEIR SUPPLY HAS RUN OUT, THEY LABOUR WITH THE *REST* OF THE SLAVES!

MY POSITION IS SECURED BY THE FACT THAT SEDRA AND I ARE THE ONLY TWO WHO KNOW THE EXACT *FORMULA* FOR MAKING BUZ...

NOT THAT THERE IS ANY REAL *DANGER* -- MOST OF THE POPULACE HAVE ENOUGH TROUBLE REMEMBERING WHAT DAY IT IS, TO BE CAPABLE OF ORGANIZING A *REVOLUTION*....

WHICH BRINGS US TO *ANOTHER* ISSUE AT HAND, *BARBARIAN!*

YOU SCALED THE WALL TO MY CITY, DISTURBED **MY** SLAVES, CHASED **MY** FEMALE...

...AND NOW, BY *GILASH'S THIRD EYE,* YOU'RE GOING TO TELL *K'COR* "WHY"!!

192

CEREBUS CAME TO **IMESH** FOR ONLY ONE REASON AND THAT WAS TO...

NEVER MIND-- I **KNOW** WHY YOU CAME.' WE HAVE A BARBARIAN COME OVER THE WALL ABOUT TWICE A YEAR! THEY'RE USUALLY IGNORANT NORTH-LANDERS IN SEARCH OF **LOOT**...

ONCE THEY SEE MY SLAVES, THEY CONVINCE THEMSELVES THAT THEY MUST HELP MY SLAVES TO REVOLT-- "TEACH THEM TO **DIE** LIKE MEN"-- WHATEVER **THAT** MEANS...

AYE! K'COR KNOWS YOU BARBARIANS TOO WELL-- WHEN MY SLAVES SHOW NO INTEREST IN REVOLTING, YOU DECIDE THAT YOU WILL AT LEAST TAKE SEDRA TO 'SAFETY' WITH YOU.

BUT, DEAR SEDRA IS NOT INTERESTED, **WITLING!** SHE CHERISHES HER PLACE AT MY SIDE, AND HAS NO INTEREST IN THE WIMS OF **BARBARIANS**...

...ISN'T THAT **RIGHT, SEDRA?**

YES, **BELOVED.**

FREEING MY SLAVES-- **IDIOCY!** FREE THEM FOR WHAT? SO THEY CAN WANDER THE SNOWS AND STARVE TO DEATH? HERE THEY HAVE LIFE, WARMTH AND **HAPPINESS!**

CEREBUS CAME TO...

I **KNOW** WHAT YOU'RE GOING TO SAY! "THEY ARE MEN AND MEN SHOULD BE FREE" A FREEMAN IS DANGEROUS TO HIMSELF AND EVERYONE ELSE. **FREEDOM** SHOULD BE LEFT TO THOSE WHO CAN PUT IT TO GOOD **USE**...

CEREBUS COULD DIE OF OLD AGE WAITING FOR PORKY THERE TO RUN OUT OF WIND...

I USED MY FREEDOM TO GET POWER! AND THEN USED MY POWER TO GET **MORE** POWER...

STILL, AFTER THE CONNIPTING, IT IS GOOD TO LISTEN TO SOMEONE CEREBUS CAN **UNDERSTAND**.

CEREBUS DOESN'T **LIKE** THIS DESPOT...

BUT CEREBUS AT LEAST **UNDERSTANDS** THIS DESPOT

YOU THINK I CARE NOTHING FOR MY **SLAVES?** DO YOU? MY PEOPLE ARE MY LIFE-- THEY SACRIFICED THEIR FREEDOM FOR A GREATER CAUSE...

AND THAT WOULD **BE?**

THE DEFENSE OF **EARTH** AGAINST THE **SECRET INVASION OF VENUSIANS!** EVEN NOW, THE SECOND PLANET FROM THE SUN IS MOUNTING IT'S FORCES.

THEY **ARE** COMING!... MAKE NO MISTAKE ABOUT IT!

MAYHAP CEREBUS IS TOO **QUICK** IN SAYING HE UNDERSTANDS THIS **LUNATIC!**

THE STRUCTURE WILL BE TWO HUNDRED FEET HIGH WHEN COMPLETED. IT'S THE SACRED SYMBOL OF THE VENUSIANS, SIGNALLING THE DEATH OF THEIR RACE.

ONE LOOK AT THIS WHEN THEY GET HERE SHOULD PUT A FEW KINKS IN THEIR **PSEUDOPODS!**

HAHAH HAHAHA HAAHAA HA AHA HAKAKA KAK-AA ≈COUGH COUGH≈

NOW DO YOU SEE THE IMPORTANCE OF MY MISSION, **INSECT?** IF YOU WERE TO FREE MY SLAVES, THE INVASION WOULD TAKE PLACE **EXACTLY AS** PLANNED...

AND WITH NONE TO RESIST THEM, THEY WOULD SOON HAVE ALL MEN OF EARTH LABOURING IN THE **AMMONIA MINES OF VENUS...**

WAIT! WAIT!

SO FAR AS CEREBUS IS CONCERNED YOU CAN FAST-FRY THOSE SLAVES AND EAT THEM, *CORPULENT ONE...*

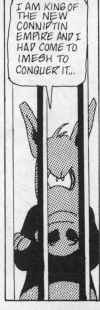

I AM KING OF THE NEW CONNIPTIN EMPIRE AND I HAD COME TO IMESH TO CONQUER IT...

AND PERSUADE YOUR MEN TO JOIN MY ARMY! HAVING SEEN YOUR MEN, CEREBUS HAS NO *INTEREST* DRAGGING THEM TO...

EH? WHAT'S *THAT?* A KING YOU SAY? OF COURSE -- OF COURSE! YOU ARE A KING WITHOUT *SOLDIERS* THEN?

CEREBUS LEFT THEM FORAGING FOR FOOD AND WATER OUTSIDE YOUR WALLS --

AS THERE SEEMS TO BE NO REASON FOR CEREBUS TO REMAIN HERE, HE WISHES TO...

CAME IN AHEAD OF THEM, *EH?* JUST TO BE SURE! HM! I *LIKE* THAT! A COURAGEOUS KING -- AS I AM A COURAGEOUS *DEMI-GOD!*

WE ARE *ADMIRABLE* FIGURES, YOU AND I !

SO, YOU HAVE COME TO TAKE MY CITY AND MY *SLAVES* FROM ME! VERY WELL -- I AM A FAIR KING -- YOU WILL HAVE YOUR CHANCE TO TAKE MY CITY AND MY SLAVES FOR YOUR OWN! I PROPOSE A WAGER OF KINGS! A *KINGLY* CHALLENGE FOR *KINGLY* STAKES...

IN A FEW MOMENTS, THOSE BARS BEFORE YOU WILL RISE! YOU WILL FOLLOW US INTO THE DOORWAY ON MY RIGHT! IF YOU CAN PASS THROUGH THE CORRIDOR *UNSCATHED* AND THEN DEFEAT MY CHAMPION, YOU WILL WIN MY CITY AND SLAVES! I WILL GIVE YOU ALL THE *BUZ* I HAVE AND SHOW YOU HOW TO MAKE IT.

WITH THAT SECRET YOU WILL CONTROL THEM -- AND IF YOU SO DESIRE...

...THEY WILL CONQUER THE *WORLD* IN YOUR NAME...

IF YOU ARE DEFEATED, YOUR MEN WILL BE WELCOMED TO A *FEAST* BY SEDRA! BY MORNING, MY POOL OF SLAVES WILL HAVE SOME NEW RESERVES...

GOOD LUCK.

DON'T YOU THINK YOU'RE TAKING AN *EXTREME* RISK WITH YOUR..... 'CRUSADE'..?

HAHAHAHAAA! WITH TARIM AND *ANTI-VENUSIANS* EVERYWHERE ON MY SIDE...

I CANNOT LOSE...

OF COURSE!

HOW STUPID OF *CEREBUS* TO FORGET...

196

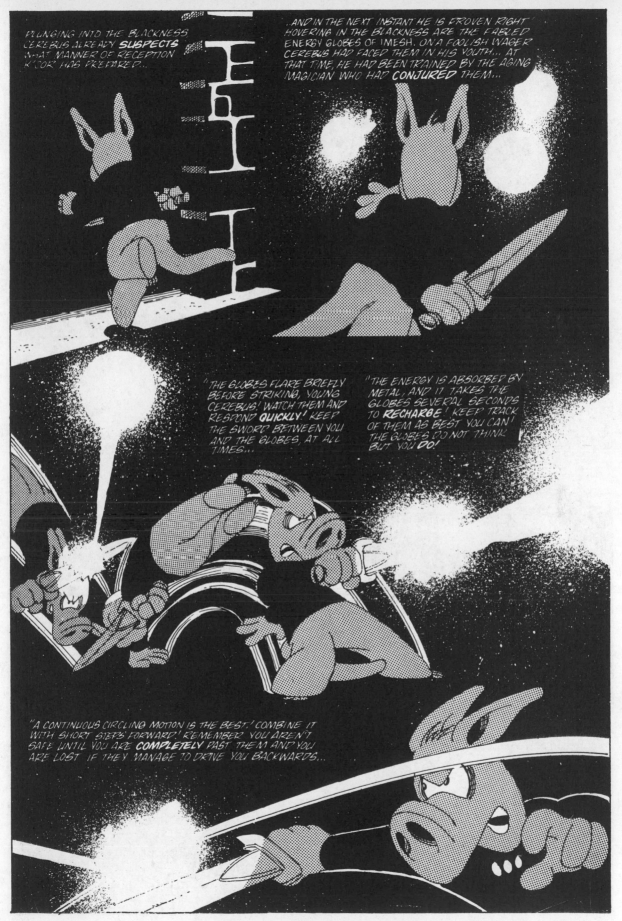

PLUNGING INTO THE BLACKNESS CEREBUS ALREADY **SUSPECTS** WHAT MANNER OF RECEPTION K'COR HAS PREPARED...

...AND IN THE NEXT INSTANT HE IS PROVEN RIGHT! HOVERING IN THE BLACKNESS ARE THE FABLED ENERGY GLOBES OF IMESH. ON A FOOLISH WAGER CEREBUS HAD FACED THEM IN HIS YOUTH... AT THAT TIME, HE HAD BEEN TRAINED BY THE AGING MAGICIAN WHO HAD **CONJURED** THEM...

"THE GLOBES FLARE BRIEFLY BEFORE STRIKING, YOUNG CEREBUS! WATCH THEM AND RESPOND **QUICKLY**! KEEP THE SWORD BETWEEN YOU AND THE GLOBES, AT ALL TIMES...

"THE ENERGY IS ABSORBED BY METAL, AND IT TAKES THE GLOBES SEVERAL SECONDS TO **RECHARGE**! KEEP TRACK OF THEM AS BEST YOU CAN! THE GLOBES DO NOT THINK BUT YOU **DO**!

"A CONTINUOUS CIRCLING MOTION IS THE BEST! COMBINE IT WITH SHORT STEPS FORWARD! REMEMBER YOU AREN'T SAFE UNTIL YOU ARE **COMPLETELY** PAST THEM AND YOU ARE LOST IF THEY MANAGE TO DRIVE YOU BACKWARDS...

THOUGH HIS COORDINATION IS **BETTER**, THOUGH HE IS FASTER THAN HE WAS IN THOSE DAYS LONG GONE, CEREBUS REALIZES THAT HE HAD BEEN FULLY RESTED FOR HIS FIRST **ORDEAL**! HE CAN FEEL THE MILES CATCHING UP TO HIM...

AND, SUDDENLY, HIS WORST FEARS ARE **REALIZED**...

EVEN AS THE EXPLOSION OF PAIN SENDS HIM TO HIS KNEES...

IT IS INSTINCT MORE THAN SKILL THAT SAVES HIM, HIS SWORD **RISING**...

HE CURSES THE FATES FOR HIS SLOW-HEALING BACK WOUND, REOPENED BY THE GLOBE... HE IS PAST THE GLOBES, EXHAUSTION FEEDING ON EVERY FIBRE OF HIS BEING! BLINKING THE SWEAT FROM HIS EYES, HE SCANS THE CORRIDOR BEFORE HIM...

FOR SOMEWHERE UP AHEAD IS K'COR'S CHAMPION, EAGER TO FACE THE EARTH-PIG...

RIGHT NOW, CEREBUS WOULD BE HARD-PRESSED TO BEAT ELROD IN HAND-TO-HAND COMBAT...

I AM LORD KOSHEM!...

YOU ARE TO BE *CONGRATULATED* FOR ESCAPING THE GLOBES... BEFORE WE BEGIN, THERE ARE SOME RULES WE MUST...

A PANROVIAN! MAYHAP CEREBUS' LUCK IS CHANGING...

YOUR ACCENT IS NOT *IMESHITE* NOBLE SIR...

NAY! I AM PANROVIAN, THE RULES WE WILL...

OH! PANROVIAN, EH? IS IT TRUE THAT PANROVIANS DERIVE SEXUAL SATISFACTION FROM SMALL WOODLAND ANIMALS...?

WHAT?!

CEREBUS HAD HEARD THAT *PANROVIAN* MEN ARE BUILT SO SMALL THAT *ANYTHING* LARGER THAN A TITMOUSE IS QUITE BEYOND THEIR...UH... *ABILITIES?*

YOUR MAJESTY! I HAVE BEEN SENT TO LOCK SWORDS WITH YOU AND I WOULD HOPE....

I SAW KING KOREM IN A TAVERN ABOUT A FORTNIGHT GONE...

KING KOREM! TARIM BE PRAISED THAT HE YET...

HE OFFERED TO DRINK THE CONTENTS OF THE *SPITTOON* IF I BOUGHT HIM AN ALE...

CEREBUS THOUGHT THAT WAS A PRETTY GROSS WAY TO MAKE A *LIVING*...

EVEN FOR A *DEGENERATE SOT* LIKE KOREM

CEREBUS HEARD THE PANROVIAN "MARCH OF VIRGINS" HAD TO BE CANCELLED...

...YOUR DAUGHTER GOT *PREGNANT*...

...AND YOUR *WIFE* REFUSED TO MARCH ALONE...

YOU THINK *PANROVY* IS A JOKE... I... WILL ...SHOW... YOU... WHAT... PANROVIANS...

CAN DO!

ACTUALLY, CEREBUS LIKES PANROVIANS

PANROVIANS WILL BE TRUSTED TO DIG LATRINES FOR THE NEW CONNIPTIN EMPIRE

YOU'RE... *EVIL!!!*

PANROVY WILL NEVER BOW TO A *TYRANT!*...

BUT CEREBUS WISHES TO KNOW MORE ABOUT YOUR *CUSTOMS*...

STOP! STOP!

IS IT TRUE THAT *PANROVIANS* HAVE A LOT OF CHILDREN...

...BECAUSE THEY FIGURE THERE'S ANOTHER *FAMINE* COMING?

NYAHHHH

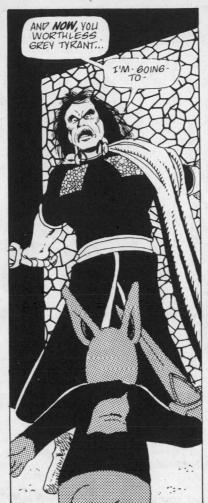

201

YOU SAY YOU HAVE FACED MY CHAMPION -- YOU HAVE *NOT!* I SAID YOU WOULD HAVE TO PASS THROUGH THE *CORRIDOR...*

AND THEN FACE MY CHAMPION! AS CHAMPION OF MY PEOPLE, I AM CHAMPION, TOO, OF MY OWN *FATE!*

WE HAVE MADE A *WAGER OF KINGS.* BUT I WILL TELL YOU SOMETHING OF KINGS, *YOUR MAJESTY...*

THEIR WAGERS USUALLY BECOME *BATTLES...*

...AND THEIR *BATTLES...*

... *WARS!*

AND *NOW,* WE SHALL SETTLE OUR WAGER...

...*AS KINGS!*

CEREBUS STARES IN STUNNED DISBELIEF AT THE SHINING BLACK ARMOUR BEFORE HIM...

HE CAN FEEL THE ACHE IN HIS LIMBS! THE *THROBBING* THAT BLURS HIS VISION SIGNALS THE ONSET OF *PHYSICAL COLLAPSE...*

IN A MOMENT, HE REALIZES THE HOPE-LESSNESS OF HIS *SITUATION!* EVEN AT HIS PHYSICAL *PEAK...*

IT WOULD TAKE HOURS TO BEAT AN ARMOURED FOE, HOURS OF *LIGHTNING* THRUSTS AND PINPOINT ACCURACY...

HOURS THE EARTH-PIG'S *RAVAGED* BODY CAN ILL-AFFORD...

THE SLASHING EDGE OF THE **BLACK SWORD** RISES AGAIN AND AGAIN IN THE EARTH PIG'S LINE OF SIGHT...

EACH MOVE IS CALCULATED, **POWERFUL!** "THIS BLUBBEROUS KING," THINKS THE AARDVARK, "IS NO MEAN, "SWORDSMAN,"

FACING ALMOST **CERTAIN** DEATH, THE AARDVARK'S BLOWS BEGIN TO GROW LESS ACCURATE...

HE HAS BEEN WITHOUT SLEEP SINCE RISING THE TWO MORNINGS BEFORE AND FRUSTRATION AND DESPAIR EAT AWAY AT HIS SPIRIT...

HE HAD SEEN MEN **FALTER** BEFORE HIM, RECOGNIZING THEIR IMMINENT DEFEAT...

THEY HAD **RECOGNIZED** A HOPELESS SITUATION AS HE DID NOW...

THERE IS A WRIST-TWISTING MOTION THAT **CEREBUS** MISSES AND THE FLAT OF THE SWORD **IMPACTS** SHARPLY WITH THE SIDE OF THE AARDVARK'S HEAD...

REELING **BACKWARD,** CEREBUS MANAGES TO RAISE HIS SWORD TO BLOCK A FATAL BLOW! IN REGAINING HIS BALANCE, HOWEVER ...

... HE IS **UNABLE** TO BLOCK THE RETURN STROKE WHICH RAKES HIS LEFT SIDE, **FRACTURING** ONE OF THE EARTH-PIG'S RIBS...

HE THINKS OF HIS OPPONENT, SWEATING AND PUFFING IN HIS ARMOUR, HIS FLESH **UNMARKED**...

AND AN **IMMENSE** RAGE BOILS UP INSIDE OF CEREBUS,

HE SWINGS **WILDLY**, FEELS THE SWORD CATCH, BRIEFLY, THEN RIP... THERE IS A BLUR OF BLACK, RED AND GREY...

...AND SUDDENLY, K'COR HOLDS THE GREAT BLACK SWORD IN HIS RIGHT HAND...!

A SLOW GRIN CROSSES THE EARTH-PIG'S FACE AND HE **SALUTES** THE GESTURE -- CEREBUS HADN'T DEMANDED HIS OWN ARMOUR...

...K'COR WILL NOT DEMAND COMPENSATION FOR THE WOUND ON HIS HAND...

NOT THAT ANY WOULD BE GIVEN...

CEREBUS DELIVERS A **BONE-RATTLING** BLOW TO THE BLACK-ARMOURED BELLY...

FIGHT, YOU **CORPULENT CRAVEN**...!

CEREBUS HAS CITIES TO **CONQUER**!

CEREBUS SEES THE KING IS **PLAGUED** BY DOUBT -- WONDERING IF CEREBUS COMES TO DO BATTLE -- OR MERELY TO WOUND HIS GOOD ARM...

CEREBUS QUICKLY DECIDES TO LEAVE THE ARM ALONE! THE KING DOESN'T KNOW THAT, HOWEVER AND THE EARTH-PIG ADVANCES...

...SMILING.

IN A WHILE K'COR WOULD DEDUCE THE AARDVARK'S INTENTIONS BUT FOR NOW, CEREBUS RELISHES THE SIGHT OF THE KING, **MINCING** DAINTILY BACKWARDS, SWORD RAISED TO DEFEND HIS ARM...

FEIGNING OUTRAGE AND ANNOYANCE AT THIS OBVIOUS COWARDICE...

HE WOULD CARRY THE CONNIPTINS ON HIS BACK IF NEED BE! THE WORLD HAD HAD ENOUGH OF FAT STRUTTING MONARCHS IN FANCY ARMOUR! A NEW EMPIRE WAS DAWNING...

K'COR CONTINUES HIS SLOW RETREAT AS CEREBUS POUNDS AT HIS BELLY...

THE NEW CONNIPTIN EMPIRE WOULD BE FORGED BY CHEERLEADERS AND DRUG ADDICTS -- PROSTITUTES AND DRUNKARDS... AND ALL THE OTHERS WHO HAD BOWED TOO LONG TO INSANE DESPOTS...

CEREBUS WAITS FOR K'COR TO TURN AND FIGHT-- IT IS ONLY A MATTER OF TIME...

A NEW AGE WAS DAWNING WHEN MEN WOULD ONCE MORE BE MEASURED BY THEIR SWORDS -- A NEW GOLDEN AGE OF WARRIORS!

AND CEREBUS WOULD LEAD THOSE WARRIORS ON GREAT AND GLORIOUS CRUSADES! HIS MEN WOULD BE ENGAGED IN THE NOBLEST OF ALL POSSIBLE PURSUITS...

...ENDLESS PILLAGING, DRINKING AND FIGHTING IN THE NAME OF CEREBUS THE KING...

STUNG BY THE LAST BLOW, K'COR RETREATS SEVERAL STEPS AND THEN PAUSES...

K'COR PAUSES, SEEMING TO CONTEMPLATE HIS NEXT MOVE A MOMENT... LATER HIS SHOULDERS SAG WITH **RESIGNATION**

AND, IN EVIDENT **DISGUST** HE FLINGS HIS SWORD AT A WALL BEHIND HIM...

YOU CEDE **CEREBUS** THE VICTORY, THEN?

GET **OUT.**

WHAT MANNER OF **JEST**...?

I POISONED ALL THE WELLS IN THE IMMEDIATE AREA A YEAR AGO TO KEEP BARBARIANS FROM STRAYING TOO CLOSE TO **IMESH**...

IF YOU **DID** LEAVE YOUR MEN LOOKING FOR FOOD AND **WATER**...

THEY ARE ALL QUITE DEAD NOW...

WHICH MEANS YOU ARE NO LONGER OF **INTEREST** TO ME...

NOW **GO!**

THE WAGER OF KINGS WAS **OVER** AS CEREBUS WATCHED THE RETREATING FIGURE OF **K'COR**...

HE WAS A KING NO LONGER-- WOUNDED, TIRED, HUNGRY

STRANDED WITHOUT FOOD, MONEY OR SHELTER IN A BARREN AND ALIEN LAND...

THE EARTH-PIG'S RAGE AND **FRUSTRATION** ERUPTS IN A PROTRACTED, PIERCING CRY...

ECHOING AND RE-ECHOING IN UPON ITSELF -- STABBING OUT INTO THE CITY WHERE POWDERY SNOW SWIRLS BETWEEN THE BUILDINGS...

BUT THE IMESHITES, ENGROSSED IN THEIR DAILY CHORES, HEAR NOTHING...

MERCHANT OF UNSHIB!

IT IS THE SEVENTH DAY OF THE *BLIZZARD!* SINCE IT HAD STRUCK WITHOUT WARNING A WEEK BEFORE, TRAVEL HAD GROUND TO A HALT AND FIVE HUNDRED PEOPLE HAD DIED OF EXPOSURE IN THE IMMEDIATE VICINITY OF IEST

UNAWARE OF THIS, CEREBUS PUSHES RESOLUTELY SOUTHWARD, ASSURING HIMSELF THAT IEST HAS ESCAPED THE POLAR SNOWS AND FREEZING *WINDS...*

HIS LEGS, PISTON-LIKE, CHURN THE POWDER-WHITE SNOW. THE *FOOTPRINTS* SEEM TO GROW FAINTER WITH EACH PASSING MILE, AND AN EMPTY PACK AND *GROWLING* STOMACH SERVE TO REMIND THE EARTH·PIG OF THE URGENCY OF HIS HUNT...

THERE IS A HANDFUL OF SCRAPS IN THE AARDVARK'S PACK, ENOUGH, HE REALIZES TO SUSTAIN HIM FOR PERHAPS HALF A DAY...

CEREBUS WINCES AS HE LOSES HIS FOOTING AND FEELS THE PAINFUL TUG ON HIS RIBS. THE FRACTURES HAD BEGUN TO HEAL, BUT WERE STILL **SENSITIVE**...

THOUGH DIZZY FROM THE PAIN, HE PRESSES ON... SUCH WAS THE NATURE OF THE STRUGGLE FOR SURVIVAL, **CEREBUS** KNEW...

...THAT OFTEN THE OUTCOME OF THE STRUGGLE WOULD HINGE ON JUST SUCH AN ACHE OR PAIN.

THE SNOW HAD DRIVEN MOST OF THE **ANIMALS** TO SHELTER. HIS KILLS HAD BECOME MORE INFREQUENT...

THE FOREST OPENS INTO A SMALL CLEARING AND CEREBUS STRAINS IN A LAST-DITCH EFFORT...

THE CHASE WAS NEARLY OVER AND CEREBUS READIES HIS SWORD ARM FOR....

IT WAS **GONE**. A SMEAR OF BLOOD MARKS THE TERMINATION OF ITS FOOTPRINTS. CEREBUS STOPS, BREATHING HARD...

HIS RIBS ACHE **ABOMINABLY** WITH EACH BREATH. AS HE SCANS THE CLEARING FOR SOME CLUE AS TO THE...

COOCHY-COOCHY-KOO!

AAAK!

SURPRISED YOU, EH? I WAS JUST OUT FOR A STROLL IN THE SNOW AND THIS FINE **JACKRABBIT** CAME HOPPING BY-- YOU LOOK **TERRIBLE!** HOW LONG HAS IT BEEN SINCE YOU'VE EATEN?

I COULD FEEL YOUR RIBS RIGHT THROUGH YOUR SHIRT!

CEREBUS-IS-NOT-GOING-TO FAINT...

ACTUALLY, I'M GLAD I RAN INTO YOU THIS WAY-- I'VE GOT SOMETHING TO **TALK** TO YOU ABOUT...

HOWZABOUT I FRY UP A QUICK BATCH OF BUNNY BURGERS AND THEN WE CAN...

CEREBUS HAS NO ...INTEREST IN SUCH SMALL GAME.

GREAT-- THEN WE'LL JUST GO TO MY TENT AND **TALK**...

CEREBUS HAS NOTHING TO SAY TO YOU...

UNFORTUNATE, BUT-- SOPHIA HAS SOMETHING TO SAY TO **YOU!**

uh-- DOES THE **BLACK BLOSSOM LOTUS** MEAN ANYTHING TO YOU?

SO YOU FOUND A FRAGMENT, EH? **CEREBUS** IS NOT IMPRESSED.

BESIDES-- THERE HASN'T BEEN AN **AUTHENTIC** FRAGMENT DISCOVERED IN NEARLY FIFTY YEARS...

THE ONE I HAVE MY EYE ON ISN'T A **FRAGMENT**, DEAR HEART...

IT'S **INTACT**.

MY TENT IS THIS WAY...

BUNNY BURGERS ... YECH!

210

THE BLACK BLOSSOM LOTUS A POWERFUL MAGIC TALISMAN CREATED BY THE WIZARD HERCES TO HONOUR THE GOD-KING OF AMSTANAT ON THE OCCASION OF HIS CORONATION! AT THE TIME OF THE RELIGIOUS WARS IN AMSTANAT, THE GRAND VIZIER HAD IT MOVED TO ESHNOSOPUR FOR SAFE-KEEPING. WHEN IT FAILED TO ARRIVE AT ITS DESTINATION, SUSPICION FELL ON THE CAPTAIN OF THE CARAVAN! HE DIED IN PRISON, STILL MAINTAINING HIS INNOCENCE! FIVE BLACK FRAGMENTS, PURPORTED TO BE PARTS OF THE MISSING LOTUS SURFACED IN THE SOUTH, SOME TWENTY TO FORTY YEARS LATER.

I MARRIED FERAS LIKE YOU TOLD ME TO... BUT HE FORGOT THAT SOPHIA WILL ONLY GIVE HERSELF TO ONE WHO HAS DEFEATED HER IN BATTLE! ON OUR FIRST ANNIVERSARY HE DIED OF EIGHT COMPOUND FRACTURES, TWELVE STAB WOUNDS AND AN ULCER...

I PUNCHED HIM IN THE JAW ONE LAST TIME, AND HE PASSED FROM THIS WORLD

YES, BUT THE LOTUS -- YOU SAY THAT THERE IS...

NOW, NOW! YOU KNOW RED SOPHIA WELL ENOUGH -- WITH ME IT'S ALWAYS PLEASURE BEFORE BUSINESS...

TARIM!

JUST MAKE YOURSELF COMFORTABLE! I'LL BE BACK IN A FEW MINUTES WITH A JUG OF WINE!

WHY DO THESE THINGS ALWAYS HAPPEN TO CEREBUS?

I'VE BEEN SAVING THIS BOTTLE OF DEHRSION BUBBLY FOR A SPECIAL OCCASION AND THIS IS...

CEREBUS?

UNH!

IN THE LAST WEEK, CEREBUS HAS HAD HIS BACK BLASTED, HIS RIBS FRACTURED AND HIS *EMPIRE* SLIPPED OUT FROM UNDER HIM BY A BLIMP IN BLACK ARMOUR. HE HASN'T EATEN OR SLEPT SINCE YESTERDAY AND WHAT LITTLE PATIENCE HE HAS IS WEARING *QUITE* THIN!

NOW! EITHER YOU TELL CEREBUS WHERE TO FIND *THE BLACK BLOSSOM LOTUS* OR HE'LL...

OOOH--YES! YES! DO IT *HARDER*, MY DARLING! YOU *SWEETHEART*, YOU! HOW DID YOU GUESS THAT I'M INTO BEING DOMINATED?

ALL RIGHT! CEREBUS KNOWS WHEN HE'S BEATEN! *KEEP* THE LOTUS FOR YOURSELF. CEREBUS HAS *HAD* IT!

DON'T *BE* THAT WAY, DARLING -- I'LL TELL YOU *ALL* ABOUT THE LOTUS -- BUT DON'T YOU THINK YOU COULD BE A *TEENSY* BIT NICER TO ME? IT'S BEEN *SO* LONG SINCE I'VE BEEN IN A MAN'S ARMS...

CEREBUS ISN'T A MAN...

CEREBUS IS AN *AARDVARK!*

"THE LEGEND IS ACCURATE UP TO THE POINT WHERE THE GRAND VIZIER SHIPS THE LOTUS TO ESHNOSOPUR-- IN ACTUAL FACT, HE HAD A DUPLICATE MADE AND SHIPPED *THAT* IN ITS PLACE. THE CAPTAIN OF THE CARAVAN WAS INNOCENT OF THE CHARGES," SOPHIA SAYS. "HOWEVER, THE VIZIER WAS WAYLAID BY THIEVES ON HIS WAY TO SELL THE STOLEN LOTUS! THE THIEVES, NOT KNOWING WHAT THE HAD, SOLD THE LOTUS TO A JEWELLER IN RESS. THE JEWELLER ADMIRED THE LOTUS VERY MUCH AND KEPT IT FOR HIMSELF UNTIL HIS DEATH ABOUT A MONTH AGO! A MERCHANT FROM LINSHIB RECOGNIZED THE LOTUS AT AN AUCTION OF THE JEWELLER'S ESTATE AND BOUGHT IT. HE'S NOW LOOKING FOR A BUYER!"

"BUT," SHE ADDS, "IF YOU'LL HELP ME, I'M SURE WE CAN SLIP THE LOTUS OUT FROM UNDER HIS NOSE AND SELL IT *OURSELVES*."

WELL?

DID YOU *LIKE* IT?

DO YOU REALLY HAVE TO *ASK* IF CEREBUS *LIKED* HAVING SALIVA SMEARED ON HIS FUR?

THIS IS GOING TO BE A LOT *TOUGHER* THAN I THOUGHT.

214

WHAT TREACHERY IS THIS, THEN?

A SCUM-SUCKING SAWED-OFF KHAIVEN! YOU CAN'T TAKE OVER OUR COUNTRY BY FORCE, SO YOU HOUND US IN OTHER LANDS!

CEREBUS-- THIS IS MEIRGEN... HE GETS THE THIRD SHARE.

MEIRGEN--SAY HELLO TO CEREBUS THE AARDVARK...

I'LL FEED YOUR HEART TO THE WOLVES, YOU STINKING KHAIVEN SCUM!

AND YOU, SOPHIA--SENDING MEIRGEN OUT TO CHECK THE CARAVAN -- WHILE YOU... LINGER... HERE WITH THAT-- THAT SCUM-SUCKING...

"...SAWED-OFF KHAIVEN." I HEARD YOU THE FIRST TIME.

SMAT

215

SORRY I DIDN'T WARN YOU THAT WE HAD *COMPANY* COMING

NOT AT ALL--*CEREBUS* IS GETTING USED TO BEATING UP COMPLETE STRANGERS WHENEVER YOU'RE AROUND...

TCAPMIN ISN'T HE?

YOU HAVE A KEEN EYE FOR *CRAZIES!* HE'S THE SON OF THE JEWELLER I TOLD YOU ABOUT. WHEN THE MERCHANT BOUGHT HIS LATE FATHER'S *LOTUS*, HE GOT SUSPICIOUS-- DECIDED TO FIND OUT WHAT HE HAD SOLD.

I PROMISED HIM "SPECIAL FAVOURS" IF HE SPLIT THE PROFITS WITH ME....

CEREBUS THOUGHT YOUR "SPECIAL FAVOURS" WERE ONLY FOR THOSE WHO DEFEATED YOU IN BATTLE.

YOU'RE NOT LISTENING! -- I SAID THAT I *PROMISED* HIM "SPECIAL FAVOURS"...

I SAID *NOTHING* ABOUT ACTUALLY, uh, "*FAVOURING*" HIM...

DO YOU WANT *CEREBUS* TO REVIVE HIM?

MMM. BETTER LEAVE THAT TO *ME*...

HE'S APT TO BE A BIT *TESTY* WHEN HE WAKES UP.

MEIRGEN! OH THANK THE GODS YOU STILL *LIVE!*

SOMEONE ...HIT ME... WITH A ... ≡*umph*≡

SOPHIA WOULD NEVER HAVE *FORGIVEN* HERSELF IF YOUR ADORABLE BRAINS HAD GOTTEN PERMANENTLY *SCRAMBLED!*

YOU REALLY ARE THE *CA-UTEST* THING! SOPHIA FEELS SAFER JUST HAVING YOU NEAR...

CEREBUS WAS HAPPIER WHEN IT WAS ONLY SNOWING *OUTSIDE*...

NOW THAT YOU'RE FEELING BETTER, I HAVE A TEENSY-WEENSY FAVOUR TO ASK... YOU WOULDN'T MIND IF WE LEFT CEREBUS BEHIND, *WOULD* YOU, *SUGAR BLOSSOM?*

unh?

OH, *I* GET IT, NOW-- YOU'RE GETTING ME CONFUSED SO I'LL DO WHAT YOU WANT!

WELL, *NOBODY* PULLS THE WOOL OVER THE EYES OF *MEIRGEN OF RESS*...

...CEREBUS GOES WITH US AND I DON'T WANT TO HEAR ANY MORE *ABOUT* IT...

AN *HOUR* LATER

LOOKS LIKE THE MERCHANT IS MAKING *SURE* HE KEEPS HIS *PRIZE*

TCAPMIN BORDER GUARDS! THOSE ARE TWENTY-YEAR DECORATIONS* ON THEIR SHOULDERS, TOO... MUST HAVE COST HIM A FORTUNE.

SIGNIFYING TWENTY YEARS OF SERVICE MANNING THE WALL OF TSI AGAINST INVASION FROM KHAIDOGE THE UNGOVERNABLE.

YOU MAY GET A FEW MONTH'S PLEASURE OUT OF FORTY GOLD PIECES! IN *TCAPMIN* ONE COULD LIVE FOR THREE *YEARS* AS A *KING!*

THOSE GUARDS COULD BE HAD FOR A HANDFUL OF SILVER COINS.

BUT, IF THEIR JOB IS TO KEEP THE LOTUS *SAFE,* NEITHER MAN NOR GOD COULD WREST IT FROM THEM.

HOLD!

HERE'S OUR STORY: SOPHIA TOLD US SHE KNEW OF SOME FINE LOOT AND TALKED US INTO TAKING A LOOK AT THE CARAVAN-- WE DON'T KNOW WHAT THE LOOT IS OR WHY SHE WANTED US TO SEE IT...

THE *TCAPMIN GUARDS* WILL BE MORE INTERESTED IN A WOMAN, ANYWAY, SO, HE'LL PROBABLY LET YOU AND ME GO...

TARIM.

WHAT BUSINESS HAVE YOU HERE?

DIDN'T YOU KNOW?

WE'RE HERE TO STEAL THE BLACK BLOSSOM LOTUS!

WELL, I GUESS NOW I HAVE TO BRIBE YOU. JOIN US AND WE'LL GIVE YOU A FULL SHARE -- *TEN-GOLD-PIECES!*

THE GUARD, WHO HAD *ALREADY* SOLD HIS LOYALTIES FOR EIGHT COPPER COINS, PAUSES AND HIS BROW DEVELOPS DEEP FURROWS.

IT WOULD MEAN LESS MONEY PER SHARE, BUT *CEREBUS* DID NOT RELISH THE IDEA OF QUARRELING WITH THE *TCAPMIN*...

THE BORDER GUARDS WERE KNOWN FOR THEIR HAIR-TRIGGER REFLEXES AND *TEMPERS*...

A SLOW GRIN SPLITS THE FEATURES OF THE GRIM BLONDE *NORTHLANDER*

TELL ME YOUR PLAN! IF I THINK IT WILL WORK I WILL JOIN.

OKAY! THIS IS OUR ONLY CHANCE TO KEEP A SHARE OF THE *LOTUS!* MAKE IT A GOOD PLAN...

CEREBUS THOUGHT YOU *HAD* A PLAN!

I *HAD* PLANNED TO TAKE THE GUARDS BY SURPRISE AND OVERPOWER THEM WHILE THEY SLEPT...

SOMEHOW I DON'T THINK HE'LL HAVE TOO MUCH *FAITH* IN THAT IDEA...

WELL?

LET'S HEAR YOUR DAMN PLAN!

219

CEREBUS RISES SLOWLY-- HIS EYES FIXED ON THE TCAPMIN'S! HIS MIND RACES, SIFTING THROUGH ALL HE KNOWS OF THE BORDER GUARDS. THE *CROSSBOW* FOLLOWS HIS RISE...

...THE POINT OF ITS ARROW AIMED DIRECTLY AT THE EARTH-PIG'S *CHEST*...

JUST DON'T MAKE HIM *ANGRY*...

CEREBUS WILL DO HIS BEST...

THE TCAPMIN GUARDS ARE *DEFENDERS*! IN TRANSIT, THEY DEFEND *EACH OTHER*! IT IS SAID TO TAKE A BOLT OF LIGHTNING TO MAKE THEM BREAK RANKS.

WE BOTH *KNOW* ALL THAT...

BUT-- IT MEANS THEY WILL BE CROSSING BRIDGES AS A *UNIT*!

WHEN THEY ARE ALL ON ONE BRIDGE, WE PLAN TO RIP OUT A FEW STRUCTURAL SUPPORTS...

...AND PICK THE *LOTUS* OUT OF THE RUBBLE THAT LANDS AT THE BOTTOM...

MEIRGEN AND SOPHIA AWAIT THE VERDICT WITH BATED BREATH...

PLEASE! KILL HIM, BUT LET *ME* GO! OH-PLEASE-PLEASE!

HAHARHAHAHAR! LONG-EARS-- I LIKE YOUR STYLE!

YOU'VE GOT A NEW *RECRUIT*!

HOWEVER, I THINK THAT WE SHOULD GET SOME *BUSINESS* OUT OF THE WAY, *FIRST.*

SINCE THIS CROSSBOW MAKES ME THE MOST *IMPORTANT* MEMBER OF THE GROUP, I THINK I SHOULD GET *TWO* SHARES--TWENTY GOLD PIECES.

BUT THE LOTUS WAS *MY* FATHER'S, AND YOU'RE ALLOWING LESS THAN SEVEN GOLD PIECES FOR EACH OF US! THAT'S COMPLETELY *UNACCEPTABLE!*

SOPHIA COULD MAKE MORE THAN *THAT* SELLING HER OLD CHAIN MAIL BIKINIS TO PERVERTS IN *IEST...*

IF YOU *PREFER* I CAN CALL OUT FOR SOME *ASSISTANCE* ...

AND YOU'LL BE *DEAD* WHERE YOU STAND!

CEREBUS IS GETTING *TIRED* OF SAYING THIS...

...BUT HE KNOWS WHEN HE'S *BEATEN.*

LET'S GO FIND A *BRIDGE.*

AMAZING HOW SOME THINGS ONLY MAKE *SENSE* WHEN YOU HAVE *SOMEONE* *EXPLAIN* THEM TO YOU.

ISN'T IT THOUGH?

CEREBUS CAN'T *BELIEVE* IT! WE'VE BEEN WALKING FOR AN HOUR?-- IT'S ALMOST DUSK...

THE BRIDGE IS JUST *AHEAD*...

AND NO *INCIDENTS* SO FAR

ALL THIS TIME I'VE JUST BEEN *WAITING* FOR THE T'CAPMIN TO SAY...

WAIT A MINUTE! I JUST HAD ANOTHER *THOUGHT*...

TWO IN ONE DAY? BEGINNER'S LUCK.

I THINK, AS LEADER OF THIS GROUP, THAT I'M ENTITLED TO SOME *FRINGE BENEFITS*...

LIKE SOPHIA, HERE! I COULD SHARE SOME OF MY GOLD WITH HER AND... *WHO KNOWS?* WE MAY FIND SOMETHING SHE CAN DO FOR ME!

THAT IS, *UNLESS* EITHER OF YOU TWO... *OBJECTS?*

NOT AT ALL...

NOW, CAN WE JUST GET TO THE...

HE DIDN'T JUST ASK *YOU*, CEREBUS...

...HE ASKED *BOTH* OF US.

222

ARE YOU *CRAZY* OR JUST PLAIN *STUPID*? HE'S A *TWENTY-YEAR-MAN!* CEREBUS COULD UNDERSTAND IF YOUR *LIFE* DEPENDED ON...

CEREBUS -- A MAN HAS TO *DO* WHAT A MAN HAS TO *DO* --

THAT'S VERY *GOOD!* DID *SOMEONE* MAKE IT UP FOR YOU OR ARE YOU JUST *CLEVER* WITH WORDS?

AND RIGHT NOW WHAT I HAVE TO DO IS...

GET YOUR FACE *PUNCHED?*

NO, NO NO...

WHAT I WAS ABOUT TO SAY WAS...

RIGHT NOW, WHAT *I* HAVE TO DO IS...

...GET YOUR *RIBS* KICKED?

JUST ... ONE ... MORE TRY...

I THINK I'M ... GETTING THE HANG OF IT...

...TELL YOU *WHAT*...

HOW ABOUT *YOU* GET SOPHIA *TODAY*... AND I GET HER *TOMORROW!*

HOW ABOUT YOU DRAG YOUR BLOODY CARCASS *AWAY* FROM HERE...

...BEFORE I *VENTILATE* YOUR WINDPIPE. HMM?

NEVER LET IT BE SAID THAT *MEIRGEN OF RESS* TURNED DOWN A COMPROMISE...

225

CEREBUS WOULD LIKE TO **BORROW** YOUR FUR -- IT IS GOING TO BE COLD TONIGHT AND HE CAN USE IT FOR A TENT...

HA! A **TENT!** DID YOU HEAR **THAT,** SOPHIA? HE WANTS TO USE MY FUR FOR A **TENT!** YOU SURE HAVE SOME **FUNNY** FRIENDS...

CEREBUS? OH, YES-- HE'S A LAUGH-A-MINUTE

I **GUESS.**

SOPHIA SMILES AT THE **EARTH-PIG** IN GRATITUDE. SHE HAD EXPECTED A FIT OF JEALOUS RAGE NOW THAT HE WAS NO LONGER HER **TRUE LOVE...**

FOR **ONCE**, THOUGH, SHE HAD **ALLIED** HERSELF WITH A **WINNER!** HENROT, FERAS AND ALL THE OTHERS WERE BEHIND HER NOW...

GOOD LUCK, **CEREBUS...**

BE **CAREFUL** THEY DON'T SEE YOU...

AND SO, THE **EARTH-PIG** DEPARTS, LEAVING SOPHIA TO HER DREAMS OF SUNKEN MARBLE BATH TUBS AND MALE ATTENDANTS...

...THE TCADMIN TO HIS DREAMS OF GOLD AND SOPHIA...

...AND MEIRGEN TO HIS DREAMS OF RIBS THAT DIDN'T **HURT** QUITE SO MUCH!

AN HOUR LATER, IN THE TCARMIN GUARDS' ENCAMPED CARAVAN

THERE'S ONLY *ONE* IN THE DECK, YOU OLD *BUZZARD* AND IT'LL COST YOU TO FIND WHETHER I HAVE IT...

ONE MORE HAND AND THAT WILL BE ALL THE *DIAMONDBACK* I CAN AFFORD TONIGHT...

YOU SAID THAT FOUR HOURS AGO,...IN OR OUT?

KHAIVEN SORCERERS! ...KHAIVEN SORCERERS!

EH?

LOOK--LOOK-- HOW THEY... CHANGED ME!

IT'S... THROGO!?

AYE: THROGO!...KHAIVEN SORCERERS... SABOTAGING BRIDGE...ONE HOUR OUT THAT WAY...WOMEN BEING RAPED,... CHILDREN...MOLESTED...FOOD PRICES SKYROCKETING...

I'LL...GUARD MERCHANT... GO...GO!

FOR THROGO!

HUNS! HUNS!

WOMEN RAPED!

FOOD PRICES SKYROCKETING!

CHILDREN MOLESTED!

AVENGE! AVENGE!

HELLO-- I'M *CEREBUS THE AARDVARK.* YOU HAVE EXACTLY FOUR SECONDS TO HAND OVER THE *BLACK BLOSSOM LOTUS*...

AND YOU'VE JUST USED UP *THREE* OF THEM...

HAVE A NICE TRIP BACK TO *UNSHIB*...

NOW, IF CEREBUS COULD ONLY SEE THE LOOK ON *THROGO'S* FACE WHEN HIS COMRADES SWOOP DOWN ON HIM...

...IT WOULDN'T BE A HALF-BAD DAY...

THE MERCHANT THE COCKROACH

CEREBUS HARBOURED THE BELIEF THAT BEDUIN EPITOMIZED THE **WORST** ASPECTS OF LOWER FELDA. ONLY IN **BEDUIN** COULD YOU DEBATE PHILOSOPHY WITH A SOLDIER BY DAY...

AND BY NIGHT, AWAKE TO FIND HIM CARVING A NEW MOUTH UNDER YOUR CHIN...THE CITY ALSO FAIRLY **REEKED** OF WINE AND PERFUME...

HE ALMOST WISHED HIS COMPANION **WAS** LEADING HIM INTO A **TRAP** SO HE COULD VENT HIS RAGE! BUT FIRST HE HAD TO SEE IF THE MERCHANT WAS SERIOUS ABOUT THE **HUNDRED GOLD COINS**...

I HOPE FOR BOTH OUR SAKES THAT YOU HAVEN'T *STUMBLED* ACROSS A *FAKE*. IN THE PAST WEEK ALONE I'VE BOUGHT MEALS FOR A *DOZEN* BAR PATRONS CLAIMING TO POSSESS *AUTHENTIC* MAGIC CHARMS

I'VE TOYED WITH THE IDEA OF OPENING A *SPARE PARTS CLINIC* FOR *LIZARDS, BATS* AND *RABBITS*...

WHY DO YOU KEEP LOOKING *AROUND?*

THERE HAVE BEEN A NUMBER OF INCIDENTS OF *VIOLENCE* IN THIS *NEIGHBOURHOOD.* A MERCHANT MUST BE *CONSTANTLY* ON HIS GUARD...

CEREBUS HAS YET TO MEET A MAN WHO *DIDN'T*...

HA HA! MERCHANT OR *OTHERWISE,* EH? WELL *PUT* MY DIMINUTIVE FRIEND...THESE *ARE* BIZARRE TIMES...

BUT, *NOW*...

I SHOULD LIKE TO SEE YOUR '*LOTUS*'...

AYE! IT IS THE *LOTUS* -- AND A BARGAIN AT A *HUNDRED GOLD PIECES!* PROBABLY THE PUREST MAGIC OBJECT IN THE KNOWN WORLD.

THERE IS BUT *ONE* THING CAN BE DONE WITH IT...

SPLASH

CEREBUS MUST HAVE *DOZED* OFF AND MISSED SOMETHING...

WHY DID YOU JUST THROW THE PUREST MAGIC OBJECT IN THE KNOWN WORLD INTO THE *FELD RIVER?*

I AM A SORCERER TURNED *BUSINESSMAN!* THE MYSTIC ARTS ARE DYING, AND THOSE LEFT IN IT ARE BUFFOONS IN NECROMANCERS CLOTHING! WERE THEY TO GET THEIR HANDS ON THE LOTUS, THESE DIME-A-DOZEN ILLUSIONISTS COULD WREAK *HAVOC,* TOPPLE EMPIRES AND BRING US *ALL* TO CRASHING RUIN...

IT IS MY ROLE-- *NAY*-- MY DUTY IN LIFE TO BUY ALL MYSTIC OBJECTS IN FELDA AND *DISPOSE* OF THEM! I WILL PERMIT NO ATTEMPTS TO UNSTEADY THE SOCIAL ORDER--

IT'S BAD FOR *BUSINESS...*

AND AS I *SAID*-- I'M A BUSINESSMAN

YOU WOULDN'T HAPPEN TO SEE MY *WRINKLE CREAM* OVER THERE WOULD YOU?

A LITTLE PINK JAR.

CEREBUS IS A **BUSINESS MAN** HIMSELF...

FROM TIME TO TIME...

AH, YES! THE MONEY!

YOU CAN **COUNT** IT IF YOU LIKE.

NO NEED.

IF THERE ARE ANY COINS **MISSING**...

CEREBUS WILL RETURN AND **DIVEST** YOU OF CERTAIN CRITICAL PORTIONS OF YOUR **ANATOMY**...

YOU'LL WANT TO SAVE SOME **RAGE** FOR MY ACCOUNTANT... HE'S THE ONE WHO FILLS THE SACKS...

BEDUIN IS A **CESSPOOL** OF DEGENERATES AND CUTTHROATS IN POWDERED WIGS...

CEREBUS WOULD NOT LIVE HERE IF THE REST OF THE WORLD TURNED TO **ORANGE SLIME!**

YOUR PHRASEOLOGY LEAVES SOMETHING TO BE **DESIRED**, BUT I TAKE IT YOU ARE OFFERING ME SOME "FRIENDLY ADVICE." MAYHAP ≡YAAAWWN≡ WE CAN DISCUSS THE MERITS OF **BEDUIN** ANOTHER TIME...

CEREBUS WAS **JUST** LEAVING...

CEREBUS OWED HIM SOME ADVICE FOR BUYING THE *LOTUS*, BUT IF HE'S GOING TO ...

MMBLE MM GRABLEM KILL 'EM ALL! HSSS! BREAK 'EM IN TWO!

I'M MMBLE KILL EVERY ONE OF 'EM! HSSS.

YOU WON'T ESCAPE, MURDERERS!

I'LL BREAK YOUR SPINES AND STOMP ON YOUR FACES MM

DO YOU **HEAR** ME?!!

I'M GOING TO KILL YOU *ALL*!

HSSS.

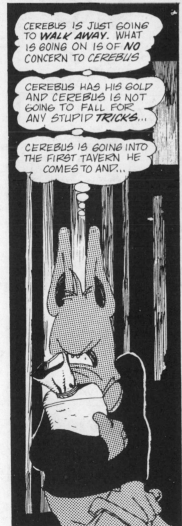

CEREBUS IS JUST GOING TO **WALK AWAY.** WHAT IS GOING ON IS OF **NO** CONCERN TO CEREBUS

CEREBUS HAS HIS GOLD AND CEREBUS IS NOT GOING TO FALL FOR ANY STUPID *TRICKS*...

CEREBUS IS GOING INTO THE FIRST TAVERN HE COMES TO AND...

ON THE *OTHER* HAND, ONE QUICK LOOK AND CEREBUS WILL LIKELY SEE THERE IS A *LOGICAL* EXPLANATION FOR ALL OF THIS...

EVIL! EVIL! EVIL!

HSSS!

THEN *AGAIN*...

234

CEREBUS DOESN'T *GET* IT...

SLINK-- *LURK!*

HE BEAT UP THE GUY WHO KILLED HIS PARENTS AND EVEN GOT A POUCH OF GOLD TO HELP *CONSOLE* HIMSELF.

SHADOWS SHADOWS!

HEE-HEE!

REVENGE! REVENGE!

SO WHAT'S HE AFTER *NOW?*

THERE'S ONLY *ONE* THING MORE IDIOTIC THAN RUNNING AROUND IN A MASK AFTER DARK IN A *SNOWSTORM*...

AND THAT'S *FOLLOWING* SOMEONE IN A MASK AFTER DARK...

...ONE FLIGHT UP ON AN *ICE-COVERED* LEDGE...

HEE-HEE! PUNCH 'EM INNA FACE!

KICK 'EM INNA *STOMACH* ≈ giggle ≈

...AND THAT GOES FOR YOUR LITTLE *DOG,* TOO! HEEHEEHEE!

237

A GOOD NIGHT'S WORK! MAYHAP ONE DAY I WILL SEE A TIME WHEN *ALL* IS GOOD AND JUST AND *COCKROACH-Y* BUT FOR NOW, I NEED REST...

YOU HEAR ME, *RED CLAW BUTCHERS?* THERE ISN'T A HOLE BIG ENOUGH FOR YOU TO HIDE FROM...

...THE *WRATH* OF...

...*THE COCKROACH!* HSSS!

CEREBUS ONLY HOPES THIS *SOLILOQUY* LASTS UNTIL I BEAT HIM *HOME!*

WITH CEREBUS' LUCK, SOMEONE STOPPED HIM TO ASK DIRECTIONS...

...IN WHICH CASE HE WON'T BE HERE FOR *DAYS!*

ONCE MORE I RETURN TO MY SECRET *ROACH LAIR!* HSSS!

AHA!

RETURN OF THE COOTIE!

MM. A CONCEALED PANEL... LOOKS LIKE CEREBUS WILL HAVE NO TROUBLE ADDING A COUPLE OF PURSES TO HIS *EARNINGS...*

SLEEP. MUST... SLEEP.

MOMENTS LATER, HIS COSTUME SECRETED BEHIND ANOTHER PANEL, THE *MERCHANT* COLLAPSES INTO A CHAIR...

REVENGE

REVENGE

MHHH

IF *CEREBUS* IS GOING TO FOLLOW LUNATICS THROUGH THE SNOW...

...HE'S GOING TO MAKE SURE HE DOESN'T DO IT FOR *FREE...*

WHAT? WHAT'S THIS?

OH YES "JUST LEAVING". WELL THANK YOU FOR THE *LOTUS*. WE'LL TALK ABOUT BEDUIN SOME *OTHER* TIME! REALLY MUST GET SOME *SLEEP*...

CEREBUS-- UH -- THAT IS...

GOOD NIGHT.

SOMEHOW, THE MERCHANT AND THE COCKROACH ARE *TWO* PEOPLE IN *ONE* BODY! WHEN CEREBUS LEFT THE *FIRST* TIME, THE MERCHANT FELL ASLEEP AND THE COCKROACH WOKE UP. WHEN THE *COCKROACH* FELL ASLEEP, THE MERCHANT WOKE UP UNAWARE OF WHAT THE COCKROACH HAD BEEN *DOING*...

WHICH MEANS THE *MERCHANT* DOESN'T KNOW THAT THERE ARE TWO PURSES HIDDEN IN THAT *SECRET PANEL*...

CEREBUS HAD BETTER GET THOSE TWO PURSES, BEFORE THE *COOTIE* WAKES UP...

...AND SPENDS THEM ON *ANTENNA POLISH* OR SOMETHING...

CEREBUS SHOULD *PROBABLY* LEAVE THE GOLD OUTSIDE WITH HIS *SWORD*...

BUT HE IS TAKING NO CHANCES OF LOSING THE ONLY MONEY HE HAS HAD IN *MONTHS*...

TARIM! ONLY IN BEDUIN WOULD A THIEF HIDE HIS PURSE IN A *BLOODY* MINE-SHAFT...

CEREBUS HOPES THE BOTTOM IS WHERE HE *THINKS* IT IS. THIS IS *ALREADY* MORE TROUBLE THAN AN EXTRA BIT OF GOLD IS *WORTH*...

DAMN! BAG OF GOLD SLIPPED OUT OF *CEREBUS'* HAND.

NOW.. WHERE DID IT....

241

AN HOUR LATER

CEREBUS HAS TO HAVE THIS GOLD -- ALL OF IT DOWN TO THE VERY *LAST* COIN...

EARTH-PIGLET DREAMS ARE *MADE* OF THIS MUCH GOLD...

BUT HOW CAN CEREBUS *MOVE* IT ALL?

WHENEVER CEREBUS THINKS OF THE MERCHANT UP THERE, COMPLETELY *UNAWARE* OF...

OF COURSE! THE *MERCHANT* IS ASLEEP!

COCKROOACH

SNFX?

AWAAKEN--COCKROACH!

I AM THE *SPIRIT* OF YOUR FATHER, *COCKROACH!*

YOU HAVE STRAYED FROM THE TRUE *PATH*, MY CHILD...

AND I HAVE COME FROM THE BEYOND TO COUNSEL YOU...

DO YOU NOT REMEMBER WHAT I TOLD YOU ABOUT *STEALING* WHEN YOU WERE A BOY!

OH, *YES,* FATHER!

YOU SAID IF I GOT *CAUGHT* YOU WOULD BEAT ME TO A PULP.

OH...OF COURSE...

THINK! THINK!

PRAISE TARIM! I AM HERE TO BRING YOU THE WORD-- THE WORD OF TARIM...

THE WORD, FATHER?

CONDOMINIUMS! TARIM HAS A CONDOMINIUM JUST FOR YOU! LUXURIOUS LIVING IN THE AFTERLIFE... IF YOU BELIEVE!

PRAISE TARIM!

I DO! I DO!!

BUT TARIM NEEDS GOLD FOR HIS GOOD WORKS AND CONDOMINIUMS! LOTS OF IT! BARRELS OF IT! WALLS FULL OF IT --ALUMINUM SIDING DOESN'T GROW ON TREES! WILL YOU GIVE YOUR GOLD TO TARIM TODAY?

YES! YES!

YOU ARE FAST BECOMING A PRIZED FOLLOWER! LET ME HEAR A 'PRAISE TARIM!'

PRAISE TARIM!

THE SPIRIT IS REALLY UPON YOU, COCKROACH MY BOY-- I'M GOING TO PUT YOUR NAME IN FOR BEACHFRONT PROPERTY AND A GARDENER

BUT RIGHT NOW, YOU'VE GOT TO GO GET A WAGON AND A TEAM OF HORSES SO WE CAN START RELOCATING TARIM'S ASSETS!

PRAISE TARIM! BUT WHERE AM I GOING TO GET A WAGON AT THIS TIME OF NIGHT?

STEAL ONE...

AND DON'T GET CAUGHT OR I'LL BEAT YOU TO A PULP!

CEREBUS RANKED THEM EASILY THE BEST THREE WEEKS OF HIS LIFE! EACH DAY, HE AND THE COCKROACH WOULD LOAD FIVE SACKS ON THE WAGON AND MOVE THEM TO A DRY WELL ABOUT A MILE OUTSIDE THE CITY. ONE TRIP A DAY SO NO *SUSPICIONS* WERE AROUSED. THEN THEY WENT ON TO NEARBY PEDRON

WHERE CEREBUS DRANK AND PLAYED *DIAMONDBACK* UNTIL THE SUN SET. IN A FEW WEEKS, HE COULD START MOVING THE GOLD TO IEST AND BUY HIS *OWN* TAVERN...

THIRTY YEARS!... COCKROACH-- MERCHANT...

OH-OH NOT *AGAIN*...

TARIM DOESN'T WANT YOU TO THINK! TARIM ONLY WANTS YOUR GOLD...

HOW MANY TIMES DOES YOUR FATHER HAVE TO TELL YOU?

NOW- STOP- THINKING!

PRAISE TARIM!

IF THAT HAPPENS ONE MORE TIME, CEREBUS IS GOING TO BE SELLING *COCKROACH FILETS* IN HIS NEW TAVERN

THERE'S THE CITY-GATES-- TRY TO NOT LOOK SUSPICIOUS, *COCKROACH*

THE *COCKROACH!*

...I...AM THE *COCKROACH*

uh -- COULD WE TALK ABOUT THIS *OUTSIDE* THE CITY GATES?

THE *COCKROACH* -- I -- *STOLE* ALL THAT *GOLD* AND NOW YOU, *TOO* ARE STEALING IT -- I'LL HAVE YOU ARRESTED! I, THE *MERCHANT* WILL USE THAT GOLD FOR *TARIM!* EVEN THE POOR WILL HAVE BEACH- FRONT *CONDOMINIUMS!*

IF CEREBUS ISN'T *CAREFUL,* HE'S GOING TO START A WHOLE NEW *RELIGION...*

MAYHAP MY BUSINESSMAN BUG HAS OUTLIVED HIS *USEFULNESS* AND IT IS TIME TO MOVE TARIM'S *PRESENT ASSETS* TO *IEST...*

CEREBUS CAN ALWAYS COME BACK FOR WHAT IS *LEFT* IN THE WALL IN A FEW *MONTHS...*

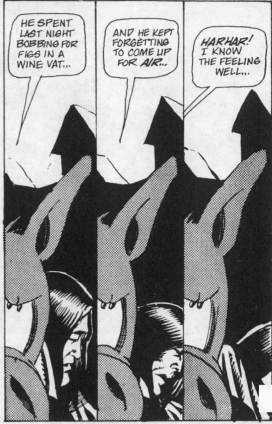

246

THE **COCKROACH HUNT** WOULD GIVE HIM AN EXTRA FEW SECONDS ONLY... THEY WOULD BE AFTER HIM NOW AS AN **ACCOMPLICE**. THE COCKROACH WOULD BE BUYING HIS FREEDOM RIGHT NOW WITH A WALL FULL OF GOLD

CEREBUS KNEW THE MILITARY GOVERNMENT WOULD BE DELIGHTED TO AT LAST BALANCE THEIR BUDGET.

FOR HIS PART, CEREBUS WOULD SEE THAT THEY DID NOT GET **ALL** THE GOLD...

SEVEN SACKS! A SUBSTANTIAL DROP FROM EIGHT FEET OF LOOT, BUT ENOUGH TO **GUARANTEE** CEREBUS ALE MONEY FOR THE DURATION OF THE SPRING...

ONE MORE MINUTE AND THE SOLDIERS WOULDN'T HAVE A PRAYER OF CATCHING HIM...

BUT EVEN AS HE LASHES THE SACKS INTO PLACE ON THE SADDLE...

...SEVEN MOUNTED SOLDIERS **THUNDER** TOWARD HIM IN A SWIRL OF DUST...

BRIEFLY, THE EARTH-PIG TURNS, **CONTEMPLATING** SOME REVENGE FOR THE LOSS OF HIS FORTUNE...

MAYHAP WHEN HE REACHES THE **HIGHLANDS**...

BUT FOR **NOW**...

...HE HAD TO REGAIN HIS LOST ADVANTAGE. ...AND *QUICKLY*...

TARIM!

ALREADY THEY ARE TOO CLOSE!

A *SACRIFICE*...

BUT THERE IS NO SACRIFICE TOO GREAT FOR KEEPING ONE'S FUR *INTACT*...

DEIDRE! COME WITH ME!

THE REST OF YOU GATHER UP THE GOLD!

CEREBUS HAD ONLY A FEW **SECONDS** TO ACT

THESE WERE NO LOCAL FARMERS IN SOLDIERS' CLOTHING. HE WOULD NEVER BEAT THEM TO THE HIGHLANDS.

HO!

DISMOUNT...

...BUT BE ON YOUR GUARD!

AYE! AND THREE MORE BAGS OF **GOLD**...

IT'S THE HORSE HE STOLE, ALL **RIGHT!**

HE MUST HAVE JUMPED RATHER THAN FACE A TRIAL AND **EXECUTION**...

I GUESS WE SHOULD HEAD BACK TO BEDUIN WITH THE GOLD...

GOLD? YOU MEAN THE THREE BAGS HE WAS HOLDING ONTO WHEN HE JUMPED?

HOLDING ONTO? BUT THEY'RE RIGHT THERE ON HIS...

OHO! I GET YOUR DRIFT...

MY BROTHER LIVES ABOUT A MILE FROM HERE... WE CAN GET HIM TO HIDE IT FOR US WHILE WE REPORT BACK...

CEREBUS IS SIMPLY GOING TO **HAVE** TO FIND A LESS **NERVE-WRACKING** WAY TO MAKE MONEY!

AT LEAST, MY FRIEND--*THE COCKROACH* WAS FINALLY STOPPED AFTER ALL THESE YEARS! LOCKED AWAY AS HE DESERVES IN THE LOWEST LEVEL OF *DARNIER PRISON* -- AND DO YOU *KNOW* WHAT THEY *FOUND?*

A WALL FULL OF *GOLD.*

ALMOST A HUNDRED SACKS OF GOLD IN A DRY WELL!

AHH-- YOU'RE DRUNK, FRIEND --NO ONE HAS THAT KIND OF MONEY!

IT'S THE *TRUTH*-- I *SWEAR* IT!

THE WALL FULL OF GOLD! *TARIM!* HE DIDN'T TELL THEM ABOUT IT...

CEREBUS LURCHED FROM HIS SEAT-- SO THE FATES HAD GRANTED HIM ANOTHER TRY AT THAT UNGODLY AMOUNT OF GOLD--STASHED BY THE COCKROACH OVER THREE DECADES

THIS TIME *CEREBUS* WOULD TAKE NO CHANCES THIS TIME HE WOULD MOVE THE GOLD ALL AT *ONE TIME...*

THIS TIME...

CEREBUS WOULD WAIT UNTIL HE WAS SOBER ENOUGH TO WALK...

IT WOULD HAVE TAKEN THE AVERAGE SAILOR FOUR HOURS TO PADDLE INTO BEDUIN. AN HOUR LATER, CEREBUS WAS WATCHING FOR THE LOOMING SHAPE OF THE *COCKROACH'S* FORMER RESIDENCE

BUT THEN THE AVERAGE SAILOR WOULD NOT HAVE HAD THE BENEFIT OF THE EARTH-PIG'S MOTIVATING FORCE....

FRUSTRATED GREED....

NO ONE IN *SIGHT*... CEREBUS PICKED A GOOD NIGHT

JUST AS CEREBUS *REMEMBERED*... THE STONE DOESN'T EXTEND ALL THE WAY TO THE BOTTOM...

AND THE WOOD LOOKS *ROTTEN* ENOUGH THAT...

SCRAMBLING ONTO THE NARROW LEDGE, CEREBUS COULD ALMOST *SMELL* HIS FORTUNE

A LITTLE *FORCE* SHOULD BRING A *CASCADE* OF GOLD INTO THE...

254

CEREBUS ENTERED THE WALL-SPACE READY TO REND, SLASH AND/OR MUTILATE ANYTHING THAT MOVED...

WHOEVER HAD ASSUMED THAT THE GOLD WAS THERE FOR THE TAKING WOULD PAY FOR THAT ASSUMPTION WITH HIS *BLOOD*...

THERE WAS JUST NO HONESTY ANYMORE TIME WAS AN AARDVARK COULD FEEL SAFE WITH HIS GOLD STASHED IN A...

BUT THEN CAME A BRIEF MOMENT OF CLARITY-- WHOEVER HAD STOLEN THE GOLD WAS LONG GONE...

CEREBUS STOOD VERY STILL, THE IDEA TURNING OVER IN HIS MIND...

THE GOLD WAS *GONE* ...

IF IT WAS TRUE HE WOULD TAKE *BEDUIN* APART BRICK BY ROTTEN BRICK UNTIL HE FOUND THE GOLD --*HIS* GOLD. NO HALF-WITTED WINE-SOAKED ...

EH? ...

WHOEVER DID THIS WILL LIVE TO REGRET NOT COVERING HIS *TRACKS*...

...BY CLOVIS' RACK AND IRONS...

OF COURSE!

A *TUNNEL!*

CEREBUS WILL HANG HIM BY HIS *THUMBS* OVER A SLOW FLAME ...DROPPING HIM SLOWLY...

THEN *DISMEMBER* HIM-- STARTING WITH THE *TOES* AND WORKING UP...

THEN A FEW RED HOT NAILS DRIVEN INTO...

ON THE OTHER HAND THIS IS NO TIME FOR *SUBTLETY*...

BETTER THAT CEREBUS JUST RUN HIM *THROUGH* WITH...

OH, NO...

KILL YOUR PARENTS WILL THEY? DON'T YOU *WORRY* -- WE'LL GET *REVENGE!* *REVENGE* =HSSS= PUNCH 'EM INNA *FACE* KICK 'EM INNA *HEAD*...

WE'LL BE LIFE-LONG *PARTNERS* AND *BOSOM BUDDIES!* I'LL TEACH YOU EVERYTHING I *KNOW*...

THAT SHOULDN'T TAKE *LONG*...

ACTUALLY *CEREBUS* CAME TO WARN YOU OF A *PLOT* AGAINST YOU

PLOT?! HA! YOU HAVE SO MUCH TO *LEARN*... *EVERYONE* PLOTS AGAINST *THE COCKROACH*...THE COCKROACH KNOWS

NYAHHAHA HAHEEHEE HOOHAHAHA HAHAHENH

HSSS

BUT GO AHEAD, *KID*-- TELL YOUR *GUARDIAN* FRIEND, MENTOR AND IDOL ABOUT THIS =HEH= *PLOT*, I'LL BET YOU I KNOW *ALL* ABOUT IT

ELROD OF MELVINBONE PLANS TO COME AND STEAL YOUR GOLD TOMORROW

AHA

AHA? YOU MEAN YOU'VE *HEARD* OF HIM

HEARD OF HIM?-- HE'S COMING *TOMORROW* TO STEAL ALL MY *GOLD!*

OH-- OF *COURSE*

CEREBUS MUST BE GETTING *ABSENT-MINDED* IN HIS OLD AGE...

NOW... WHAT DO I *DO* ABOUT IT? I COULD-- uh *NO*, THAT WOULDN'T WORK I COULD...I COULD...

uh...

WE COULD MOVE THE GOLD BEFORE HE *GETS* HERE ...

I'VE *GOT* IT!

WE'LL MOVE THE *GOLD* BEFORE HE GETS ...

YOUR ABILITY TO THINK THROUGH A *PROBLEM* IS *AMAZING* ...

HA-HA--THAT'S WHY EVERYONE ELSE IS *OUT THERE* AND THE COCKROACH IS *IN HERE!*

YUP-- THAT'S WHAT WE'LL DO -- WE'LL MOVE THE GOLD

WE'LL SHOW THAT CRUMMY ELROD OF MELBABONE

TRY AND STEAL MY GOLD, WILL HE? WE'LL JUST SEE ABOUT...

uh -- HOW ARE WE GOING TO MOVE IT...

CEREBUS HAS A BOAT WAITING ON THE RIVER...

THANK YOU, OLD CHUM!

I'LL PAY YOU BACK --SOME DAY WE'LL HAVE A LOVELY BIG HOUSE --LUXURIOUS SURROUNDINGS

THE FINEST SILK ROBES -- A BUTLER, AND FLOWERS -- OH YES! LOTS AND LOTS OF FLOWERS...

CEREBUS IS STARTING TO WONDER ABOUT THIS BUG...

I KNOW IT'S A PAINFUL SUBJECT, BUT CAN YOU TELL ME HOW YOUR PARENTS DIED?

MOM AND DAD WERE CIRCUS PERFORMERS --ACROBATS

THE RED CLAW CULT CUT THROUGH THEIR TRAPEZE ROPES...

THE ROPES SNAPPED IN MID-AIR AND THEY FELL...

THEN, ONE OF THE RED CLAW CLIMBED UP TO THE SAFETY NET AND BEAT THEM TO DEATH WITH A CLUB...

TRAGIC...

JUST TRAGIC...

I KNOW, BUT IT WAS THE BEST CEREBUS COULD DO ON THE SPUR-OF-THE MOMENT...

THERE WAS ONE CHANCE! *SIMULTANEOUS* WITH THE THOUGHT, CEREBUS PLUNGES INTO AN ALLEYWAY...

ONE WAY OR ANOTHER, THE COCKROACH WOULD HAVE TO BE PUT BACK IN HIS CELL...

...AND *SOON!*

THE *COCK AND BULL TAVERN!* IF HIS MEMORY WASN'T FAULTY AND HE COULD REACH THE MEZZANINE IN TIME...

SORRY --WE'RE...

AAAK

OUT OF MY WAY, *DOLT!!*

YOU *CAN'T*...I'LL CALL THE *WATCH!*

HE'S WELCOME TO *TRY...*

...THINKS HE CAN CATCH *CEREBUS* ...

IF THERE'S A SOLDIER IN *BEDUIN* ...

TARIM! NO SIGN OF HIM ON THE *RIVER...*

CEREBUS CAN ONLY HOPE HE'S *DIRECTLY UNDER* THE...

261

DO YOU HAVE *ANY* IDEA HOW HARD IT'S GOING TO BE TO *ROW* THIS THING *UPSTREAM*--FULL OF *GOLD*!!?

DO YOU?!!

NOW-GIVE-ME-THAT-OAR!

CEREBUS FORGOT TO *MENTION*...

IT LOOKS *BAD* NOW, *OLD CHUM* BUT, IF YOU LOOK ON THE *BRIGHT* SIDE...

IF YOU SAY ONE *WORD*--HE'S GOING TO USE *YOU* FOR AN OAR...

THEIR PROGRESS IN THE FIRST TEN MINUTES COULD BE MEASURED IN *INCHES*! CEREBUS KNEW HE WOULD HAVE TO ROW A GOOD QUARTER MILE TO REACH QUIETER WATER

CEREBUS, BOY!...

I'D--I SAY-- I'D KNOW THAT *BUNNY-SUIT* ANYWHERE!

OH, TARIM, NO!

WELL, I'LL BE WRAPPED IN *HAM-FAT* AND PICKLED FOR THE *HOLIDAYS* ...

IT *IS* YOU!

SAY SOMETHING, BOY... DON'T TELL ME YOU'VE *FORGOTTEN* ELROD THE ALBINO -- SAY -- WHO'S YOUR FRIEND WITH THE *CURB-FEELERS* IMBEDDED IN HIS *SKULL?*

ELROD?

DID HE SAY -- *ELROD?!*

YES! YES! THAT'S WHAT HE SAID -- NO DOUBT AT ALL -- IT'S *HIM!*

HSSSS!

HEH-HEH! MY *REPUTATION* -- I SAY -- MY *REPUTATION* PRECEDES ME, EH? DON'T FREEZE UP, SON...

THIS MIGHT BE YOUR *ONLY* CHANCE TO MEET A *GENUINE* LAST RULER OF A DYING RACE

CEREBUS IS JUST GOING TO LET THE *COOTIE* MAKE MINCE- MEAT OUT OF HIM...

CEREBUS ALREADY KNOWS ELROD WOULD BE HARD-PRES- SED TO BEAT AN *EGG* *

* SEE CEREBUS #4

REVENGE HSSS

STAND WHERE YOU ARE *MORTAL!*

FOR I AM THE *COCKROACH* AND...

COCKROACH? PLEASED TO MEET YOU, SON! NAME'S ELROD, ACCENT ON THE 'EL'

SAY-- PURPLE IS YOUR COLOUR, BOY! WHAT-- I SAY-- WHAT'S YOUR LINE OF WORK?

I DEDICATE MYSELF DAILY TO FACING THE *CRIMINAL ELEMENT* ON THEIR OWN TERRITORY IN *MORTAL COMBAT*

SORT OF A COMBINATION SOCIAL WORKER AND *HOODLUM,* EH?

YOUR UNIFORM'S ALL *WRONG,* SON...

MY... UNIFORM?

YOUR *HEADGEAR,* SON... IT'S ABOUT AS USEFUL AS A *BOREALAN* AT A BANQUET!

IMPRACTICAL, THAT IS

ON THE OTHER HAND -- CEREBUS HAS WAITED A *LONG* TIME FOR THIS...

AS LONG AS *ELROD* IS GOING TO GET BEATEN TO A *PULP* CEREBUS MIGHT AS WELL...

NO NO! *DOWN*, BOY!

HEEL-- I SAY-- *HEEL*, SON!

HALT! YOU'RE GOING BACK TO YOUR CELL, COCK-ROACH! THE *GOLD'S* BEEN REMOVED TO MAKE MORE ROOM FOR YOU...

SO!-- ELROD'S CRONIES!

ELROD? WHO'S *ELROD?*

YO!

NO TIME TO *DIG OUT* THE *SWORD!*

WELL, CEREBUS HAS FOUGHT WITH A LOT LESS USEFUL WEAPONS THAN AN *OAR*...

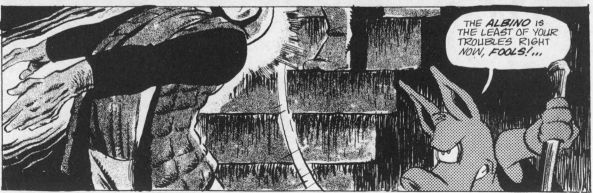

THE *ALBINO* IS THE LEAST OF YOUR TROUBLES RIGHT NOW, *FOOLS!*...

CEREBUS HAD **ALREADY** INVESTED THE BETTER HALF OF TWO MONTHS IN THE GOLD! IF THE FATES DEMANDED THAT HE GET NO MORE THAN A BOATLOAD, SO **BE** IT, BUT NO SECOND-RATE SOLDIERS WERE GOING TO GET IN HIS...

....WAY.

TWANG

THAKT!

268

KRAK

DOOOF

KLANK

WELL *DONE*, SHORT, GREY WONDER! WE MAKE A PRETTY GOOD *TEAM!*

OF COURSE IT PROBABLY WOULDN'T HAVE TAKEN *ME* AS LONG TO BEAT THEM, BUT I WANTED TO SEE...

THAT'S FOR LOSING MOST OF *CEREBUS'* GOLD!

SOMETHING YOU WANT TO *SAY*, ALBINO?

JE SUIS NON HABLE, PARDONEZ-MES...

HE WOULD HEAD FOR ONE OF THE SMALLER TOWNS BORDERING BEDUIN AND BUY THE *TAVERN* HE HAD BEEN THINKING ABOUT...

SOME DAY-- I SAY, SOME *DAY*, SON, WE'RE GOING TO HAVE TO HAVE A *LONG* TALK...

AND YOU CAN EXPLAIN WHAT IN THE HECK JUST *HAPPENED* HERE...

AS HE DRIFTS OUT OF THE TUNNEL, CEREBUS LOOKS UP TO SEE THE SUN *RISING*...

THE LONG BEDUIN NIGHT WAS OVER

...AND THE GOLD WAS HIS...

WITH THE SUN COMES A WAVE OF *EXULTATION* AND A STRANGE NEW SENSE OF OPTIMISM...

ABRUPTLY, CEREBUS' WORLD SHATTERS AND QUICKLY *REFORMS* AS A MONTAGE OF IMAGES-- MURKY WATER, SPLINTERED TIMBERS AND AN ELUSIVE TWINKLING VANISHING BELOW HIM...

LET THEM SEND MORE SOLDIERS --A WHOLE *ARMY*! HE WOULD FIGHT THEM OFF, TOO -THE-GOLD- WAS-HIS!!

A BOATFUL OF IT!!

CEREBUS' HEAD BREAKS THE SURFACE AND HE GULPS LUNGS-FUL OF *AIR*-- AIR THAT SOMEHOW NO LONGER SMELLED AS SWEET AS IT HAD BARE *MOMENTS* BEFORE...

HE SWIMS TO THE SHATTERED FRAME OF THE *BOAT!* HIS INTENTION WAS TO ESCAPE BEFORE THE SOLDIERS *AWOKE*

THERE WAS NO TIME FOR REGRET OR SELF-RECRIMINATION...

IF ANYTHING, HE IS GRATEFUL THAT THE WEATHER IS WARM AND THE CURRENT *SWIFT*...

WITH A MINIMUM OF EFFORT HE WOULD BE OUTSIDE OF BEDUIN'S WALLS WITHIN THE HOUR IN SEARCH OF SHELTER FOOD AND ALE

"ALL THINGS CONSIDERED," MUSES THE EARTH-PIG...

"IT'S BEEN ONE HELL OF A LOUSY *TWENTY-SEVENTH* BIRTHDAY..."

THE FIRST BREATH OF SUMMER IN LOWER FELDA...

A SOLITARY BIRD, WINGS OVER THE LUSH FARMING LAND FOLLOWING THE COURSE OF THE CLEAR BLUE FELD RIVER ...

AND WHETHER IT IS COGNIZANT OF THE FACT OR NOT...

IT BECOMES YET ANOTHER LINK IN THE CHAIN OF MISFORTUNE WHICH HAS RECENTLY HOUNDED A CERTAIN EARTH-PIG BORN!

UNHH?

BLACK MAGIKING

CEREBUS IS NO CREATURE OF *SORCERY*

CEREBUS CONTEMPLATES RUSHING THE LEADER RESTRAINED ONLY BY HIS KNOWLEDGE OF FELD FARMERS...

...AS THE RAW MATERIAL FOR FELDWAR ARMIES THEY ARE RUGGED AND VICIOUS COMBATANTS!

THEN EXPLAIN YOUR PRESENCE HERE...

...NOW!

CEREBUS HAS JUST BEEN...

LYING DEVIL SPAWN!

CEREBUS BRACES AS THE BULKY FORM HURTLES TOWARD HIM, STAFF RAISED...

THE EARTH-PIG IS NOT ALTOGETHER UNPREPARED FOR THE ATTACK

DISCUSSIONS IN LOWER FELDA HAVE, IN HIS EXPERIENCE, A DISTURBING TENDENCY TO TURN PHYSICAL IN THE BLINKING OF AN EYE...

THE ATTACKING FARMER, OVERCONFIDENT WITH HIS SIZE ADVANTAGE, WIELDS HIS HEAVY, WOODEN STAFF LIKE A FLYSWATTER...

...PREDICTABLE.

THE RESULTS OF THIS ERROR IN JUDGEMENT, AS WOOD IMPACTS WITH EARTH-PIG PALMS, IS...

AS HIS FOE STRUGGLES TO HIS FEET, THE EARTH-PIG TOSSES THE STAFF TO ONE SIDE...

...CEREBUS INTENDS TO BEAT THE FARMER TO A PULP-- NOT POLE-VAULT OVER HIM!

ENOUGH!

THIS IS A MATTER FOR THE CHURCH OF TARIM TO DECIDE...

SEIZE HIM AND WE'LL TAKE HIM TO THE PRIEST!

THE PRISONER IS ACCUSED OF CONSORTING WITH DARK DEMONS, HIGH CRIMES AGAINST NATURAL LAW, MAKING THE CROPS MOULDY, NOT LOOKING LIKE THE REST OF US...

...AND ANYTHING ELSE THE CHURCH OF TARIM CAN THINK OF IN THE COURSE OF THIS TRIAL...

HOW DOES THE PRISONER *PLEAD?*

CEREBUS *DEMANDS* THAT YOU RELEASE HIM OR HE'LL CALL UPON HIS DARK MASTERS TO TURN YOU INTO A FLOCK OF PIOUS PINK TOADS...

THAT'S NOT A HALF-BAD DEFENCE.

HE'S *BLUFFING.*

TRUST ME.

HMPH!

I SAY WE SHOULD EXECUTE HIM *NOW* AND HAVE THE TRIAL *AFTER* THE FESTIVAL OF VIRGINS!

I DON'T KNOW ABOUT *YOU* BUT I DON'T INTEND TO SPEND THE FESTIVAL OF VIRGINS PICKING PINK WARTS OFF MY BACKSIDE

WAIT A MOMENT-- I THINK I HAVE A WAY TO KILL TWO BIRDS WITH ONE STONE...

TARIM HAS LISTENED TO THE CHARGES AND DECLARES NOW THAT *JUSTICE* MUST BE SERVED...

AS PRIEST OF *THEYR* I SHALL SEE TARIM'S WILL IS DONE

EH?

SOME SORT OF...

PRAISE TARIM AND HIS *INFINITE* MERCY!

...SIGNAL...

SOME TIME LATER, THE PRIEST APPEARS MOVING AWAY FROM THE VILLAGE AND IT'S FIELDS -- HIS EXPRESSION GRIM AND DETERMINED...

...HE IS FOLLOWED BY ONE OF THE FARMERS WHO CARRIES AN INERT GREY BUNDLE ON ONE SHOULDER...

ABRUPTLY THE GRASSES END. ABRUPTLY THE WINDS DIE AND THERE IS NOTHING SAVE THE COLD GREY ROCK AND THE UNNATURALLY LOUD RUSTLING OF PRIESTLY ROBES...

IT IS CALLED BY MANY NAMES, THIS PLACE OF DARK SILENCE "HELL'S GATE" "HOB'S HOLLOW" -- BUT THE VILLAGERS OF THEYR KNOW IT AS...

...THE CASTLE.

LODGED IN THE VALLEY OF MISTS IT IS DARK AND UNHOLY HOME TO **NECROSS THE MAD** REPUTED TO BE THE MOST EVIL AND CUNNING OF THE BLACK SORCERERS...

HIS EVIL IS LEGENDARY IN LOWER FELDA, CAUSING CATASTROPHE AFTER CATASTROPHE --THE BLACK DEATH, THE AVALANCHE AT SAN TREMAIN, THE GREAT FIRE OF BEDUIN

NOT TO MENTION THE PREGNANCY OF ALANNE THE MILK-MAID...

WHO DIDN'T RELISH THE IDEA OF BEING FORCED TO MARRY GUMS, THE VILLAGE IDIOT...

YOUR EMINENCE *PERHAPS* IT IS TOO *DANGEROUS* FOR US TO...

THE CHRONICLES OF TARIM ARE QUITE *CLEAR*, DESPUESS...

YOU HOLD IN YOUR HAND THE KEY TO OUR RELEASE FROM THE THREAT OF *NECROSS THE MAD!*

BUT HE IS *POWERFUL* YOUR EMINENCE

POWERFUL, YES, BUT THIS HELL-SPAWNED "SAVR-A-BUSS" IS A CREATION OF HIS DARK MAGIC

THE CHRONICLES DESCRIBE IN DETAIL THE CLEANSING RITES WHICH WILL AID US IN TURNING HIS MAGIC AGAINST HIM...

DON'T *DAWDLE* DESPUESS!

BUT WHAT IF...

TARIM FORBID

THE CREATURE IS *NOT* OF MAD NECROSS' OWN?

THE CREATURE IS GREY AND FURRY?

YES, YOUR EMINENCE

THE MOULD ON OUR CROPS IS GREY AND FURRY?

YES YOUR EMINENCE.

AND WHO CAUSED OUR CROPS TO TURN GREY AND FURRY?

ARE YOU READY, DESPUESS ... FAVOURED SON OF THE LIVING TARIM?

DESPUESS?

SO, MAD NECROSS! YOU SEEK TO ABDUCT A FOLLOWER OF THE LIVING TARIM!

PREPARE YOURSELF NECROSS! VENGEANCE -WILL-BE- MINE!!

AS SOON AS I CAN FIND SOMEONE TO GO IN AFTER DESPUESS...

283

CEREBUS COULDN'T SAY -- SIXTEEN-FOOT PAPERWEIGHTS AREN'T ORDINARILY REGARDED AS PROOF OF SANITY!

PAPERWEIGHT? *PAPERWEIGHT?* EVEN FOR A SHORT, GREY FURRY PERSON YOU'RE UNUSUALLY *NAIVE!*

THIS IS *THRUNK!* MY GREATEST CREATION

SOMEDAY, I'LL BREATHE LIFE INTO MY STONE *THRUNK*

...AND THEN

AND THEN!

AND THEN *WHAT?*

I HAVEN'T THE *FOGGIEST*

THAT'S WHY I'M A LITTLE RELUCTANT TO BREATHE LIFE INTO HIM...

CEREBUS ALWAYS FEELS OUT-OF-PLACE ASKING INTELLIGENT QUESTIONS IN *LOWER FELDA*...

THE PRIEST WHO BROUGHT YOU HERE WILL BE BACK-- YOU CAN COUNT ON IT!

SEEKING TO DESTROY ME WITH HIS CHANTS AND INVOCATIONS...

THE FOOLS! ALWAYS BLAMING ME FOR THEIR EARTHQUAKES, THEIR FIRES -- ALWAYS BLAMING ME FOR THEIR INSIGNIFICANT TRAGEDIES

DO YOU CAUSE THEM?

288

FOOLS! I'LL CRUSH YOU ALL!!

STOMP STOMP

WELL? DID YOU GUYS GET HIM OR...AAAK!

SAY-- IT'S AWFULLY GORY IN HERE!

LET ME SEE! LET ME SEE!

THIS TIME, CEREBUS HAD DEFINITELY HAD *ENOUGH!* EVERYONE--*EVERYONE* IN LOWER FELDA WAS IN-BLOODY-SANE...

HE HAD WASTED THE BETTER PART OF FOUR WRETCHED MONTHS IN THIS OPEN-AIR *SANITARIUM...*

THE PRIEST! BRING ME THE PRIEST!

THE PRIEST? ISN'T HE THAT RED BLOT ON THE FLOOR OVER THERE?

NAW-- THAT'S D'MITRI!

I GET HIS SHARE OF THE CROPS WHEN WE GET BACK TO THE VILLAGE...

WELL *NO MORE!* BROKE OR NOT, HE WOULD BE OUTSIDE THE BOUNDARIES OF THE FELDWAR STATES INSIDE OF A WEEK OR *DIE* IN THE ATTEMPT...

HE HAD CHASED A SIX-FOOT COOTIE ACROSS BEDUIN... GRAPPLED WITH SOLDIERS ON TWO OCCASIONS, BOTH TIMES LOSING A FORTUNE IN GOLD...

WHAT DO YOU MEAN *YOU* GET HIS SHARES OF THE CROPS, PORK BREATH

HE WAS MY BROTHER!

BRING ME THE PRIEST OR YOU'RE ALL DEAD!

YOU KEEP OUT OF THIS, GRANITE FACE...

HE HAD SPENT FOUR DAYS ADRIFT ON THE FELD RIVER ONLY TO BE WAYLAID BY A BUNCH OF FARMERS WHO LIVED IN MORTAL FEAR OF A HERMIT MAGICIAN WHO SCULPTED SIXTEEN FOOT PAPERWEIGHTS IN HIS SPARE TIME...

GRANITE FACE?! WHO ARE YOU CALLING GRANITE FACE?

YOU, YA BIG STIFF!

YEAH-- WH... DO YOU THINK YOU...

STOMP STOMP

TARIM! CEREBUS WAS THE ONLY NORMAL CREATURE IN THE WHOLE DAMNED COUNTRY

293

Cerebus THE AARDVARK

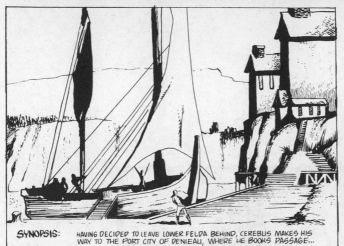

SYNOPSIS: HAVING DECIDED TO LEAVE LOWER FELDA BEHIND, CEREBUS MAKES HIS WAY TO THE PORT CITY OF DENIEAU, WHERE HE BOOKS PASSAGE...

ON THE TRADING VESSEL *CUTTER* BOUND FOR HOME -- THE CITY-STATE OF PALNU

"IT IS A RARE SUMMER'S DAY" CRIED THE SICKENINGLY CHEERFUL SON OF THE DIRECTOR OF TRADE AT PALNU.

"IT HAS THE SMELL OF NEW ADVENTURE TO IT" SMILES YOUNG LORD SILVERSPOON TURNING HIS FACE TO THE SUN

"AND A HOLD FILLED WITH WINE AND SPICES" HE CHUCKLES." FATHER WILL BE SO PROUD!"

"BUT *NOW*, WE SET SAIL FOR THE *BAY OF SUNSHEE* -- AND WHO KNOWS WHAT PIRATES AND BRIGANDS WE SHALL ENCOUNTER IN OUR TRAVELS?" HE BUBBLES FLINGING OUT HIS ARM, CARELESSLY.

"SURE THING" MUTTERS THE EARTH-PIG "HOW ABOUT A SEA SERPENT WHILE WE'RE THERE, YOU SNOTTY ARISTOCRATIC BRAT"

DAVE SIM

NEXT WEEK: SEA SERPENT

"GREAT TARIM," CRIES THE CREW IN UNISON, "IT IS A SEA SERPENT!"

"ONE SIDE, EARTH-PIG," CRIES SILVER-SPOON, "THIS IS MY SPECIALTY"

"SOMEONE HELP ME GET THE ROWBOAT INTO THE WATER," HE ADDS, "AND BRING ME A SWORD"

"WHAT ON EARTH IS THAT THING" QUERIES CEREBUS, "IT'S MOSTLY MADE OF ANIMAL FAT AND PLASTER AND SNAKE SKIN," ANSWERS DHLIFU, ONE OF THE MERCHANTS. "WE MAKE A HABIT OF DROPPING IT INTO THE WATER AT LEAST ONCE PER VOYAGE, SO THAT HIS LORDSHIP HAS THE ADVENTURE HE SEEKS"
"BUT ISN'T THIS A RATHER TIME-CONSUMING WAY TO HUMOUR HIM?" ASKS THE EARTH-PIG, AS SILVERSPOON HACKS A LARGE PIECE OUT OF THE 'SERPENT.'
"POSSIBLY, BUT IT'S EASIER TO LIVE WITH THAN HIS LORDSHIP'S OTHER INTEREST."
"WHICH IS WHAT?"

"ENGAGING ONLIU PIRATE VESSELS IN EXTENDED NAVAL BATTLES AND FIGHTING TO THE LAST MAN" COMES THE REPLY."

"YES," AGREED CEREBUS "I CAN SEE HOW THIS IS A LESS DANGEROUS HOBBY FOR A YOUNG NOBLE"

NEXT WEEK· ONLIU PIRATE VESSEL

297

Cerebus THE AARDVARK

SYNOPSIS: WITH BARELY A HALF DOZEN ARMED SOLDIERS, CEREBUS DIRECTS THE DEFENCE OF THE TRADING VESSEL CUTTER, UNDER ATTACK FROM ONLIU PIRATES.

ABRUPTLY, "THEY HAVE A CATAPULT! FIREBALLS COMING THIS WAY--"

"I CAN'T BLOW THEM OUT FROM UP HERE! KEEP FIRING," SNARLS THE EARTH-PIG.

THE ARROWS, HOWEVER, CONTINUE TO FALL FAR SHORT OF THEIR INTENDED TARGET

AND, INSIDE OF AN HOUR, A MAKESHIFT BUCKET BRIGADE FIGHTS A LOSING BATTLE AGAINST THE INFERNO RAGING AMIDSHIPS

"ABANDON SHIP" BELLOWS THE AARDVARK-- "GRAB ALL NECESSARY PROVISIONS"

"YOU HEARD HIM," WHINES SILVERSPOON "SOMEONE GET MY CASE OF CHATEAU DEHRSION '26"

NEXT WEEK: SHIPWRECKED

298

CEREBUS WATCHES AS THE *CUTTER* SINKS BENEATH THE WAVES, BILLOWING STEAM MINGLING WITH OILY, BLACK SMOKE AS THE TRADE SHIP VANISHES FROM SIGHT. THOUGH HE LOOKS CAREFULLY FOR IT, THERE IS NO SIGN OF THE ONLIU PIRATE SHIP.

THE CREW, ELECTING TO ATTEMPT THE LONG VOYAGE TO PALNU IN OPEN BOATS, HAS TURNED WEST...

FEELING THE RISK TO BE TOO GREAT, CEREBUS CHOOSES A SMALL SUB-TROPICAL ISLAND AS HIS IMMEDIATE DESTINATION.

THOUGH UNSURE OF HIS OWN PLANS HE IS AT LEAST *GRATEFUL* TO BE RID OF THE ARROGANT AND INSUFFERABLE YOUNG SILVERSPOON

DOUBTLESS, HE HAS JOINED THE *CUTTER* IN ITS WATERY GRAVE. CEREBUS COULD PICTURE HIM, CLINGING TENACIOUSLY TO HIS WINE AND SPICE CRATES...

"WELL, IT'S ABOUT TIME SOMEONE *SHOWED UP,*" COMES THE FAMILIAR NASAL WHINE. "I WAS BEGINNING TO THINK I WOULD HAVE TO GO FORAGING FOR MY OWN FOOD, FOR HEAVEN'S SAKE!"

DAVE SIM

NEXT: DIVISION OF LABOUR

Cerebus THE AARDVARK

"IF YOU THINK I INTEND TO FORAGE FOR YOUR MEALS AS WELL AS MY OWN," SNARLS THE EARTH-PIG.

SILVERSPOON CUTS HIM OFF. "NATURALLY MY FATHER WILL PAY YOU WHEN WE REACH PALNU - - SHALL WE SAY A HUNDRED GOLD PIECES?"

"TWO HUNDRED!" SNAPS CEREBUS. "AGREED," SMILES SILVERSPOON.

AS HE MOVES OFF IN SEARCH OF SUSTENANCE, CEREBUS WONDERS IF HE HAS WON THE ARGUMENT -- OR LOST IT.

A NORTHERNER SINCE BIRTH, CEREBUS SOON FINDS FORAGING A MORE DIFFICULT TASK THAN HE HAD EXPECTED.

HE COULD SEPARATE THE POISONOUS FROM THE EDIBLE BASED ON SHADES OF GREEN AND BROWN, BUT WAS STYMIED BY THE RAINBOW COLOURED VEGETATION

"AT LEAST" MUTTERS THE EARTH-PIG TO HIMSELF "THAT EXPLAINS WHY HUMANS NEVER SETTLED ON THIS ISLAND.."

NEXT: NATIVES

"FROM WHAT I GATHER, THEY WANT US TO GO WITH THEM TO THEIR VILLAGE," SAYS THE EARTH-PIG.

"TELL THEM WE'LL BRING OUT THE BEADS AND THE TRINKETS AFTER WE'VE EATEN," SAYS SILVERSPOON, WAVING OFF THE INTERRUPTION.

"I DON'T THINK THEY WANT TO WAIT THAT LONG" SAYS CEREBUS, RAISING HIS VOICE SLIGHTLY.

"OH, PIFFLE, YOU'RE NOT GOING TO LET THESE IGNORANT SAVAGES PUSH YOU AROUND ARE YOU?" ASKS SILVERSPOON, "TELL THEM TO SHOO!"

"CRAK!" SAYS A ROCK AND SILVERSPOON'S FOREHEAD IN UNISON.

#6   DAVE SIM

"NOW WHY DIDN'T I THINK OF THAT?," PONDERS CEREBUS ALOUD.

NEXT: FUN AND GAMES

SILVERSPOON RETURNS TO CONSCIOUSNESS OVER A PERIOD OF SEVERAL MINUTES, AT LAST RECOGNIZING THE BUZZING IN HIS EARS AS CEREBUS' VOICE "WE'VE BEEN TAKEN CAPTIVE, BRAT," GROWLS THE EARTH-PIG, "TRY NOT TO MAKE THEM ANY ANGRIER, OKAY

"RAGGA RAGGA NUMU LUM TUM DIDDY YAH-YAH," SUGGESTS ONE OF THE NATIVES.

"UM TUT SUT LIM LUM BUBBA BUB BUBA BOO," DISAGREES HIS COMPANION.

"SHA-BOOM SHA-BOOM," OPINES A THIRD MEMBER OF THE GROUP.

"WHAT ARE THEY SAYING?" ASKS SILVERSPOON. "THEY'RE BETTING ON WHAT WILL GET US FIRST -- EXPOSURE OR STARVATION," ANSWERS CEREBUS.

NEXT: A STICKY WICKET

SYNOPSIS: CEREBUS AND SILVERSPOON HAVE BEEN TAKEN CAPTIVE BY NATIVES WHO HAVE TIED THEM SIDE-BY-SIDE IN THE OPEN. THE TEMPERATURE SOARS EACH DAY AS THE SUN MAKES ITS INFINITELY SLOW CIRCUIT ACROSS THE SKY.

LATE EVENING BRINGS THE POUNDING OF MIDSUMMER RAINS, DRENCHING THE LANDSCAPE AS THE SUN SINKS FROM VIEW.

THEN, THE LONG HOURS OF NIGHT AND NEAR-FREEZING TEMPERATURES UNDER A STAR-FILLED SKY...

AS THE SUN BEGINS ITS RISE ONCE MORE INSECTS FEED ON HUMAN AND AARDVARK FLESH...

FOUR DAYS! CEREBUS WAS USED TO SUCH HARSH CONDITIONS BUT WHAT OF THE CITY-BRED BRAT? HOW LONG COULD HE LAST?

"CHATEAU DEHRSION '26," GASPS YOUNG SILVERSPOON, FROM BETWEEN PARCHED LIPS, "CHATEAU DEHRSION '26."

DAVE SIM

"HE MAY BE ON THE VERGE OF DEATH," MUSES CEREBUS "BUT HIS BREEDING IS IMPECCABLE."

NEXT: DADDY

OUR STORY: CEREBUS WAKES TO THE SOUND OF SPLINTERING BAMBOO. ARMED SOLDIERS ARE BREAKING INTO THE SMALL VILLAGE, THE BRONZE-SKINNED NATIVES DROPPING LIKE FLIES IN THE FACE OF SWORDS AND CROSSBOWS. "HEY, BRAT," GRUMBLES THE EARTH-PIG, "VISITORS." "DADDY" CRIES SILVERSPOON, HIS EYES SHINING WITH DELIGHT.

DAVE SIM

"DADDY?" QUERIES THE EARTH-PIG. "OF COURSE, SILLY" REPLIES THE YOUNG HEIR, "IT'S DADDY AND HIS TROOPS COME TO RESCUE ME."

"OVER HERE, DADDY," CRIES SILVERSPOON. CEREBUS CAN HARDLY BELIEVE HIS GOOD LUCK! SOON HE WOULD BE RID OF THE BRAT AND HAVE HIS REWARD FOR SAVING THE BOY'S LIFE!

"HE'LL PROBABLY KILL YOU WHEN I TELL HIM HOW YOU KIDNAPPED ME." INTONES SILVERSPOON AS A SLENDER MAN APPROACHES...

NEXT: OUT OF THE FRYING PAN

Cerebus THE AARDVARK

OUR STORY: SILVERSPOON'S FATHER ARRIVES WITH ARMED SOLDIERS TO RESCUE THE YOUNG HEIR. AS HIS BONDS ARE SEVERED, HE RELATES A GRIM (AND ENTIRELY FICTITIOUS) TALE OF HIS KIDNAPPING BY CEREBUS THE AARDVARK.

"HE REALLY DID, DADDY, I PROMISE. REALLY! LET ME EXECUTE HIM, PLEASE! PLEASE! I HAVEN'T EXECUTED ANYONE IN WEEKS." WHINES YOUNG SILVERSPOON.

DAVE SIM

"UH-- HOW ABOUT IF WE WAIT UNTIL THIS LITTLE SITUATION IS ALL CLEARED UP BEFORE WE..."

"NO NO NO!" SHRIEKS SILVERSPOON STAMPING AN ARISTOCRATIC BOOT ON THE GROUND. "YOU'RE JUST STALLING! YOU NEVER LET ME HAVE ANY FUN ANYMORE! IT'S NOT FAIR! IT'S NOT FAIR! IT'S NOT..."

"NICE THROWING" SAYS LORD JULIUS TO ONE OF HIS MEN. "GLXXP" SAYS SILVERSPOON JUST BEFORE LAPSING INTO UNCONSCIOUSNESS.

NEXT: PEACE and QUIET

Cerebus THE AARDVARK

OUR STORY: CEREBUS WATCHES AS SILVERSPOON IS LOADED ABOARD THE SHIP SOON TO BE BOUND FOR PALNU. HIS FATHER, LORD JULIUS, HAS OFFERED TO GIVE CEREBUS FREE PASSAGE ON THE VESSEL AND PROMISES THAT A REWARD AWAITS THE EARTH-PIG WHEN THEY REACH PORT "WHAT WILL HAPPEN TO THE BR... uh... SILVERSPOON WHEN HE WAKES UP," ASKS CEREBUS.

"I HADN'T REALLY THOUGHT ABOUT IT," ADMITS LORD JULIUS, "I SUPPOSE I'LL SEND HIM TO A BOY'S MILITARY SCHOOL..."

"BUT SILVERSPOON HAS TRAVELLED THE WORLD," VENTURES CEREBUS "WON'T A BOY'S SCHOOL BE A LITTLE BIT...WELL...BORING?"

DAVE SIM

"YOU KNOW, YOU'RE RIGHT," AGREES JULIUS --"MAYBE I'LL SEND HIM TO A GIRL'S SCHOOL INSTEAD..."

NEXT: A NEW ADVENTURE

SYNOPSIS: AFTER LEAVING LOWER FELDA, CEREBUS BOARDS A TRADING VESSEL BOUND FOR PALNU! WHEN THE SHIP IS WAYLAID BY ONLIU PIRATES, CEREBUS AND THE SON OF THE DIRECTOR OF TRADE (AND ELECTED RULER) OF PALNU ARE SHIPWRECKED ON A DESERT ISLAND! RESCUED BY THE BOY'S FATHER AND HIS TROOPS, CEREBUS IS PROMISED A REWARD FOR SAVING THE YOUNG HEIR'S LIFE! THREE WEEKS LATER, THEY ARRIVE IN PALNU TO A TUMULTUOUS HERO'S WELCOME...

THE WALLS OF
Palnu

CEREBUS' EARS STILL RING WITH THE CRIES OF THE CROWDED STREETS AS HE SETTLES INTO JULIUS' OFFICE...

I'LL COME STRAIGHT TO THE *POINT!* AS A REWARD FOR SAVING MY SON'S LIFE, I'D LIKE YOU TO BE IN CHARGE OF MY SECURITY FORCES...

YOUR OFFICIAL TITLE WILL BE *"KITCHEN STAFF SUPERVISOR"*

WHY NOT *"DIRECTOR OF SECURITY FORCES"?*

IMPOSSIBLE -- THAT'S THE TITLE I GAVE TO THE SECRETARY OF THE NAVY...

BUT, IF HE'S THE SECRETARY OF THE NAVY, WHY DID YOU GIVE HIM ...?

WHEN YOU'RE RUNNING A BUREAUCRACY, THE BEST WAY TO SAFEGUARD YOUR JOB IS TO MAKE SURE YOU'RE THE ONLY ONE WHO KNOWS HOW THE WHOLE THING WORKS...

SO WHAT DOES THE SECRETARY OF THE NAVY *DO?*

HE MEETS TWICE A WEEK WITH THE COOK TO PLAN *MILITARY STRATEGY*

AND WHAT IS CEREBUS SUPPOSED TO DO?

AS I SAID, YOU'LL BE IN CHARGE OF MY SECURITY FORCES! YOU'LL MAKE SURE THAT NO ONE *ASSASSINATES* ME ...

IF THEY DO, YOU'RE FIRED.

HOW MANY MEN WOULD CEREBUS HAVE AS... KITCHEN STAFF SUPERVISOR?

HOW MANY MEN?!

I GIVE YOU A POSITION HALF OF DALNU WOULD KILL THEIR *GRANDMOTHERS* FOR AND YOU WANT *MEN* AS WELL...?

I'M NOT AS STUPID AS I *LOOK*, MY BOY! SUPPOSE I PUT YOU IN CHARGE OF *FIVE* MEN? SOON, IT'LL BE SIX... THEN *TEN*! INSIDE OF SIX MONTHS, YOU'LL BE COMMANDING MORE MANPOWER THAN THE SENIOR AIDE TO THE FILE CLERK!

AND A FINE KETTLE OF FISH *THAT* WOULD BE!

OH NO! I CATCH YOU EMPLOYING EVEN ONE FREELANCE SPY AND I'LL HAVE YOU REDUCED TO EXECUTIVE SECRETARY OF THE INTERIOR SO FAST YOU WON'T REMEMBER WHAT A KITCHEN LOOKS LIKE...

CEREBUS FINDS THIS *VERY* CONFUSING...

LORD JULIUS THE REPRESENTATIVES OF THE SATELLITE CITIES OF PARMUC, CIHNU, AVERS, *ENIATH* AND JYLCEW AWAIT YOUR BIDDING...

I WOULDN'T BID A HALF-PIECE FOR THE *LOT*, BUT SHOW THEM IN, ANYHOW...

VERY GOOD, M'LORD!

MOMENTS LATER...

GENTLEMEN--AND I USE THE TERM ADVISEDLY--SINCE IT TOOK FOUR HOURS TO FUMIGATE AFTER YOUR LAST VISIT, I'LL MAKE THIS SHORT AND SWEET...

I AM ASKING EACH OF YOU TO PROVIDE A FORCE OF ONE THOUSAND FIGHTING MEN TO ASSIST IN REPELLING ONLIU'S ANNUAL ASSAULT ON OUR FAIR BORDERS...

IMPOSSIBLE

UNREASONABLE

OUT OF THE QUESTION

IF YOU REFUSE, I'LL HAVE NO CHOICE BUT TO CALL UPON YOUR INTIMATE KNOWLEDGE OF THE SITUATION AND PRESS YOU INTO SERVICE AS FRONTLINE MILITARY ADVISORS...

PATRIOTISM KNOWS NO LIMITATIONS!

NATURALLY, PARMOC WILL DO ITS BEST!

IS A FORTNIGHT TOO SOON?

THANK YOU GENTLEMEN...

DON'T SLAM IT ON YOUR WAY OUT

NOW, WHERE WERE WE?

CEREBUS WAS ABOUT TO ASK-- WHAT'S IN THIS DEAL FOR HIM?

AMAZING! SIMPLY AMAZING!

YOU'VE ONLY BEEN IN THE CITY TWO HOURS AND ALREADY YOU SOUND LIKE A NATIVE...

YOU'LL BE GIVEN YOUR OWN ROOM HERE IN THE TRADE BUILDING, ALL THE FOOD, WINE AND ALE YOU CAN CONSUME AND MORE SPARE TIME THAN YOU'LL KNOW HOW TO HANDLE...

AND IF YOU HAVE ANY QUESTIONS, ASK SOMEONE ELSE! THERE'S A RUMOUR GOING AROUND THAT I'M VERY BUSY RIGHT NOW.

FOLLOW ME, SIR. I WILL SHOW YOU TO YOUR ROOM.

CEREBUS HAD NEVER BEEN TO PALNU, BUT, IN THE COURSE OF HIS TRAVELS, HAD HEARD MUCH ABOUT IT! MOST OUTLANDERS DWELT AT SOME LENGTH ON ITS SIZE AND WEALTH! SINCE HE HAD DECIDED TO REMAIN HERE, HE WOULD NEED TO KNOW MORE! THERE WAS AN EXPRESSION IN SERREA; "WHEN THE DRUNKARD SPEAKS THE SOBER MAN LEARNS MUCH." WITHIN THE HOUR, CEREBUS HAD LOCATED A SUITABLE BUREAUCRAT AT THE "FROG AND DUCK" AND, FOR THE PRICE OF A FEW TANKARDS, IS SOON UP TO HIS MEDALLIONS IN INFORMATION

THE ARISTOCRACY HAD ALL BUT VANISHED IN PALNU! BOUND AS THEY WERE TO THEIR ENORMOUS ESTATES, THEY WERE NO COMPETITION FOR THE THRIVING MERCHANT CLASS WHOSE ASSETS NOW GENERATED UNDREAMT-OF INCOME. THERE WERE FIVE DOMINANT MERCHANT "HOUSES" WITHIN THE CITY WALLS. THESE HOUSES EMPLOYED "CLIENTS," EACH CITIZEN OF VOTING AGE BEING A CLIENT, THEIR LIVING EXPENSES PAID BY THE HOUSE "LORD" IN EXCHANGE FOR THEIR VOTE! THE LORD, BY PAYING FOR THESE VOTES, ASSURED HIMSELF OF A PLACE ON THE "GRAND COUNCIL OF PALNU." THE LORD WHO OWNED THE MOST CLIENTS, AND, HENCE, VOTES WAS MADE 'GRANDLORD' OF THE CITY AND ITS SURROUNDING TERRITORY! AT THE MOMENT, THIS WAS LORD JULIUS! THE WRINKLE THAT JULIUS HAD ADDED TO THIS IDEA WAS THE SELLING OF TITLES FOR ADDITIONAL REVENUE! THE LORDS OF THE NOUVEAU-RICHE MERCHANT HOUSES, HAVING, SOME TIME BEFORE, RUN OUT OF THINGS TO BUY, NOW FILLED JULIUS' COFFERS IN EXCHANGE FOR THE TITLE OF THEIR CHOICE! THESE THEY HANDED OUT LIKE PARTY FAVOURS TO CONCUBINES, FAMILY BODYGUARDS, ACCOUNTANTS, NIECES, NEPHEWS AND, OF COURSE, THEMSELVES. JULIUS HIMSELF WAS GRANDLORD-SUPREME, BARON OF THE HOUSE OF TAVERS, RIGHT HONOURABLE PRIME MINISTER OF PALNU, PRESIDENT OF PARMOC, COUNT OF CIHNU...

THERE WERE A NUMBER OF OTHER TITLES HE HAD PAID FOR, BUT CEREBUS HAD FORGOTTEN ANOTHER SERREAN EXPRESSION;

"WHEN THE BUREAUCRAT SPEAKS, THE SOUND OF SNORING SOON FILLS THE ROOM."

THE ENSUING WEEKS PASS LIKE MOLASSES THROUGH AN HOURGLASS! CEREBUS HAS KNOWN ADVERSITY AND HARDSHIP, HAS FACED DEATH IN COUNTLESS GUISES AND FORMS; NONE CAN COMPARE WITH THE LIVING DEATH OF BOREDOM AT THE CORE OF A BUREAUCRACY...

GENTLEMEN OF THE HOUSE OF TAVERS -- WE ARE HERE TODAY TO DISCUSS A GRAVE AND PRESSING SITUATION... I AM, OF COURSE, REFERRING TO THE CINNAMON CRISIS! THERE ARE THOSE AMONG YOU WHO ASK "WHAT CINNAMON CRISIS?"

OUR SUPPLY OF CINNAMON FROM THE ESHTANNIN WILDERNESS HAS BEEN DRASTICALLY CURTAILED BY COWARDLY ONLIU NAVAL ATTACKS! THERE IS EVERY INDICATION THAT BY LATE FALL, WE WILL BE COMPLETELY AND IRREVOCABLY CINNAMON-LESS...

IF I WAIT 'TIL HE'S THROUGH, I'LL STARVE!

THERE ARE THOSE AMONG YOU ASK "SO OUR BELOVED LEADER CAN'T HAVE CINNAMON TOAST WITH HIS HOT CHOCOLATE BEFORE BEDTIME -- WHY CAN'T HE BE A MAN ABOUT IT AND DO WITHOUT?"

MAYBE JUST ONE BITE.

THERE ARE PROBABLY THOSE AMONG YOU WHO SAY AS...

EEEER

WELL -- THAT WASN'T IN THE SPEECH, BUT IT'S NOT A BAD ATTENTION-GETTER.

LORD JULIUS -- THIS FOOD IS POISONED!

THAT'S FUNNY -- I'VE BEEN SAYING THE SAME THING FOR YEARS...

THERE'S ONLY ONE THING TO DO -- EXECUTE THE COOK...

BUT, THE COOK MAY BE INNOCENT!

YOU'VE OBVIOUSLY NEVER HAD TO EAT ONE OF HIS STUFFED TOMATOES!

THE ASSASSIN HAD MADE A FATAL ERROR IN HIS ATTEMPT ON JULIUS' LIFE... THE POISON WAS EXOTIC FOR THIS PART OF THE WORLD, BUT CEREBUS HAD RECOGNIZED IT INSTANTLY! A FEW INQUIRIES LED HIM TO A NEARBY SHOP...

GLEPIE
IMPORT and EXPORT

GOOD MORROW -- A SHIPMENT HAS JUST ARRIVED FROM ESHNOSOPUR?

OOH -- YES! YES INDEED!

A FINE YEAR FOR WHEAT -- IT WILL MAKE A LOAF FIT FOR THE GODS!

CEREBUS WAS THINKING MORE OF A VIAL OF PENTAZIN...

A TOXIN NATIVE TO THAT COASTAL CITY...

I BUY ONLY WHEAT FROM ESHNOSOPUR! I'M AFRAID YOU'LL HAVE TO TRY....

IT WAS QUITE FASHIONABLE A FEW YEARS AGO... ADDED TO -- SAY -- A BIT OF POULTRY IT WAS FLAVOUR-LESS, BUT VERY SWIFT IN ITS...

SMASH

CEREBUS CURSED HIMSELF FOR A PANROVIAN... HE HAD UNDERESTIMATED THE EFFECT HIS ACCUSATION WOULD HAVE ON QIEPIE. THE MAN KNEW NOW THAT HE WAS BEING HUNTED AS A TRAITOR...

THOUGH A MERE HANDFUL OF SECONDS HAD ELAPSED...

ALREADY THE STREET HAD SWALLOWED UP HIS CORPULENT QUARRY...

AN HOUR LATER...

ONE OF MY IMPORTERS -- AN ASSASSIN?

SEND FOR THE ARMY!

WAIT!

LORD JULIUS -- THESE MATTERS ARE BEST HANDLED QUIETLY...!

SEND FOR THE ARMY AND HAVE THEIR FEET WRAPPED IN COTTON!!

WAIT! A LARGE FORCE WILL JUST DRIVE HIM UNDERGROUND! CEREBUS WILL INVESTIGATE ALONE!

THIS MAY NOT BE A RANDOM ATTEMPT ON YOUR LIFE...

YOUR ENEMIES MAY BE ORGANIZED...!

THAT WOULD PUT THEM A JUMP AHEAD OF MY ARMY, ALL RIGHT!

VERY WELL, MY POINTY-EARED FRIEND-- I'LL GIVE YOU A CHANCE...

BUT, REMEMBER THE WORDS OF NEAFON THE GREAT WHO ONCE SAID "IF AT FIRST YOU DON'T SUCCEED"...

"YOU BETTER START LOOKING FOR A NEW EMPLOYER..."

IT HAS BEEN THREE DAYS AND STILL NO SIGN OF GIEPIE! CEREBUS WAS CONVINCED THAT THE IMPORTER WOULD NOT LEAVE HIS POSSESSIONS UNGUARDED MUCH LONGER!

AN ODD SHIFTING OF SHADOWS IN THE ALLEYWAY OPPOSITE HIM ATTRACTS THE EARTH-PIG'S ATTENTION

IT IS THE FIGURE OF A MAN MOVING VERY CAUTIOUSLY TOWARD THE FRONT DOOR OF THE IMPORT SHOP.

IT WOULD APPEAR THAT CEREBUS' SUSPICIONS THAT GIERIE ISN'T IN THIS ALONE WERE *WELL-FOUNDED...*

THIRTY SECONDS TO FIND WHAT YOU SOUGHT AND PACK IT IN A VALISE...

CEREBUS IS NOT SO MUCH INTERESTED IN *WHAT* YOU ARE CARRYING AS HE IS ...

IN *WHO* YOU PLAN TO DELIVER IT TO!

CLOVIS' *BURIAL MOUND!* THIS IS THE *TRADE BUILDING!* IS IT POSSIBLE THAT *JULIUS* SENT FOR GIEPIE'S BELONGINGS?

THAT IDIOT! HE'LL RUIN ALL OF CEREBUS'...

HUH?

NOK NOK NOK

NOK NOK

ENTER! THE MEETING IS ABOUT TO BEGIN!

MEETING?

317

A.M... THE POUNDING OF RUNNING FEET, CEREBUS HEARS THE UNMISTAKABLE RASP...

...OF A SLIDING PANEL OF WOOD!

THE MECHANISM WAS NEVER INTENDED FOR ANYTHING MORE STRENUOUS THAN CONCEALMENT...

IT RESISTS, HUMMING ANGRILY, FOR A MOMENT! IN THE NEXT INSTANT, HOWEVER...

...AARDVARKIAN MUSCLES PREVAIL!

I AM CEREBUS, THE KITCHEN STAFF SUPERVISOR -- HALT IN THE NAME OF LORD JULIUS...

THERE'S NOWHERE TO RUN!

THE CHASE CONTINUES UP THREE FLIGHTS OF DARKENED STAIRS LEADING, FINALLY TO AN OPEN WINDOW! WAS IT POSSIBLE THE MAN HAD JUMPED?

AS CEREBUS LOOKED OUT AND DOWN, HE DREW A SHARP BREATH -- ALREADY THE MAN WAS MAKING HIS WAY... DOWN THE FACE OF THE BUILDING!

CEREBUS HAD FORGOTTEN THE ORNATE DESIGN OF PALNU'S BUILDINGS! THERE WERE SUFFICIENT HANDHOLDS FOR A GOOD CLIMBER TO ESCAPE ALONG FIVE CITY BLOCKS WITHOUT ONCE TOUCHING PAVING STONES...

IF CEREBUS LOST HIM NOW, THERE WERE COUNTLESS HIDING PLACES IN A CITY OF THIS SIZE...

AND THE DEADLY GAME BEGINS...

AS HE CLIMBS, CEREBUS LOOKS FOR ANY UNEXPECTED CHANCES -- FOR, NOT ONLY DOES HE HAVE TO CLIMB DOWN SAFELY...

...HIS MIND MADE UP, CEREBUS BEGINS HIS PURSUIT...

BUT HE MUST ALSO FIND SOME WAY TO MAKE UP THE DISTANCE BETWEEN HIMSELF AND HIS QUARRY!

JOIN US!-- THE REVOLUTION HAS NEED OF TRUE *PATRIOTS* WHO WISH TO RESTORE PALNU TO HER FORMER GREATNESS!

YOUR PLEAS FALL ON DEAF EARS, *STRIPLING!*

CEREBUS HAS A JOB TO DO... NO MORE AND NO LESS... THE PRICE WAS RIGHT, HE WOULD FOLLOW A WOOD FAERIE IN A RELIGIOUS CRUSADE AGAINST THE ONLIU...

THE LEADER YOU FOLLOW-- THE LEADER WHOSE *GOLD* YOU ACCEPT SO *WILLINGLY...*

HOW'D YOU BOYS LIKE TO GO PLAY SOMEWHERE *ELSE* -- I HAVE SOME TRADE AGREEMENTS THAT I HAVE TO...

OH! IT'S *YOU!*

TELL ME -- HOW'S EVERY LITTLE THING IN THE KITCHEN?

CEREBUS HAS FOUND YOUR ASSASSIN...

WELL, WELL, WELL SO YOU HAVE

I'D ASK YOU BOTH IN FOR A DRINK BUT IT'S GETTING AWFULLY LATE AND I HAVE TO GET UP FOR WORK TOMORROW...

HOW CAN YOU WORK FOR HIM -- THE MAN IS AN *OBVIOUS* SHAM -- A *FRAUD!*

HOW *DARE* YOU, SUH! -- I PAID GOOD MONEY TO BECOME WHAT I AM TODAY

YOU *SEE?* THERE IS ONLY ONE COURSE OPEN TO US -- YOU AND I -- *ONE CHANCE TO SAVE THIS CITY!*

WE MUST KILL THIS FOOL -- *NOW!* THE PEOPLE WILL FOLLOW US -- I *KNOW* THEY WILL!

NO.

I DON'T SUPPOSE ANYONE WANTS TO HEAR *MY* OPINION.

BUT *WHY?* IN THE NAME OF *TARIM* -- *WHY?!!*

BECAUSE YOU'RE *BOTH* IDIOTS! THE ONLY DIFFERENCE IS THAT *HE'S* FILTHY RICH AND *YOU'RE* DIRT POOR!

I'M NOT SURE, BUT I THINK I *RESENT* THAT LAST REMARK!

IF YOU'LL NOT JOIN ME IN *REVOLUTION*, THEN, *BY THE GODS*, YOU WILL JOIN ME...

HEY!

WHAM

...IN *DEATH!!*

SAY-- IT'S NOT OFTEN YOU GET HIGH QUALITY ENTERTAINMENT RIGHT OUTSIDE YOUR BEDROOM WINDOW...

NGGHH! NGGHH!

OR OUTSIDE YOUR BEDROOM, *PERIOD*, FOR THAT MATTER.

PRE...PARE ...TO.....D... .....DIE!!

THAT EITHER MEANS THAT HE'S ABOUT TO KILL YOU...

...OR HE'S REMINDING YOU OF THE IMPORTANCE OF MAKING OUT A WILL.

NGHH NGHH

DON'T MENTION IT.

RGRRNHH! RGRRNH!

MNRGHH MNRGHH

ATTABOY-- HE MAY BE TALLER AND STRONGER THAN YOU, BUT REMEMBER-- YOU'RE *SHORTER* AND *GRAYER!*

ONLY A FEW SECONDS REMAINED BEFORE THE WEIGHT OF THE MAN CARRIED THEM OVER THE EDGE TOWARD CERTAIN DEATH...

FOCUSSING THE REMAINDER OF HIS STRENGTH, CEREBUS PULLS HIS SNOUT IN TIGHT TO HIS FACE...

AND, IN THE NEXT INSTANT, MANAGES TO TWIST INTO THE NECESSARY POSITION!

EARTH-PIG NECK, SHOULDER AND BACK MUSCLES STRAIN AND TENSE BENEATH THE GRAY-FUR AND...

POOMP

UNH?!

PLEASE! ...I...I...

PLEASE!!

WHAP

I'D ASK YOU TO TEACH THAT TRICK TO THE TROOPS, BUT I DON'T THINK THEY HAVE THE *EQUIPMENT* FOR IT...

WELL, THIS CERTAINLY HAS BEEN QUITE A NIGHT OF ADVENTURE! -- I ≶SNIFF≷ I GUESS -≶SNIFF?≷

IT'S CEREBUS' FUR--THAT ALWAYS HAPPENS WHEN IT GETS WET...

THANK HEAVEN!

I THOUGHT THE ONLIU WERE INVADING!

YOU KNOW -- CEREBUS AGREES WITH HIM -- YOU CAN'T KEEP THIS CITY RUNNING IF NO ONE WORKS

WELL -- YOU CAN REST ASSURED THAT I'LL GIVE THE MATTER ALL THE ATTENTION I FEEL IT DESERVES...

THAT'S WHAT CEREBUS WAS AFRAID OF...

CEREBUS IS GOING TO BED...

SO SOON?

YOU CALLED, LORD JULIUS?

CIRCULATE A MEMO...

"ANY MEMBER OF THE HOUSEHOLD STAFF ALLOWING CEREBUS WITHIN TEN FEET OF LORD JULIUS ON A RAINY DAY IS TO BE *EXECUTED!*"

VERY GOOD, SIR!

LORD JULIUS -- FORGIVE THIS *INTRUSION!* SHALL I CALL THE...

LET HIM GO!

I'LL ADMIT IT'S NOT VERY *LIKELY*...

BUT HE MIGHT HAVE SOMETHING INTERESTING TO SAY...

I AM *HERE* LORD JULIUS BECAUSE IT HAS COME TO MY ATTENTION THAT, IN A *FORTNIGHT*...

... YOU INTEND HAVING *ANOTHER* OF YOUR *DRUNKEN DEBAUCHERIES!*

SORRY -- THE GUEST LIST IS ALREADY SET FOR *THAT* DRUNKEN DEBAUCHERY!

BUT I'LL SPEAK TO MY SOCIAL SECRETARY AND WE'LL TRY TO SQUEEZE YOU IN SOMEWHERE

YOU -- YOU *DARE* TO JEST IN THIS MANNER WITH A PRIEST OF MY *STANDING...?!*

STANDING?

I'M AFRAID THAT'S *IMPOSSIBLE*...

THE ONLY ROOM WE'LL HAVE IS FOR SOMEONE LYING DOWN...

GAH!

WE'LL PENCIL YOU IN FOR *THREE* CUSHIONS BY THE WINE VAT...

AND YOU CAN GIVE US AN ANSWER IN A DAY OR SO...

SEEMED LIKE A DECENT SORT -- WHAT DID YOU THINK?

VERY PRIESTLY. ANY CHANCE HE'LL SHOW UP AT YOUR FESTIVAL?

PROBABLY NOT -- IT'S COUPLES ONLY...

LORD JULIUS...?

SPEAKING.

LORD JULIUS THE MINISTER FOR EXECUTIVE PLANNING REQUESTS AN AUDIENCE...

NOT A CHANCE--THE LAST TIME I GAVE HIM AN AUDIENCE, HE JUST STOOD THERE AND STUTTERED UNTIL EVERYONE WALKED OUT ON HIM...

NO, NO -- HE WISHES TO SPEAK WITH YOU, LORD JULIUS...

WELL, WHY DIDN'T YOU SAY SO...?

CANCEL THE AUDIENCE AND SHOW HIM IN...

MINISTER FOR EXECUTIVE PLANNING?

ONE OF MY STENOGRAPHERS... THE CABINET TITLE IS STRICTLY HONORARY...

... IN HONOUR OF WHAT?

IN HONOUR OF HIS PAYING TWO HUNDRED PIECES A MONTH TO USE IT...

I SENT HIM TO THE TORTURE CHAMBER TO RECORD ANY INFORMATION WE CAN SQUEEZE OUT OF THOSE REBELS...

THE MINISTER FOR EXECUTIVE PLANNING, M'LORD!

BASKIN, MY BOY...

COME IN, COME IN!

READ ME WHAT YOU HAVE SO FAR...

"AAAGH"

"NO, NO, NO"

"AIEEEEE OH-NO, AAG AAAAAH"

"AAAAAAA AAAAGGH!"

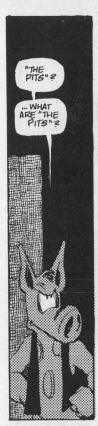

"THE PITS"?

...WHAT ARE "THE PITS"?

THE PITS?

WHY... THE PITS ARE...

WHEN YOU BOYS ARE THROUGH PLAYING "STUMP THE STENOGRAPHER"...

...LET ME KNOW AND I'LL ORGANIZE SOME NEW GAMES...

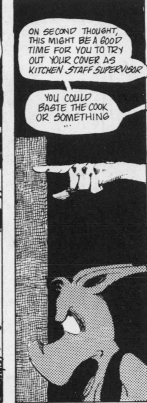

ON SECOND THOUGHT, THIS MIGHT BE A GOOD TIME FOR YOU TO TRY OUT YOUR COVER AS KITCHEN STAFF SUPERVISOR...

YOU COULD BASTE THE COOK OR SOMETHING...

I SHOULD HAVE WARNED YOU... LORD JULIUS DOES NOT PERMIT HIS EMPLOYEES TO SPEAK TOGETHER EXCEPT THROUGH HIM...

HE BELIEVES THAT IT CAUSES MUCH DISSATISFACTION IN THE CITY...

HOW DOES ANYTHING GET DONE?

THIS IS A BUREAUCRACY, SIR... NOTHING IS SUPPOSED TO GET DONE!

LORD JULIUS' TANTRUM POSED A PROBLEM FOR CEREBUS. IF HE WAS TO FIND OUT ABOUT "THE PITS" FROM ONE OF THE INNUMERABLE BUREAUCRATS, HE WOULD HAVE TO WAIT 'TIL DUSK WHEN THEY WOULD BE THROUGH PASSING PAPER BACK AND FORTH FOR THE DAY...

"WHERE" MUSED THE EARTH-PIG "CAN I FIND SOMEONE OUTSIDE THE BUREAUCRACY WHO CAN SPARE A FEW MINUTES FOR AN INTERVIEW?"

BLASPHEMERS!

YOU ARE ABOMINATIONS IN THE EYES OF THE LIVING TARIM...

REPENT...!

I LOOK ABOUT ME...

AND WHAT IS IT I SEE?

332

AH! THE PITS! A FOUL PLACE! FOUL, INDEED

BENEATH THE CITY THEY ARE!

"HIDDEN FOREVER FROM THE EYES OF MEN! REMNANTS OF THE OLD CITY AND ITS OLD WAYS... IT'S A STORY THAT *BEGAN* WHEN THE FIRST LORDS OF PALNU UNTAPPED MYSTERIES OF THE ANCIENT WORLD! THERE WERE RUMOURS OF STRANGE UNHOLY EXPERIMENTS ...ALCHEMY AND OTHER FORBIDDEN DISCIPLINES..."

"FOR A TIME, THE CHURCH OF TARIM STRUCK PALNU FROM THEIR MAPS, AND ALLOWED NO PRIEST TO VENTURE WITHIN A HALF-MILE OF IT."

"AND THEN... ABOUT A CENTURY AGO..."

"AN EARTHQUAKE SWALLOWED UP THE CITY; A GIFT FROM THE INFINITE MERCIES OF THE LIVING TARIM... THOUSANDS DIED, VIRTUALLY IN THE BLINKING OF AN EYE! FULLY NINETY PERCENT OF THE CITY DISAPPEARED BENEATH THE SURFACE. EVEN TODAY, MANY OF THE OLD STREETS LIE INTACT BENEATH THE CITY..."

"IT IS THESE PASSAGE-WAYS WHICH ARE CALLED..."

"...THE PITS!"

"THOUGH MOST REGARD THEM AS AN AMUSING BIT OF FOLKLORE, POPULATED BY MYTHICAL BEASTS, DREAMED UP TO FRIGHTEN CHILDREN"

"THEY ARE UNAWARE THAT MUCH EVIL MANIFESTED IN THE OLD CITY YET LIVES IN THOSE DARK CAVERNS"

AND WHAT KIND OF EVIL IS IT THAT STILL LIVES AFTER A...?

BLASPHEMY! UNHOLY! UNCLEAN!

JEWELRY! ADORNMENTS! GRAVEN IMAGES!

OH NO

...CEREBUS THANKS YOU FOR YOUR HELP...

A PRIEST OF TARIM LIVES ONLY TO SERVE.

WASH THAT EVIL PAINT FROM YOUR FACE, UNBELIEVER!!

CAST OFF THESE-- DEMONIC ORNAMENTS!

...AND BEG THE LIVING TARIM FOR FORGIVENESS!

TWAK

BE NOT UNCONSCIOUS BUT OPEN THINE EYES TO THY WICKED WAYS!

TWAK

BE UNCONSCIOUS, THEN, BUT BE NOT DEAD -- OR I SHALL SURELY FACE A MURDER RAP...

CEREBUS MUST SPEAK TO LORD JULIUS ABOUT PRESSING THESE PRIESTS INTO SERVICE AS SHOCK TROOPS...

THE AARDVARK MAKES HIS WAY TO THE ANTE-CHAMBER OF JULIUS' OFFICE, LADEN WITH MAPS, PLANS AND SCROLLS...

EVEN A CURSORY GLANCE THROUGH THE MATERIAL CONFIRMS THE EXISTENCE OF THE PITS! THE PLANS SHOW THE KNOWN PASSAGE-WAYS AND ACCESS ROUTES INTO THEM...

IF CEREBUS' SUSPICIONS PROVED CORRECT, HE KNEW HE WOULD NEED AS COMPLETE A KNOWLEDGE OF THOSE HIDDEN CORRIDORS AS WAS POSSIBLE BEFORE HE EXPLORED THEM...

AH! JUST THE PERSON I WAS LOOKING FOR...

LORD JULIUS-- CEREBUS HAS FOUND SOMETHING ON ALL THESE REVOLUTIONARIES ...

YOU KNOW, THIS ALWAYS HAPPENS WHEN IT'S MY TURN TO STAGE A FESTIVAL...

THE PROBLEM IS, OF COURSE, TO FIND OUT WHERE THEY'RE HIDING...

WHEN YOU'RE SURROUNDED BY BUREAUCRATS, YOU HAVE NO TROUBLE GETTING HALF A TON OF PAPER SHUFFLED FROM ONE END OF THE CITY TO THE OTHER...

TAKING INTO ACCOUNT THEIR MOBILITY, THEIR HIT-AND-RUN TACTICS AND THEIR ORGANISATION ...

BUT ASK THEM TO COME UP WITH AN IDEAL LOCATION FOR *THE FESTIVAL OF PETUNIAS*...

...AND THESE ARE THE SUGGESTIONS I PAID GOOD MONEY FOR...

THERE'S ONLY ONE PLACE IN THE CITY THAT COULD CONCEAL THAT MANY PEOPLE...

"THE BALLROOM... THE BALLROOM ...THE CENTRAL PLAZA... THE BALLROOM.,.,THE BALLROOM..."

THROWING CAUTION TO THE WIND I THOUGHT MAYBE YOU MIGHT HAVE AN IDEA...

...THE PITS!

OF COURSE! *THE PITS!*

OH, MOTHER! WHAT AN IDEA! OLD LEOPOLD THOUGHT NO ONE WOULD EVER TOP HIS FESTIVAL OF GROUNDHOGS IN A LIVE VOLCANO!

WHAT A PARTY THIS WILL BE!

PARTY?

LORD JULIUS -- CEREBUS WAS TALKING ABOUT...

"THE PETUNIAS IN THE PITS!"

I WONDER IF IT'S TOO LATE TO WALLPAPER!

WELL, NO TIME LIKE THE PRESENT TO CHECK OUT WHAT WE HAVE TO WORK WITH...

OH, *BASKIN!*

M'LORD?

SAY-- WHAT ARE YOU DOING BACK THERE?

YOU FORGOT TO DISMISS ME THIS AFTERNOON AFTER I READ MY NOTES, M'LORD...

THAT EXPLAINS WHY THE MATTRESS WAS LUMPY WHEN I TOOK MY NAP...

WELL, NEVER MIND THAT! I'LL NEED YOU TO TAKE DICTATION WHEN I CHECK OUT THE PITS...

YOU BOYS WAIT HERE WHILE I SLIP INTO SOME LESS-EXPENSIVE SHOES...

VERY GOOD, M'LORD!

CEREBUS DOESN'T THINK YOU LOOK VERY WELL...

FRIGHTENED OF THE PITS? WHY THE VERY IDEA! DO YOU TAKE ME FOR A CHILD--? PTOO! I SPIT ON THE SHADOW-CRAWLER-THOSE ARE JUST STORIES TO FRIGHTEN CHILDREN! DEVOURING MEN IN ONE BITE! WHO COULD PICTURE SUCH A THING?

LORD JULIUS-- CEREBUS WILL BE NEEDING A SWORD...

I MEAN THE WHOLE IDEA IS SILLY ISN'T IT? HAHAHAA? ISN'T IT? HUH ...WELL?

YOU CAN USE MINE ...

GUARD IT WITH YOUR LIFE-- THERE'S THE JUICE OF A THOUSAND GRAPEFRUIT ON THAT BLADE...

JUICE...YES!

GRAPEFRUIT!

HAHAHA!

FIND OUT WHAT HE'S BEEN SMOKING...

AND HAVE A FEW OUNCES SENT TO MY CHAMBER...

337

HE WAS JUST TELLING CEREBUS SOME FOLK TALES ABOUT *THE PITS* HE REMEMBERED FROM HIS CHILDHOOD...

SILLY -- YES! SILLY -- SILLY FOLK TALES

ABOUT-THE-PITS...

MOMENTS LATER, THE TRIO DESCENDS INTO A DARKNESS AS SUF-FOCATING AS IT IS SILENT...

FIRST OF ALL, WE'RE GOING TO NEED A WORK-CREW TO SCRAPE THIS GRAY SLIME OFF THE WALLS...

WASN'T IT PARMOC THAT SENT US THE MESSAGE OF A POSSIBLE FOOD SHORTAGE THIS WINTER?

YES M'LORD

HAVE THE SLIME GARNISHED WITH FRUIT SLICES AND DELIVERED BY CARAVAN WITH MY COMPLIMENTS...

SOMETHING IS AMISS!

NO -- I'M PRETTY SURE...

FRUIT SLICES WITH GRAY SLIME... NO DOUBT ABOUT IT...!

THAT DOOR... ON THE PLANS IT WAS MARKED AS BEING BLOCKED BY TEN FEET OF RUBBLE ....

THIS IS AN *OUTRAGE!* YOU MEAN, SOMEONE HAS STOLEN TEN FEET OF *MY* RUBBLE?

...OR...

...EATEN IT. "

DON'T BE *ABSURD!* THE PEASANTS ARE HUNGRY...

...BUT THEY'RE NOT *THAT* HUNGRY...

COME ALONG, BASKIN! IF THAT RUBBLE THIEF IS STILL AROUND, HE'S GOING TO RUE THE DAY HE TANGLED WITH US!

STAY CLOSE TOGETHER-- THIS MAY BE A TRAP...

M-MAYHAP WE SHOULD TURN BACK

I DON'T LIKE TO DISILLUSION YOU BOYS, BUT ANYONE STUPID ENOUGH TO STEAL RUBBLE COULDN'T BE SMART ENOUGH TO CONSTRUCT A REALLY SOPHISTICATED...

CLANG

CLANG

HELP.

ABRUPTLY, TORCHES FLARE TO BRILLIANT LIFE, BLINDING THE TRIO...

GREETINGS...

WHEN THEIR VISION CLEARS, THEY ARE IN A LONG TUNNEL OF ROUGH STONE BLOCKS--THE SIDE WALLS ILLUMINATED BY TWO ROWS OF TORCHES...

...AS THE LEADER OF THE "EYE OF THE PYRAMID" I BID WELCOME TO THE SOON-TO-BE-DEPARTED *LORD JULIUS* OF PALNU AND HIS...

...COMPANIONS.

MAYHAP YOU HAVEN'T NOTICED....

BUT ONE OF YOUR RABBITS ISN'T IN HIS HUTCH...

INTENTIONAL, I ASSURE YOU ...WHEN I SAW YOU CARRYING A SWORD, I ASSUMED YOU WERE LORD JULIUS'...

...CHAMPION?

LORD JULIUS' EMPLOYEE ...

...IF YOU COME DOWN HERE IT WILL SAVE CEREBUS THE TROUBLE OF DISMANTLING THAT WALL ...

FOR A THOUSAND YEARS HAS THE PYRAMID SURVIVED...

AND, FOR A THOUSAND YEARS...

THERE HAS BEEN BUT ONE FATE FOR THE UNBELIEVER...

THE SHADOW-CRAWLER'S HIDE SEEMED VULNERABLE ENOUGH-- LIKE A SYNTHESIS OF LEATHER AND SNAKE SKIN. EVEN AS THE CREATURE LUNGES, CEREBUS CROUCHES LOW...

...AND DIVES UNDER THE ATTACK...

USING HIS FORWARD MOMENTUM, THE EARTH-PIG FLIPS ONCE...

...AND LANDS ON HIS FEET! ARMS RIGID, AND GRIPPING THE SWORD WITH BOTH HANDS, HE DELIVERS A TREMENDOUS BLOW TO THE CREATURE'S EXPOSED FLANK...

THE NET RESULT OF WHICH IS A SHOOTING PAIN IN THE AARDVARK'S RIGHT WRIST AND A SOMEWHAT ANGRIER SHADOW-CRAWLER...

HIS SWORD AT THE READY, CEREBUS PREPARES TO STRIKE AGAIN...

THIS TIME AT THE UNBLINKING RIGHT EYE...

WHICH, IF ANYTHING, PROVES TO BE TOUGHER THAN THE HIDE...

THE EARTH-PIG'S REFLEXES BUY HIM ANOTHER SECOND OF LIFE...

...AND HIS MIND RACES...

...THE CREATURE IS SORCEROUS...

...ITS HIDE IS IMPENETRABLE...

...IT HAS NO WEAKNESS...

THE TORCHES FORM TWO LINES ON THE TUNNEL WALLS...

AND IT IS THIS LAST THOUGHT WHICH GIVES CEREBUS THE KEY TO THEIR ESCAPE...

HIS SWORD WAS OF NO USE...

...FOR GOOD OR ILL...

...THREE LIVES NOW HINGED...

...ON TWO SLIM TORCHES!

FOR CENTURIES, THE CRAWLER HAD PERCEIVED LITTLE IN HIS ENVIRONMENT, SAVE THE DOUBLE ROW OF TORCHES WHICH INVARIABLY LED HIM TO FOOD...

...THIS TIME AS HE LUNGES...

...ONE OF THE TORCHES *MOVES!*

AT THE LAST INSTANT, WITHIN INCHES OF THE FLAME, THE CREATURE VEERS AWAY...

IN THAT INSTANT, CEREBUS IS ON THE CREATURE'S BACK... NOW *TWO* TORCHES BEGIN TO MOVE...

FOR A MOMENT, THE SHADOW-CRAWLER IS CONFUSED -- UNTIL CEREBUS MOVES THE FLAMES INTO POSITION ...

...ON EITHER SIDE OF THE MASSIVE HEAD... INSTINCTS TAKE OVER AND THE CRAWLER ABRUPTLY ACCELERATES...

...TOWARDS ITS PREY!

AND CEREBUS HOPES, AS THE WALL LEAPS FORWARD...

NO!

...THAT THE IMPACT WILL BE SUFFICIENT...

NO!

...TO KNOCK THE BEAST SENSELESS!

NOO!

AAAAH!

BAM

TOO BAD THE BARS DIDN'T GO BACK WHERE THEY CAME FROM UNTIL YOU HIT THE WALL...

OTHERWISE I COULD HAVE HELPED YOU WITH THAT OVERSIZED PORTION OF FISH-BAIT!

THAT RUMBLING!

SPEAKING OF FISH -- IT LOOKS LIKE EVERYONE'S FAVOURITE REVOLUTIONARY AND SNAKE FETISHIST IS DEPARTING THE PREMISES...

WE'LL HAVE TO WORRY ABOUT HIM LATER, LORD JULIUS...

CEREBUS SEEMS TO HAVE LOOSENED A PIVOTAL PIECE OF ARCHITECTURE...

THE SHORT EXPANSE OF FLOOR STRETCHES BEFORE THEM AS STONE CONTINUES TO DROP IN EVER-LARGER PIECES...

AND JUST AS THE CEILING SHRUGS AND GIVES UP IN ITS CENTURIES-OLD COMPETITION WITH GRAVITY...

...THEY ARE OUTSIDE OF THE TUNNEL...

...EACH, MORE OR LESS, ALIVE...

345

346

synopsis:

THE ATTACKS ON THE BUREAUCRACY BY THE REVOLUTIONARIES KNOWN ONLY AS THE EYE OF THE PYRAMID HAVE BECOME EVEN MORE FREQUENT! AS THE FESTIVAL OF PETUNIAS NEARS, CEREBUS IS FACED WITH MAKING THE PITS INTO A SAFE LOCATION FOR THE FESTIVITIES! HE INSISTS, OVER LORD JULIUS' GRUMBLING THAT THE GUEST LIST AND FESTIVAL AREA BE CUT IN HALF AND ONLY ONE ENTRANCE BE LEFT UNSEALED! EVEN WITH THESE PRECAUTIONS, THERE IS NO GUARANTEE OF SAFETY! IF A POTENTIAL ASSASSIN WAS **ON** THE GUEST LIST, HE COULD EASILY STRIKE DOWN THE GRANDLORD OF PALNU AND ESCAPE IN THE CONFUSION! IT IS THE EARTH-PIG'S HOPE THAT JULIUS HAS HEEDED HIS WARNINGS AND WILL KEEP HIMSELF AT A REASONABLE DISTANCE FROM THE CROWD OF PARTY-GOERS...

WHAT ARE YOU SUPPOSED TO *BE* ANYWAY...?

AN AARDVARK WEARING A FURRY BLACK SHIRT...

WELL, YOU'VE GOT MY VOTE FOR *"MOST AUTHENTIC COSTUME"*...

CEREBUS KNEW THAT, BARELY A HUNDRED YARDS AWAY, MEN WERE STILL SEARCHING THE RUBBLE FOR THE REBEL LEADER'S CORPSE. THE EARTH-PIG WAS CERTAIN THEY WOULDN'T FIND IT...

AH! LORD AND LADY WYNDMEL-SMITH...

...YOU'VE MET *CEREBUS*, MY KITCHEN STAFF SUPERVISOR...?

WHY... *NO!*

...WE HAVEN'T HAD THE PLEASURE ... *HOW DO YOU DO?*

CEREBUS HAS NO TIME FOR *FAT LADIES*...

THERE MAY BE REBELS ABOUT...

I'VE BEEN THINKING THAT HE MIGHT BE A CANDIDATE FOR THAT DIPLOMATIC LIASON POST IN DANROVY...

YOU DON'T SAY...

I...I ...UH...I

IF YOU'LL EXCUSE ME, I'M GOING TO TRY TO CATCH UP TO HIM BEFORE HE GETS ME INTO A WAR ...

BY ALL MEANS...

AND I'LL SEE IF I CAN FIND SOMEONE TO GET ARISTONNIA'S HEART STARTED AGAIN...

THERE YOU ARE!

YOU HAVEN'T TALKED TO ANYONE, HAVE YOU?

JUST SOME WOODEN-HEADED BUREAUCRAT WITH A LISP ...

uh -- WAS HE WEARING A FALCON'S HEAD?.

AYE! CEREBUS TOLD HIM WHAT TO DO WITH HIS BEAK...

WELL, ESHNOSOPUR NEVER WAS THAT GOOD AN ALLY ...

LORD JULIUS...

...THERE IS MENACE IN THE AIR HERE...

THAT'S JUST THE HERRING-AND-ONION DIP... TRY FACING AWAY FROM THE AIR DUCTS...

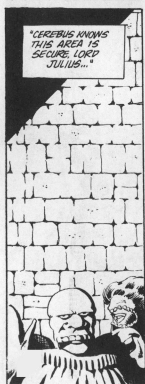

"CEREBUS KNOWS THIS AREA IS SECURE, LORD JULIUS..."

"THOSE GUARDS WON'T LET ANYONE IN WITHOUT AN INVITATION"

"BUT CEREBUS CAN'T HELP FEELING..."

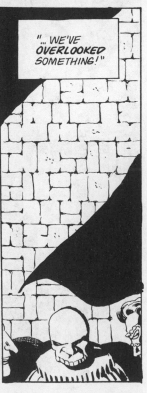

"... WE'VE OVERLOOKED SOMETHING!"

E'LASS! IT'S HIM! IT'S THE-KILLER-WHO-LOOKS-LIKE-A-BUNNY!

SH! THESE TWO INVITATIONS TOOK THE LAST OF OUR MONEY!

IF YOU GET US THROWN OUT, WE LOSE OUR CHANCE AT THE WYNDMEL DIAMOND

AND WITHOUT THAT DIAMOND WE DON'T HAVE ANY MONEY FOR FOOD...

BUT E'LASS... WHAT IF HE RECOGNIZES ME? HE DOESN'T LIKE ME -- I CAN TELL BY THE WAY HE PUNCHES ME WHENEVER I GET NEAR HIM...*

* CEREBUS #6

JUST KEEP THAT MASK ON, DON'T TALK...

... AND TRY NOT TO MOVE AROUND...

WITH ANY LUCK HE'LL FIGURE YOU'RE A BABY ELM THAT SOMEONE DRESSED UP AS A JOKE...

WHY, LORD JULIUS -- WHAT AN ADORABLE COSTUME...

THE SITUATION WAS HOPELESS THE EARTH-PIG HAD DECIDED ...

THIS OLD THING? I HAD IT PATTERNED ON THE BURIAL COSTUME OF DESERAN THE GAUCHE...

THEY SAY HALF OF THE FUNERAL PARTY WAS NAUSEOUS FOR A WEEK...

... EVEN IF THE LEADER OF THE REVOLUTION WAS HERE, HE COULD BE WEARING ...

TEE-HEE! YOU SAY THE CUTEST THINGS...

DON'T I THOUGH?

UNH?

IT'S HIM!

HE'S EVEN WEARING THE SAME ROBES!

351

CEREBUS PAUSED.

PERHAPS IT WAS A TRICK...

...A DECOY IN BLACK ROBES TO DRAW HIM AWAY FROM LORD JULIUS...

THE EARTH-PIG SUDDENLY FELT **VULNERABLE** ...THEY WERE IN THE MIDST OF THE CROWD, FAR FROM THE STONE WALLS AND STAIRWAY...

TACTICALLY, THEIR POSITION WAS A **DISASTER**...

A MOTION TO THE RIGHT CATCHES CEREBUS' ATTENTION...

GRADUALLY HE BECOMES AWARE THAT THERE ARE ABOUT A DOZEN AMONG THE GUESTS WATCHING HIM INTENTLY...

EACH IS CARRYING A SWORD, AND STEP-BY-CAUTIOUS-STEP, ...

...EACH IS GETTING CLOSER AND CLOSER TO HIM...

HE OPENS HIS MOUTH TO CALL THE GUARDS FROM THEIR POST AT THE ENTRANCE...

UNTIL HE SEES THEM IN THE CROWD, SIDE-BY-SIDE WITH THE REBELS, THEIR SWORDS DRAWN AND SMILES OF BARELY CONCEALED AMUSEMENT ON THEIR FACES

I DON'T WISH TO INTERRUPT LORD JULIUS BUT ARMED REBELS ARE ADVANCING ON US...

WELL, DON'T JUST *STAND* THERE -- *DO* SOMETHING...

CEREBUS IS OPEN TO SUGGESTIONS

HIS SWORD WOULD BE USELESS AGAINST A DOZEN OPPONENTS! HIS ONLY CHANCE WOULD BE TO GET THE FESTIVAL GUESTS TO TURN ON THE ARMED REVOLUTIONARIES SOMEHOW...

BUT CEREBUS HAD SEEN ENOUGH OF RICH CITY-DWELLERS TO KNOW THAT THEIR INSTINCTIVE REACTION TO ANY WARNING OF DANGER WOULD BE A MINDLESS, FULL-SCALE PANIC...

AND, OUT IN THE OPEN LIKE THIS, A MASS EXODUS TO THE STAIRWAY WOULD FINISH THEM AS SURELY AS THE REBELS' SWORDS...

EVEN IF HE *COULD* ROUSE A FEW OF THE JADED MERCHANTS TO AID HIM, THE MATERIAL IMMEDIATELY AVAILABLE WAS NOT EXACTLY INSPIRING...

HEMMED IN NEXT TO THE REFRESHMENT TABLES, CEREBUS BEGINS TO THINK THAT THE LAST SOUND HE WOULD EVER HEAR WOULD BE THE GRINDING OF MOLARS...

TARIM! IT WOULD TAKE A CROWBAR TO PRY THEIR FEEBLE MINDS AWAY FROM THAT FOUL-SMELLING...

A MOMENT LATER A SLOW GRIN SPREAD ACROSS THE EARTH-PIG'S FEATURES

AND HE PLACED THE SWORD BETWEEN HIS FEET...

ATTENTION, EVERYONE! LORD JULIUS HAS ARRANGED A LITTLE DIVERSION FOR ALL OF US!

I HAVE?

OBOY! A GAME!

A GAME! A GAME!

I LOVE GAMES!

HE HAS ENGAGED SOME PROFESSIONAL ENTERTAINERS TO JOIN THE FESTIVAL ...THEY'RE THE ONES CARRYING THE SWORDS ...

SAY -- WHAT THE HELL IS THIS?

THE OBJECT OF THE GAME IS SIMPLE --

YOU HAVE TO COVER THE ENTERTAINERS FROM HEAD TO FOOT WITH HERRING-AND-ONION DIP!

THE FIRST COUPLE WITH AN EMPTY BOWL WILL BE DECLARED KING AND QUEEN OF PETUNIAS...

THE CLOSEST REBEL MUTTERS AN OATH AND RESUMES HIS STEALTHY ADVANCE ...

RECENTLY ARRIVED IN PALNU, HE, QUITE NATURALLY, IS UNAWARE OF JUST HOW LITTLE IT TAKES TO AMUSE THE CREAM OF PALNU'S MERCHANT CLASS

PLOOP!

IN SECONDS, THE REBELS ARE THROWN INTO CONFUSION AS THE AIR FILLS WITH BLOBS OF THE FOUL-SMELLING MIXTURE AND BEGINS TO COAT THEIR SKIN AND THEIR CLOTHING...

KEEP THROWING, SWEETHEART --ONLY HALF A BOWL TO GO...

I GOT ONE!

SPLAT

PLOOP! PLAP

ZIPPPP

SPLOP

SPLAD

WHIZ

ZOOOP

IT'S ONE OF LORD JULIUS' TRICKS...

GUARD THE EXIT, BROTHER JANUS!

SLOPP

GUARD THE EXIT?

YOU MORON--

I CAN'T EVEN SEE THE EXIT!

PLOOP

WHILE, ACROSS THE ROOM, LADY WYNDMEL-SMITH IS STILL RECOVERING FROM HER MEETING WITH A PREOCCUPIED EARTH-PIG...

THE IMMIGRATION LAWS SIMPLY MUST BE TIGHTENED, LUCIUS...!

YES, MY DEAR...

...PERHAPS YOU'D BE BETTER TO JUST PUT IT OUT OF YOUR MIND...

MARK MY WORDS! IF SOMETHING ISN'T DONE SOON, WE'RE ALL GOING TO BE HIP-DEEP IN SHORT, ILL-MANNERED FOREIGNERS!

YES, MY DEAR...

WILL YOU BE ALL RIGHT WHILE I GET YOU SOME BRANDY?

KITCHEN STAFF SUPERVISOR! THE IDEA! WHAT MUST LORD JULIUS HAVE BEEN THINKING OF?!

PERHAPS I COULD GET YOU SOME OF THAT *DIP* WE HAD EARLIER...?

LUCIUS! THE *DIP!* NOW I KNOW WHAT THE WRETCHED CREATURE HAS PLANNED—HE'S GOING TO *POISON* US ALL!

HE PROBABLY STIRRED IT WITH THOSE LICE-INFESTED HANDS OF HIS... AND ...I...I..... ...ATE....

OOOOOOOOOOH

PERHAPS JUST THE *BRANDY*, THEN...

DON'T GO AWAY, MY DEAR...

ELASS CHEWED HIS LIP NERVOUSLY BENEATH HIS MASK... HE TRIED TO PUSH ALL THOUGHTS OF LORD JULIUS' BOARD OF JUSTICE FROM HIS MIND ...

THE INFREQUENT INCIDENTS OF CRIME IN PALNU WAS DUE IN LARGE PART TO THIS AUGUST BODY RENOWNED FOR THEIR WISDOM, EXPERIENCE...

..AND UNBLEMISHED RECORD OF THREE THOUSAND TWO HUNDRED AND EIGHTY-ONE CONVICTIONS IN THREE THOUSAND TWO HUNDRED AND EIGHTY-ONE TRIALS...

GINGERLY LIFTING THE DIAMOND WITH ONE HAND, HIS RESOLVE CRUMBLES! WHAT IF SOMEONE WAS WATCHING HIM? HE HADN'T PLANNED THOROUGHLY ENOUGH--BETTER TO GET OUT *NOW!* IF THEY NEEDED MONEY, TURG WOULD JUST HAVE TO GET A ...

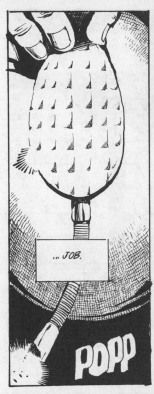

...JOB.

POPP

THE BUTTERFLIES IN HIS STOMACH BECAME FANGED LIZARDS... HE HAD SEEN LORD JULIUS' GUARDS AT THE ENTRANCE...

LORD WYNDMEL MIGHT RETURN AT ANY MOMENT

THERE WAS SIMPLY NO TIME TO REATTACH THE GEM...

HE BECAME EVEN MORE CONVINCED SOMEONE WAS WATCHING HIM! "THAT'S RIGHT, HE TOOK IT RIGHT OFF HER WRIST!" "HE'S NOTHING BUT A LITTLE THIEF! OFF WITH HIS HEAD!"

TURG IS SWIFTLY FORGOTTEN AS HE CASTS ABOUT WILDLY FOR SOME OTHER EXIT...

IT WAS SAID THAT LORD JULIUS' GUARDS WERE TRAINED TO RECOGNISE THE SCENT OF GUILT SEVERAL FEET AWAY...

CEREBUS SCANNED THE CROWD THROUGH A HERRING AND ONION BLUR... WITH THE FAILURE OF HIS ASSASSINS, THE REBEL LEADER WAS DOUBTLESS EVEN NOW CRAWLING BACK UNDER SOME CONVENIENT ROCK...

LORD JULIUS! OVER THERE!

EH? OVER...

OHO!

A FEELING BEGINS TO GNAW AT E'LASS' NERVES THAT THERE **WAS** ONLY ONE EXIT...

LADY WYNDMEL WAS ALREADY STIRRING ON HER COUCH! E'LASS WHIMPERED...THERE JUST **HAD** TO BE...

...A WAY OUT...

I GUESS IT'S **TRUE**...

TARIM **DOES** HELP THE PURE OF HEART...

LOCKED IN CONVERSATION, CEREBUS AND LORD JULIUS FAIL TO SEE THE SECOND FIGURE SLIP QUIETLY AWAY FROM THE FESTIVITIES...

WELL?

AREN'T YOU GOING **AFTER** HIM?

CEREBUS THINKS YOU BETTER COME ALONG, TOO

ME? WHY?

BECAUSE THOSE ASSASSINS ARE GOING TO BE A TRIFLE PEEVISH WHEN THE CROWD RUNS OUT OF DIP...

AND THEY'VE **ALREADY** BEEN ORDERED TO KILL YOU...

SAY-- DO YOU MIND IF I COME ALONG?

CEREBUS WOULD BE MOST *PLEASED* ...

USING HIS COSTUME TO CONCEAL HIS SWORD FROM THE CROWD, CEREBUS LEADS LORD JULIUS TO THE SLIDING STONE PANEL...

E'LASS CONFRONTS THE STONE CORRIDOR BEFORE HIM WITH APPREHENSION... BARELY A DOZEN FEET AWAY IS INKY BLACKNESS

HIS MIND MULLS OVER THE POSSIBILITY OF RETURNING TO THE FESTIVAL AND DROPPING THE DIAMOND ON THE FLOOR --THEN PRAYING NO ONE SEES HIM DO IT...

...BUT IN THE FEW SECONDS IT TAKES TO WEIGH HIS OPTIONS...

THROUGH HERE-- HE'S ONLY HAD A FEW SECONDS HEAD START...

THE DECISION IS MADE FOR HIM...

WHY NOT JUST LET HIM GO? WE CAN BRING A DOZEN MEN IN HERE TOMORROW TO DESTROY ANYTHING THAT MOVES...

HE'S MADE A *FOOL* OF CEREBUS FOR THE LAST TIME... CEREBUS IS GOING TO FOLLOW HIM...

...AND *ONE* OF ISN'T COMING OUT OF HERE ALIVE...

OH, MIGHTY TARIM -- YOUR HUMBLE SERVANT BESEECHES YOU TO BE MERCIFUL AND STRIKE DOWN HIS ENEMIES WITH MASSIVE CORONARIES ...

SO TURG HAD BEEN RIGHT... IT HAD TAKEN MORE THAN A YEAR, BUT IT SEEMED CEREBUS WAS JUST AS ANGRY AS HE...

E'LASS COULD BARELY CONTAIN HIS AMAZEMENT! THEY HAD GONE RIGHT PAST HIM, AS IF IT HAD NEVER OCCURRED TO THEM THAT HE MIGHT BE HIDING...

E'LASS FELT HIS HEART SWELL WITH PURITY... IN A FEW SECONDS, THEY WOULD BE GONE... LOOKING FOR HIM!

WITH HIS NEWLY-DEVELOPED BOND WITH TARIM, E'LASS WAS CONVINCED HE COULD WALK PAST JULIUS' GUARDS WITHOUT A ...

THOOM

TARIM! WHAT WAS THAT?

THE SLIDING PANEL...

AYE!

CLOSED TIGHT...

UNDOUBTEDLY, A SIGN THAT OUR QUARRY SEEKS A CONFRONTATION AS MUCH AS CEREBUS DOES...

NO! NO! I DON'T! REALLY -- WE COULD BE FRIENDS! I'LL EVEN GIVE BACK THE DIAMOND...

AS THE SOUND OF FOOT-STEPS FADES TO A DISTANT ECHO, ELASS STEALS ONCE MORE FROM HIS HIDING PLACE...

PLEASE, TARIM!

YOU DID IT ONCE--JUST OPEN THE PANEL...

I'LL USE THE DIAMOND TO BUILD CHURCHES --MONASTERIES

PLEASE OPEN IT.... PLEEEASE!

HE HAD COME THIS FAR... HE REFUSED TO GIVE UP! HE FORCED HIS MIND TO SLOW DOWN AND THINK...!

SOMEWHERE UP AHEAD THERE HAD TO BE A DOORWAY OR TUNNEL THAT WOULD LEAD HIM TO THE SURFACE...

CLENCHING HIS TEETH HE RESOLVES TO FIND IT...

AND WHEN HE FOUND IT -- WITH OR WITHOUT TARIM'S HELP...

HE WOULD BE A VERY WEALTHY MAN...

YOU REALLY THINK HE KNOWS WE'RE CHASING HIM?

WE'RE NO LONGER CHASING HIM, LORD JULIUS ...

WE'RE BEING LED!

LED? BUT HOW COULD HE...?

FROM THE TIME WE CAME THROUGH THAT *PANEL*, WE HAVEN'T ONCE BEEN FACED WITH A CHOICE OF PATHS TO FOLLOW...

THERE HAVE BEEN NO SIDE-TUNNELS, NO DOORWAYS, NO BRIDGES...

IT IS VERY MUCH UNLIKE THE PREY TO LEAD YOU TO HIS HIDING SPOT

BUT IT IS *NOT* SO UNLIKE THE PREDATOR...

HE IS UP AHEAD -- SOMEWHERE -- WAITING FOR US!

THERE WEREN'T ANY SIDE TUNNELS! HE HAD WALKED FOR THE EQUIVALENT OF FIVE CITY BLOCKS! WHAT IF THE TUNNEL ENDED UP AHEAD? THEY MIGHT ALREADY HAVE TURNED BACK! IF SO, HE WAS *TRAPPED!*

I'D PROBABLY BE ABLE TO HANDLE THIS BETTER IF MY STOMACH DIDN'T HURT SO MUCH...

GREETINGS, GENTLE-MEN -- I'VE REALIZED THAT THE SHADOW-CRAWLER WAS A --uh-- MISTAKE...

LARGE, POWERFUL, BUT IN *ESSENCE* LITTLE MORE THAN A TRIBAL MASCOT THAT PROVED UNSUITED TO ITS TASK... *

* CEREBUS #15

NO-- THERE IS ONLY ONE WAY TO SETTLE THIS SITUATION! UNTIL YOU ARE *DEAD* LORD JULIUS, MY FORCES WILL BE LITTLE MORE THAN THE DREGS OF YOUR OWN SOCIETY-- THE MALCONTENTS!

WILL FEAR NO LONGER! I WILL *TRAMPLE* YOUR DAMN BUREAUCRACY INTO *DUST!*

...WITH YOU DEAD, PALNU WILL NEED A NEW *LEADER*... THOSE WHO NOW FEAR YOUR POWER AND INFLUENCE...

IN A FEW WEEKS LORD JULIUS' REIGN WILL BE LITTLE MORE THAN A BAD DREAM...

IN THE MINDS OF THE PEOPLE OF PALNU...

...MY PEOPLE.

YOU ARE ALL THAT STANDS IN MY WAY, *CEREBUS!* STEP FORWARD AND FIGHT FOR WHAT LITTLE HONOUR YOUR MASTER STILL RETAINS...

WHAT ARE YOU WAITING FOR...?

DON'T YOU KNOW IT'S *IMPOLITE* TO KEEP A PSYCHOTIC WAITING?

CEREBUS IS TIRED OF CITIES... PALNU, BEDUIN THEY ARE ALL THE SAME!

CEREBUS NEEDS MORE THAN MODIFIED ANT-HILLS CAN OFFER...

THIS IS A HELL OF A TIME TO DECIDE TO ASK FOR A *RAISE!*

CEREBUS WILL FIGHT YOUR BATTLE, BUT CEREBUS WANTS EIGHT BAGS OF GOLD AND A HORSE SO HE CAN GET OUT OF THIS...

DO YOU HAVE ANY IDEA OF THE DENT THAT WOULD PUT IN MY PETTY CASH VAULT? I *REFUSE!*

THE PSYCHOTIC'S QUARREL IS WITH *YOU!* IF YOU PREFER, CEREBUS WILL GO NOW, *EMPTY-HANDED...*

...AND LEAVE YOU TWO TO SETTLE YOUR DIFFERENCES...

IT'S A GOOD THING FOR YOU I'M AS BIG A COWARD AS I AM

BUT CEREBUS HAS ALREADY MOVED ONTO THE NARROW TILTED BRIDGE...

BUT, BEFORE YOU DIE, LORD JULIUS, IT IS ONLY FITTING THAT YOU SHOULD KNOW WHO WILL SUCCEED YOU!

GAZE THEN UPON THE VISAGE OF...

...YOUR SOCIAL SECRETARY!

HAHAHA! YES, LORD JULIUS -- ALL ALONG YOUR GREATEST ENEMY WAS RIGHT UNDER YOUR VERY NOSE!

HOW EASY IT WAS TO CONFOUND YOUR FEEBLE PLANS! HOW YOU MUST HAVE WONDERED AT THIS ENEMY WHO SEEMED TO READ YOUR EVERY...

SSKRAK

...THOUGHT...

THAT WASN'T EXACTLY FAIR, WAS IT? I MEAN...

...HE THOUGHT YOU WERE GOING TO FIGHT TO THE DEATH WITH SWORDS!

365

LORD JULIUS WATCHES THE HORSE AND RIDER PASS FROM SIGHT...
"WHERE DO YOU THINK YOU'LL GO?" "NORTH.. SOUTH... IT MATTERS
LITTLE WHEN YOU'RE RICH" AND THAT WAS IT, TOO BAD, REALLY...
WHO KNOWS WHAT HE MIGHT HAVE BEEN ABLE TO DO FOR
PALNU...? AS A GENERAL, HE COULD POSSIBLY HAVE...

MESSAGE FOR YOU, LORD JULIUS...

HAVE YOU GOT CHANGE FOR A GOLD PIECE?

OH, YES, SIR!

GOOD, THEN YOU WON'T NEED THIS COPPER BIT I WAS GOING TO GIVE YOU

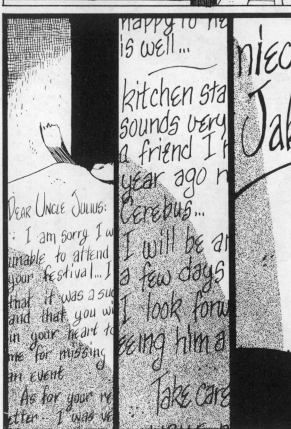

DEAR UNCLE JULIUS:

I am sorry I w
unable to attend
your festival... I
that it was a suc
and that you wi
in your heart to
me for missing
an event

As for your re
tter. I was ve

happy to h
is well...

kitchen sta
sounds very
a friend I
year ago

Cerebus...
I will be ar
a few days
I look forw
being him a

niece,
Jaka

Take care

HEY!

OH, WELL...

IT PROBABLY WASN'T IMPORTANT ....

368

BAM BAM BAM BAM

SHOW YOUR EMACIATED FACE, PEASANT... I AM CEREBUS THE AARDVARK!

AND I WISH TO BUY YOUR CRUMBLING HOVEL!...

NO LODGINGS *HERE*, DWARF...THERE'S AN INN TEN MILES DOWN THE ROAD...

CEREBUS DOES NOT WISH TO *RENT* LODGINGS....CEREBUS WISHES TO *BUY* A *HOVEL!*

NOW

HAH! I OWN AN ACRE AND A HALF OF PRIME PARMOC VINEYARDS...

WHERE WOULD AN UGLY FREAK LIKE YOU GET ENOUGH MONEY TO...

FOUR PIECES OF GOLD...

TAKE IT OR LEAVE IT...

THE HINGED WOOD PANEL SNAPS SHUT! FROM WITHIN, CEREBUS HEARS RUSTLING NOISES AND WONDERS BRIEFLY WHETHER HIS OFFER HAS BEEN REFUSED OR...

BUT, MY *HUSBAND* IT IS RAINING AND LITTLE *THEOPHELES* HAS A BROKEN LEG ...

SILENCE, WOMAN -- IT IS ONLY TEN MILES TO THE INN ...

...THE WALK WILL DO HIM *GOOD*...

...*THREE* ...*FOUR*...

A PLEASURE DOING BUSINESS WITH YOU, IMPOVERISHED ONE...

HE HAD LEFT *PALNU* THREE WEEKS BEFORE, AND IN THAT TIME HE HAD SPENT *TWENTY* GOLD PIECES OUT OF HIS *EIGHT* BAGS OF...

ACHTUNG, CITIZEN!-- VE HAFF A BUSINESS DEAL FOR YOU...

OPEN THE DOOR AND IT VILL NOT BE NECESSARY TO *REMOOF* YOUR ARMS AND LEGS ...

VE CAN BE *VER-RY* FRIENDLY IF YOU DO NOT *ANG-KER* US...

TARIM! IF IT'S NOT ONE THING, IT'S *ANOTHER!*

CEREBUS IS *BUSY*...

GO AWAY...

AH!

GUT *MOR*-RNING TO YOU! IF IT WOULT NOT BE TOO MUCH *TR*-ROUBLE, MIGHT WE USE YOUR HOFEL FOR A *HEAD*QUARTERS?

OUR *AR*-RMY ISS SOON ATTACKING PALNU ANT WE NEET SOME PLACE TO WORK ON OUR PLANS...

FIND YOUR OWN HOVEL!

TARIM! THE NERVE OF SOME OF THESE BACK-WATER MERCENARIES *...*

WANTING TO MOVE INTO CEREBUS' HOVEL! *...* I DON'T CARE IF THEIR ARMY *IS* ABOUT TO ATTACK...

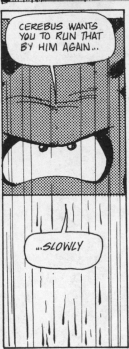

CEREBUS WANTS YOU TO RUN THAT BY HIM AGAIN...

...SLOWLY

AH! YOU ARE *INTR*-RIGUED! DIS IS GUT! WE COME INSIDE AND DISCUSS IT... *NEIN?*

CEREBUS PONDERS THE OFFER BRIEFLY...THE ACCENT AND INFLECTION WAS T'GITAN AND HE DIDN'T RELISH ENDURING AN INTERMINABLE HARANGUE ON THE VIRTUES OF FOREST LIVING...

DO YOU HAVE ANY **FOOD?**

I AM AFRAIT ALL WE HAFF ISS A FEW POUNTS OF BEEF UND MUTTON AND A FEW LOAFS OF **FR-RESH** BREAT...

ON THE OTHER HAND, MUSES CEREBUS ONE CAN NEVER FIND OUT TOO MUCH ABOUT OTHER CULTURES...

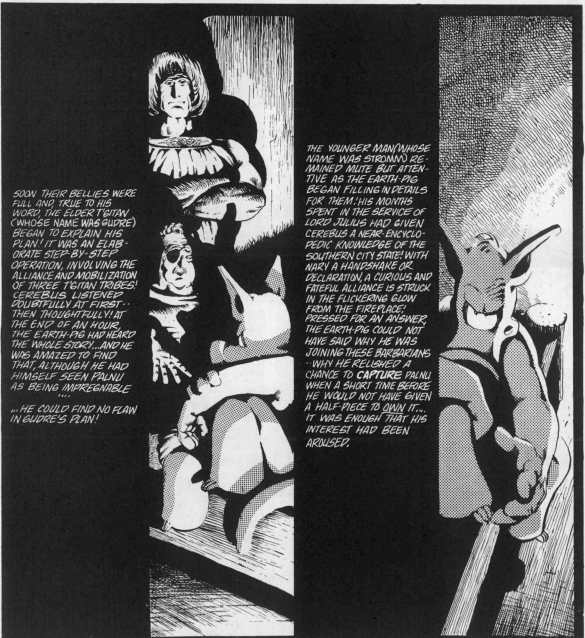

SOON THEIR BELLIES WERE FULL AND, TRUE TO HIS WORD, THE ELDER T'GITAN (WHOSE NAME WAS GUDRE) BEGAN TO EXPLAIN HIS PLAN! IT WAS AN ELABORATE STEP-BY-STEP OPERATION, INVOLVING THE ALLIANCE AND MOBILIZATION OF THREE T'GITAN TRIBES! CEREBUS LISTENED DOUBTFULLY AT FIRST-- THEN THOUGHTFULLY! AT THE END OF AN HOUR, THE EARTH-PIG HAD HEARD THE WHOLE STORY...AND HE WAS AMAZED TO FIND THAT, ALTHOUGH HE HAD HIMSELF SEEN PALNU AS BEING IMPREGNABLE ....

...HE COULD FIND NO FLAW IN GUDRE'S PLAN!

THE YOUNGER MAN(WHOSE NAME WAS STROMM) REMAINED MUTE BUT ATTENTIVE AS THE EARTH-PIG BEGAN FILLING IN DETAILS FOR THEM.' HIS MONTHS SPENT IN THE SERVICE OF LORD JULIUS HAD GIVEN CEREBUS A NEAR-ENCYCLOPEDIC KNOWLEDGE OF THE SOUTHERN CITY STATE! WITH NARY A HANDSHAKE OR DECLARATION, A CURIOUS AND FATEFUL ALLIANCE IS STRUCK IN THE FLICKERING GLOW FROM THE FIREPLACE! PRESSED FOR AN ANSWER, THE EARTH-PIG COULD NOT HAVE SAID WHY HE WAS JOINING THESE BARBARIANS --WHY HE RELISHED A CHANCE TO **CAPTURE** PALNU WHEN A SHORT TIME BEFORE HE WOULD NOT HAVE GIVEN A HALF-PIECE TO OWN IT... IT WAS ENOUGH THAT HIS INTEREST HAD BEEN AROUSED.

I MUST ASK YOU TO *NOT* SAY THAT NAME AROUND STROMM... ZENZITIVE HE ISS ZINCE THE INZIDENT AT...

...GHETTY'S POINT!

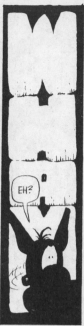

WHAP

EH?

VOT A *RELIEF!*...

NO *PR-*OPERTY DAMATCH THIS TIME!

I DO, HOWEFER, APOLOGIZE FOR THE DENT IN YOUR COW...

"HE ISS OUT OF RANGE" WHISPERS GUDRE, "NOW VE CAN TALK! SOME YEARS AGO AT THE GHETTY'S POINT ARMY CAMP, MY SON HAT THE BAD LUCK OF SPILLINK A DRINK ON KRULL. IT VAS PURELY AN ACCIDENT, BUT KRULL HASS NEVER BEEN THE FORGIFFING SORT.. AND HE WAS DRUNK. HE DEMANTED THAT STROMM APOLOGIZE. MY SON REFUSED..."

"AND KRULL HAD HIS TONGUE CUT OUT ON THE SPOT"

MMMM. GRIM BUSINESS THAT...

GRIM? ACH! GRIM IS NOT THE WORD FOR IT...!

FOR MONTHS, STROMM DID NOTHING EXCEPT SIT AROUND ALL DAY MOUTHING OBSCENITIES...

375

THE NEXT DAY DAWNS RADIANT AND CLEAR...

UNFORTUNATELY, BY THE TIME CEREBUS AND GUDRE ARE WENDING THEIR WAY THROUGH THE WOODS IT IS WET AND MISERABLE AGAIN...

CEREBUS JUST THOUGHT OF SOMETHING. IF STROMM HASN'T GOT A TONGUE, HOW DO THE ORANGE CREAMS CALM HIM DOWN?

IT ISS THE TEXTURE HE REMEMBERS...SORT OF MAKES THINKS EASIER FOR ME...

IF I'M OUT OFF ORANCHE CREAMS, I USE ZUMTHINK ELTZE...

AN OFER*RIPE* BANANA CHUNK, A LUMP OF SOGGY OATMEAL; YOU NAME IT. IF IT'S SOFT UND SQVISHY IT VILL CALM HIM DOWN.

GUDRE.

HAIL STROMM GOTT OF THUNDER!

ZO! VOT DEFENSIS HASS KRULL COME UP WITH TO TRY UND...

NONE.

NONE?

I CANNOT BELIEF IT MYSELF ALMOST.

I KNOW.

BUT THERE ARE NO GUARTS ON THE WALLS --NO FORTIFICASHUNTS ON DER GATES. I HAFF SEEN TREE-FORTS THAT ARE BETTER DEFENTED...

HAIL STROMM.

SOD OF THUNDER?

SOMETHING ISS *RRANCID* IN DAVIN...

KRULL KNOWS THAT VE ARE AMASSING AN ARMY-- WHERE ARE HISS *TR-RICKS?* SURELY HE DOES NOT INTENT TO GIFF UP MITOUT A FIGHT?

I DO *NOT* UNTERSTAND THIS...

NO GUARTS -- NOTHINK MOVINK IN THE CITY AT ALL...

LIKE EFRYONE HASS GONE

AN EFACUATION? HOW MANY PEOPLE HAF LEFT THE CITY ZINCE...

IT ISS WINTER. THE ROAD WILL BE EMPTY FOR SEFERAL MONTHS YET...

I SAW TWO PRIESTS LEAVE THE CITY EARLY THIS MORNINK, BUT NO ONE ELTZE HASS LEFT WHILE I...

PRIESTS? DID YOU SAY TWO *PRIESTS?*

JA! PRIESTS ...VHY DO YOU ASK?

THESE ARE THE HIGH HOLY DAYS -- FROM MIDWINTER TO CONCORDANCE EVE...

NO PRIEST IS ALLOWED TO EAT SALTED NUTS...

COMMENT ON THE WEATHER..

OR *LEAVE* HIS PLACE OF MEDITATION

THEN WHO..?

CEREBUS IS WILLING TO BET IT'S KRULL AND SOME ASSISTANT

BUT... VHY?

YOU SAID LORD JULIUS WAS MOVING HIS TROOPS TO THE ONLIU BORDER -- DO YOU KNOW THE ROUTE THEY ARE USING?

JA... ABOUT TWENTY MILES SOUTH OFF HERE ...AN OFERLAND ROUTE...

AND THESE 'PRIESTS' YOU SAW WERE HEADING SOUTH AS WELL?

JA. BUT I DON'T SEE...

ONE OF THEM IS KRULL FOR SURE, THEN.

HE'S HEADING SOUTH TO DIVERT SOME TROOPS TO FLUROC... HE'LL COUNTERMAND JULIUS' ORDERS IF NECESSARY...

PERHAPPS YOU ARE RIGHT...

BUT HE VILL BE TOO LATE...VE ARE ALMOST READY TO ATTACK...AT THIS MOMENT STROMM ISS....

BUT THAT'S THE POINT...HE'S QUITE WILLING TO LET YOU TAKE THE CITY...

FOR A WHILE!

YOU'LL SLAUGHTER SOME ARISTOCRATS AND MERCHANTS --IN KRULL'S MIND THEY'RE EXPENDABLE...

MEANWHILE HE'LL BE HEADING NORTH WITH HAND-PICKED TROOPS

YOUR PLANS FOR CONQUEST ARE SOLID AS FAR AS CEREBUS CAN SEE...

...BUT YOUR FORCES CONSIST MOSTLY OF RAW RECRUITS...

IF KRULL RETURNS WITH EVEN FIVE OR SIX THOUSAND PALNAN MERCENARIES THIRSTY FOR BLOOD, CEREBUS WOULD GIVE YOU TWO CHANCES OF HOLDING THE CITY FOR A NIGHT ..

...SLIM AND NIL!

CEREBUS HAS NEED OF YOUR SWIFTEST HORSE!

THAT CAMP VE PAST ON THE VAY HERE...

BUT WHERE ARE YOU GOINK?

CEREBUS HAS A PLAN!

BUT VE SHOULT DISCUSS IT!

DISCUSS IT, THEN

YOU CAN LET CEREBUS KNOW YOUR DECISION WHEN HE GETS BACK

HE HASS NO SWORT -- NO AR-RMOUR-- NOT EFEN A SKINNINK KNIFE

VHAT DO YOU THINK?

I THINK I WOULT NOT LIKE TO BE IN KRULL'S SHOES RIGHT NOW...

JA! I THINK SO, TOO!

I DON'T MEAN TO *PRY*, SIR, BUT WHAT MADE YOU DECIDE TO WRITE YOUR MEMOIRS?

YOU KNOW OF THE TIME I DEFENDED FLUROC'S GATE WITH ONLY TWO DOGS AND A CRIPPLE AT MY SIDE?

HOW I HAD AN ARROW IN MY SHOULDER AND EVEN THOUGH I WAS *DELERIOUS* FOR A WEEK, HOW THE FOUR OF US HELD OFF THE CREAM OF GALFANN'S ARMY?

YES, SIR...

AND YOU'VE HEARD OF THE TIME I WAS CRUCIFIED OUT IN THE DESERT...

HOW I WAS WITHOUT FOOD AND WATER FOR TWELVE DAYS...

HOW A CAMEL CAME BY TO SNIFF ME AND I RIPPED OUT ITS THROAT WITH MY TEETH AND ATE IT...

OH, YES SIR...

WELL...

I'M HOPING MY MEMOIRS WILL SHOW PEOPLE THAT EVEN MY LIFE ISN'T *ALWAYS* THAT GLAMOROUS...

NOW WHERE WAS I...?

AH!

"KRULL STARED INTO THE STYGIAN GLOOM OF THE SURROUNDING FOREST..."

"HIS NOSTRILS FLARED AND A LOW, MENACING ANIMALISTIC GROWL..."

"RRRRRR..."

"RUMBLED IN HIS THROAT! HE KNEW THE WAYS OF THESE..."

UNH?!

GREETINGS TO YOU, O SONS OF THE LIVING TARIM...

WHAT? OH... eh... AND GREETINGS TO *YOU*, O INCONVENIENT OBSTACLE! I BID YOU LET US PASS FOR WE DOTH HAVE BUSINESS MOST PRESSING...

SO!...

YOU CHOOSE TO NOT RETURN THE SACRED GREETING OF THE *GRAUZWERG*

YOU ARE AWARE OF THE *PENALTY* FOR THIS INSULT..?

SIR--DO YOU KNOW WHAT HE'S...

SHH--SOME KIND OF PRIEST-TALK --LET ME HANDLE THIS IDIOT...

WELL?

eh-- I FEAR MY MIND IS MOST FUZZY AND I AM...uh...*VEXED* WOULDST THOU *REMINDETH* MY MOST UNWORTHY SELF OF THE PENALTY?

FORGIVE ME, TARIM...!

FORGIVE ME TARIM...!

FORGIVE ME, TARIM!

BUT...

...BUT...

FORGIVE ME, TARIM!

SIR-- HE WANTS ME TO...

JUST DO WHAT HE TELLS YOU GRIMES-- I'M WORKING ON A PLAN...

FORGIVE...

CRUNK

MUNH!

NICE SHOT, KID...

CEREBUS THINKS THERE MIGHT BE A POSITION FOR YOU IN OUR ORGANIZATION

TARIM...

384

A WEEK LATER, IN LORD JULIUS' PRIVATE OFFICE IN PALNU...

LORD JULIUS! I BRING YOU GRAVE NEWS...!

YOU MEAN *BESIDES* THE MUD YOU'RE TRACKING ALL OVER MY NEW BROADLOOM?

FLUROC HAS FALLEN! THE BARBARIANS OF T'GITA HAVE TAKEN THE CITY-- THOUSANDS DIE EVEN AS WE *SPEAK*!

FLAMES SCORCH THE SKIES THE COLOUR OF *BLOOD*! HORDES OF SLAVERING, GODLESS...

IS THIS A MILITARY REPORT OR AN AUDITION?

LORD JULIUS-- WHAT ARE WE TO *DO*?!

YOU KNOW, I HAD A *PREMONITION* YOU WERE GOING TO ASK ME THAT...

I SAY WE SHOULD *SUE* FOR PEACE.

SUE FOR...? BUT, LORD JULIUS --THESE...

...THESE ARE BARBARIANS!

MY BOY, HAVING LIVED TO THIS RIPE OLD AGE, THERE ARE THREE BASIC TRUTHS ABOUT LIFE I CAN VOUCH FOR...

ONE; YOU CAN'T TELL A BOOK BY ITS COVER. *TWO;* YOU CAN'T TELL A *DIPLOMAT* ANYTHING. AND *THREE;*

THE BARBARIAN HASN'T BEEN BORN YOU CAN'T *BUY OFF* WITH A WARM ALE, RAW MEAT AND SOME BEADS...

YOU DON'T UNDERSTAND -- THEY'VE *CUT* OUR NORTHERN SUPPLY LINE! THEY'RE MASSING ON THE BORDER, ON THE ROAD, AT THE RIVER ...EVEN AT THE *AKSHUN* CROSSING!

MASSING IN *AKSHUN?*

OF COURSE THEY REALIZE THIS MEANS *WAH!!*

SEND IN THE ARMY!

BUT, *SIR* -- YOU SENT THE ARMY TO THE *ONLIU* BORDER ...

YOU SAID THAT ALL OF OUR OTHER BORDERS WERE *SECURE!* YOU SAID...

OH -- SO NOW IT'S *MY* FAULT...

THE BUCK STOPS *HERE*, EH?

I'LL HAVE YOU KNOW THAT IT HAS BEEN THE GOAL OF MY ADMINISTRATION FROM THE BEGINNING TO SEE THAT THE BUCK STOPS HERE, THERE AND EVERYWHERE

SIR?

FORGIVE ME, I WAS OVERCOME BY A WAVE OF *RHETORIC...*

HOW LONG DO WE HAVE TO *RAISE* AN ARMY?

THE T'GITANS WILL BE PREPARED TO MOVE SOUTH IN A FORTNIGHT, SIR

BRING ME A LIST OF MY POLITICAL ENEMIES IN *VESSARIAT* -- I WANT THE TOP-RANKING BUREAUCRATIC PEST PLACED IN CHARGE OF RAISING AND LEADING THE ARMY

YES, SIR -- BUT *WHY?*

IF ALL THE REPORTS FROM THE FIELD ARE GOING TO BE THIS *GRIM*, I'M GOING TO NEED SOMETHING TO CHEER ME UP WHEN MY COMMANDER GETS KILLED...

YES, SIR! ANYTHING *ELSE?*

YES...

START PRAYING THIS IS MORE THAN A *TWO-PART STORY!*

FLUROC

THE EASTERN GATE STOOD OPEN AS THE SUN DRIFTED DOWN TO THE HORIZON! IT HAD BEEN THREE DAYS SINCE THE T'GITAN HORDE HAD RUSHED THAT GATE...

ZERBUTZ!

...THREE DAYS SINCE THE LAST OF FLUROC'S RESIDENTS HAD FALLEN BEFORE THE KNIVES, SWORDS AND WEIGHTED SPEARS OF THE PAINTED, HALF-NAKED SAVAGES. THERE IS NO SOUND OF CONQUERING FOOTSTEPS...

ALMOST ALL OF THE VICTORIOUS T'GITANS HAVE RETURNED TO THE SURROUNDING WOODS, THERE TO GAMBLE THEIR LOOT (SUCH AS IT WAS) AND DRINK MORE WINE AND BEER, SO RECENTLY 'LIBERATED' FROM PALNU'S MOST NORTHERLY-PLACED BASTION...

...WHILE INSIDE THE WALL BARELY A HANDFUL REMAIN, SIFTING THROUGH THE DEBRIS IN SEARCH OF ANOTHER KIND OF LOOT....

ZERBUTZ?

DOWN HERE, GRAUS...

THE STENCH OF DEATH HANGS HEAVILY IN THE HUMID WINTER AIR, BUT THE T'GITAN SMELLS NOTHING. HE HAS BEEN A WARRIOR FOR THE LAST TWELVE SEASONS, AND HAS SEEN, SMELLED AND CAUSED ENOUGH DEATH TO BE ALMOST TOTALLY INSULATED FROM ITS IMPACT...

WHILE AT THE OTHER EXTREME A CERTAIN EARTH-PIG IS RELIVING OLFACTORY EXPERIENCES...

CEREBUS BETTER FIND WHAT HE'S LOOKING FOR SOON-- HE CAN FEEL HIS NOSTRIL HAIRS STARTING TO CURL

HAIL STROMM!

...THAT WOULD BE BETTER LEFT UN-LIVED IN THE FIRST PLACE...

THE ODD SALUTATION REMINDS CEREBUS OF THE FIRST TIME HE HEARD IT, AT THE TIME HE HAD BEEN TOO PREOCCUPIED TO THINK MUCH ABOUT IT, BUT NOW HIS CURIOSITY WAS GENUINELY AROUSED.

WHAT DO YOU KNOW ABOUT STROMM, GRAUS?

"STROMM? GRAUS KNOW EFERYTHINK ABOUT STROMM! SON OF TARIM-- GOTT OF THUNTER-- FALL OUT OF CLOUDS! ADOPT T'GITANS AS HIS CHILDREN."

"STROMM SMART-- STRONG! GRAUS SEE HIM BREAK WINE BOTTLE OPEN WITH TEETH! GRAUS SAY TO SELF 'SELF--ISS MAN YOU BE PROUD TO FOLLOW!'..."

"ISS GOOD LIFE AS FOLLOWER OF THUNTER GOTT--MUCH LOOTING, FREE BEER, STAY UP LATE AS GRAUS WANT"

WHAT ABOUT *GUDRE?*

GUDRE IS STROMM'S FIRST FOLLOWER. STROMM SAFE GUDRE FROM MANY LIONS... STROMM STARE AT LIONS, LIONS STOP.

STROMM WAVE ARMS IN AIR-- NEAREST LION GROWL AND COME TOWARD STROMM

...CLOSER...

...CLOSER!

STROMM BARES HISS TEETH! LION LEAP!'... BUT STROMM HASS ALREATY HISS SWORD OUT...

SHUMP!

SWORD CUTS OFF LEG!

SHUMP!

SWORD CUTS OFF HET!

SWORD BECOMES BLUR...LIONS DROPPINK LIKE FLIES

SOON ALL ARE *DET...*

'THANK YOU, THANK YOU,' SAY GUDRE

STROMM MAKE GUDRE LIFE-LONK COMPANION UND MALE SECRETARY...

NOW GUDRE SPEAK FOR STROMM IN GREAT COUNCIL

GUDRE BRINGS US STROMM'S WORD...

STROMM DOESN'T TALK MUCH HIMSELF DOES HE?

STROMM NOT TALK AT *ALL!* --THUNTER GOTT SAY VUN WORD UND HE WUT KNOCK WHOLE BUILTING OFER-- HE SAY *"GUT MORNINK"* UND MOUNTAIN RANGE WUT *CR*-RUMPLE...!

STROMM VERY CAREFUL-- THUNTER GOTT MUST NOT EFEN *BELCH*-- COULT DESTROY HALF OFF ARMY BY *AC*-CIDENT...

NEIN?

CEREBUS HAD NO IDEA THE LIFE OF A THUNDER GOD WAS SO...

...COMPLICATED.

CEREBUS MARVELS AT GUDRE'S HANDI-WORK-- HE HAD EFFECTIVELY MADE STROMM THE FOCUS OF ALL OF THE WARRIORS' ATTENTION...

...AND LEFT HIMSELF UNHAMPERED BY POLITICAL DEBATES IN THE PROCESS

WHAT DO YOU SUPPOSE STROMM HAS PLANNED?

GUDRE SAY *"STROMM REST."* STROMM NEET TIME TO GATHER STRENGTH FOR TRIAL AHEAT...

STROMM TELL US HISS PLAN VHEN TIME ISS RIGHT...

IN THE MEANTIME, GUDRE WOULD BE LEFT ALONE TO PLAN THE COMING ASSAULT ON PALNU, MUSES THE EARTH-PIG, WHILE STROMM'S WARRIORS WAIT PATIENTLY...

AND WHEN GUDRE TELLS YOU THAT STROMM IS RESTED...?

GRAUS VILL BE READY. FOLLOW STROMM -- DO VHAT HASS TO BE DONE...

GRAUS NOT UNTERSTANT VHY YOU STAY IN CITY-- NO MORE LOOT... VOMEN ARE ALL COLD UND BLUE UND STIFF...

CEREBUS AND GUDRE ARE SEARCHING THE WEALTHIER HOMES FOR *BOOKS*... THERE'S A GOOD POSSIBILITY WE COULD FIND SOME INFORMATION ON *PALNU* IN THEM...

SPECIFICALLY, WE'RE LOOKING FOR BOOKS ON *PREVIOUS* ATTEMPTS TO CONQUER THE CITY, IN THE HOPE THAT WE MIGHT FIND SOMETHING HELPFUL TO *US*...

UNFORTUNATELY, WHOEVER OWNED THIS COLLECTION SEEMS TO HAVE HAD A *BIZARRE* INTEREST IN STARS AND THE SUN AND THE MOON! IT'S GOING TO TAKE SOME TIME TO WADE THROUGH ALL OF THE *DRIVEL* TO FIND SOMETHING *INTERESTING*...

GRAUS *STILL* NOT *UNTERSTANT*...

GUDRE SAY "WE NEED MAGIC TO BEAT PALNU! WE GO LOOK"

MAGIC HERE SOMEWHERE! CEREBUS LOOK FOR *STRONG* MAGIC!

WHEN WE FIND MAGIC, SMASH PALNU INTO SMALL PIECES.

NO ONE GET AWAY!

NOW GRAUS UNTERSTANT.

VHY YOU NOT SAY SO IN FIRST PLACE?

LORD JULIUS -- **LORD GORCE** OF VESSARIAT HAS ARRIVED AS YOU ORDERED...

I DISTINCTLY REMEMBER ORDERING HIM 'WELL-DONE'

THIS MAN WOULD BARELY QUALIFY AS *'HALF-BAKED'*

I AM HERE TO DO YOUR *BIDDING*, M'LORD

FEEDING ME STRAIGHT LINES ISN'T GOING TO GET YOU OFF THE HOOK, MY GOOD FELLOW!

THE PEOPLE SAY THAT *FLUROC* HAS BEEN CAPTURED -- THAT COMMANDER KRULL HAS FALLEN INTO ENEMY HANDS. THE PEOPLE FEAR THAT PALNU IS NEXT...

AND WHAT ABOUT YOU?

WHAT DO YOU KNOW OF THE MENACE TO THE NORTH?

THE FEARS OF THE PEOPLE HAVE NEVER BEEN MY *CONCERN...*

WRITE THAT DOWN...

...I MAY WANT TO USE IT IN MY FAREWELL ADDRESS TO THE CITIZENS...

YES, SIR!...

I HAVE SOME BAD NEWS FOR YOU, *GORCE* -- THE RUMOURS ARE *TRUE!* FURTHERMORE, OUR MILITARY FORCES ARE CONCENTRATED ON THE ONLIU BORDER AND THERE ISN'T THE *SLIGHTEST* CHANCE OF THEIR REACHING PALNU IN TIME TO SAVE US...

...THERE IS ONLY *ONE* MAN I WOULD ENTRUST WITH RAISING AN ARMY AND LEADING US TO VICTORY IN THIS OUR DARKEST HOUR...

AND THAT MAN IS *YOU!*

M-ME, LORD JULIUS?

I KNOW...

IT'S MORE OF AN HONOUR THAN YOU EVER *DREAMED* WOULD BE BESTOWED UPON YOU WHEN YOU ARRIVED HERE...

IF THE TRUTH BE KNOWN, I HAD HOPED TO LEAD OUR NEW ARMY AGAINST THESE GODLESS HEATHENS...

BUT THERE IS LAST-MINUTE PACKING TO BE DONE, ALAS! AND SO, MY PLACE IS *HERE* WITH THE WINE STEWARDS AND TRAVEL AGENTS ...

B-B- BUT...!

I KNOW YOU WILL LIVE UP TO ALL EXPECTATIONS -- MY AIDE WILL, OF COURSE, GIVE YOU AN ADDRESS WHERE YOU CAN REACH ME! WHEN ALL OF THIS IS HISTORY, WE *MUST* HAVE LUNCH AND ENGAGE IN A MEANINGFUL *DIALOGUE*...

B-B- BUT...!

BUT FOR NOW, MAY TARIM SPEED YOU ON YOUR WAY TO THE GREATER GLORY TO WHICH YOU COMMIT YOURSELF. THESE ARE TIMES WHICH CALL FOR EACH OF US TO DEDICATE OURSELVES WITH *RENEWED VIGOUR* TO THE TASK AT HAND...

YOUR NAME SHALL BE AS A SHINING BEACON TO ALL PALNU, FOR THINE IS THE KINGDOM AND THE POWER AND THE GLORY...

IS HE GONE?

YES, SIR...

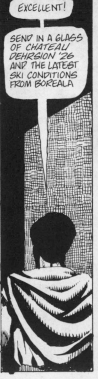

EXCELLENT!

SEND IN A GLASS OF CHATEAU DEHRSION '26 AND THE LATEST SKI CONDITIONS FROM BOREALA

LORD GORCE?

I AM AFRAID LORD JULIUS HAS JUST DROPPED A RATHER SUBSTANTIAL MESS IN MY LAP, *HARKER*...

WHAT ARE YOU GOING TO *DO*, SIR?

DO? I'M GOING TO RAISE AN ARMY, DEFEAT THE I'GITANS, RALLY THE MERCHANT CLASS TO MY SIDE, TOPPLE THE BUREAUCRACY, TRY LORD JULIUS IN PUBLIC FOR HIGH TREASON AND SEIZE THE REIGNS OF POWER...

YES, SIR...

AND THEN I'M GOING TO MAKE SOME *LONG*-RANGE PLANS...

CER-REBUTZ, MY FRIENT-- I HOPE YOU HAFF FOUNT SOME-THINK...!

A PASSAGE IN ONE BOOK-- NOTHING MORE...

ACH...

I AM AFRAIT I HAFF MATE A GRAFE ERROR IN CHUDGEMENT-- FLUROC'S WEALTH HASS BEEN GR-REATLY OFERESTIMATED!

HAVING EXAMINT DER LOOT THAT VAS TAKEN, IT ISS MY CONSIDERT OPINION THAT VE VILL BE LUCKY IF VE ARE ABLE TO AFFORT TO HIRE ONE CAVALRYMAN...

AND THEN ONLY IFF HE PROVIDES HISS OWN HORSE...

CEREBUS HAS MARKED THE PLACE...

...THE INFORMATION MAY BE USEFUL IF IT ISN'T OUT OF DATE...

JA...PR-RETTY BLEAK...

A BLEAK SITUATION, THEN?

HAIL STROMM!

HAIL STROMM!

YOU HAFF ZUMTHING TO TELL ME ABOUT, *KRAUFTIG*?

OUTSIDE NORTH WALL -- MANY MEN, SOLDIERS TOO -- FUNNY CLOTHES

SMELL LIKE *FLOWERS*.

VOT DO YOU *THINK*?

SOUNDS LIKE MERCHANTS! FLUROC IS -- *WAS* -- A MAJOR TRADING CENTER...

THEY STANDINK OUT-SIDE -- YELLINK AT WARRIORS ON WALL

SOUND LIKE "GIBBLE GIBBLE GIBBLE" TO KRAUFTIG...

YELLING? YELLING WHAT?

FOREIGN MERCHANTS AT THAT...

MAYHAP WE SHOULD SEE WHAT THEY WANT...

VELL?

N'GAMIN MERCHANTS... THE CHAPS WITH THE SHIELDS AND SHORT JAVELINS ARE THEIR MERCENARY GUARDS... THEY WANT TO KNOW IF SOMETHING IS *WRONG*...

WE'RE IN LUCK...

THEY'VE BROUGHT FURS AND JEWELRY... THEY WANT TO KNOW WHY WE DON'T LET THEM IN SO THEY CAN SHOW US...

CEREBUS SHOUTS IN THE T'CAPMIN LANGUAGE FOR SEVERAL MINUTES... SUDDENLY THE VISITORS BEGIN MOANING AND SHIFTING NERVOUSLY ABOUT...

I TOLD THEM THAT WE ARE INTERESTED IN SEEING THEIR JEWELRY AND THAT WE HAVE MUCH MONEY...

I ALSO TOLD THEM ABOUT *THE PLAGUE* ...

PLAGUE?!

AYE! IT STRUCK ABOUT FOUR OR FIVE DAYS AGO... WIPED OUT MOST OF OUR POPULATION... *TRAGIC!* JUST TRAGIC. ONE MINUTE YOU'RE WALKING AROUND AND THEN... *POOF!*...PUNCTURE WOUNDS APPEAR IN VITAL ORGANS; YOUR THROAT BURSTS OPEN OR YOUR CHEST AND YOU BLEED TO DEATH ...

AH!--DER BODIES, NEIN?

OUR VISITORS WILL BE LESS THAN EAGER TO EXAMINE THE LATE RESIDENTS OF *FLUROC*...

THEY'LL BE MULLING OVER THEIR NEXT MOVE FOR A WHILE. I SUGGEST WE GET ALL THE T'GITANS IN HERE DRESSED IN *PALNAN GARB*

VOT DO YOU HAFF IN MIND?

CEREBUS THINKS HE MIGHT BE ABLE TO TALK THEM INTO LEAVING THEIR GOLD HERE ...WE'LL HAVE TO BE CAREFUL! NOW THAT THEY'VE HEARD "*PLAGUE*" WE'LL BE FACING THEIR MOST FEARLESS MERCENARIES AND THEIR GREEDIEST MERCHANTS...

KRULL * IS STILL SECURE, I HOPE--

...IT WOULDN'T DO TO HAVE HIM SUDDENLY SHOW UP...

JA GRIMES LEFT HISS POST TO GET AN ALE YESTERDAY, VHICH LET TO A SMALL INZIDENT...

* COMMANDER KRULL, THE MILITARY "CHAMPION OF FLUROC" CAPTURED BY CEREBUS LAST ISSUE...

HE VAS GONE BUT FIFE MINUTES UND VHEN HE RETURNT, KRULL HAT SMASHT HISS IRON MASK AGAINST DER VALL TIL IT OPENT-- RIPPT OFF HISS MANACLES VISS HISS TEETH, SNAPPT DER ROPES VISS HISS CHEST UND BICEPS...

AND VASS IN DER PR-ROCESS OF PULFERIZINK THE CEMENT ENCASING HISS FEET MIT DER BALL-UND-CHAIN ATTACHED TO HISS VAIST...

EVERYTHING IS ALRIGHT NOW?

ACH, JA!-- VE HAT FORTY OFF OUR BEST MEN STANTING BY SO VE HAT HIM SUBTUED IN A MATTER OF HOURS...

398

I··I SEE WHAT YOU MEAN. AND WE *HAVE* COME SUCH A LONG WAY...

SHALL WE GO INSIDE...

AND MAKE OUR-SELVES MORE COMFORTABLE?

OH NO...

EH? VASS ISS? ≡SNIFFF≡

FAUGH! SMELL LIKE PANROVIAN WHOREHOUSE...!

GUDRE MUST HAVE *MISSED* THIS ONE...

"A T'GITAN MARAUDER! STAY BACK, GENTLEMEN" CRIES CEREBUS IN TCAPMIN, "THEY CAN BE QUITE DANGEROUS!"

AH, *ZERBUTZ!* THESE ARE FRENTS OFF YOURS?

"IS IT NOT ENOUGH THAT I HAVE TO WATCH MY PEOPLE SQUIRT? MUST I ALSO ENDURE THESE CONSTANT BARBARIAN ATTACKS?" CONTINUES THE EARTH-PIG...

ISS FUNNY··COULT HAFF SWORN YOU USED TO SPEAK SAME LANGUAGE AS ME...

"TAKE *THAT!*"

"AND THAT!"

I SUGGEST THAT YOU HAVE HIM REMOVED -- AND, IF *POSSIBLE*, WE SHOULD DOUBLE HIS RATIONS FOR THE NEXT MONTH...

I THINK HE VILL BE MOST PLEAST VITH THAT -- HOW-EFFER, PERHAPS YOU SHOULT EXPLAIN YOUR *JUSTICE* TO ....*THEM!*...

THE T'GITANS STOOD WITH EYES RIVETED ON THE *EARTH-PIG!* HIS PERFORMANCE HAD WORKED WONDERS WITH THE *N'GAMIN* WHO JABBERED EXCITEDLY ABOUT HIS BRAVERY AND QUICKNESS...

THE *DISGUISED* T'GITANS, HOWEVER, HAD JUST SEEN ONE OF *STROMM'S* CHOSEN OFFICERS BERATE A WARRIOR IN A FOREIGN TONGUE... AND THEN BATTER HIM INTO *UNCONSCIOUSNESS!*

FOR HIS PART, *GUDRE* WAS LOOKING FORWARD TO YET ANOTHER DISPLAY OF THE EARTH-PIG'S INGENUITY! HIGH QUALITY ENTERTAINMENT WAS HARD TO COME BY...

CEREBUS PUNISH *SCHWAGERIN*...

SCHWAGERIN STEAL WINE SKIN FROM CEREBUS...

THAT NOT SCHWAGERIN ...

THAT *LIEBSCHAFT!*

MMM.

CEREBUS MAKE BIG MISTAKE. CEREBUS MUCH SORRY...

CEREBUS GIVE LIEBSCHAFT *TWO* WINE-SKINS WHEN HE WAKE UP...

NOW IT WAS THE TURN OF THE T'GITANS TO ENTHUSE ABOUT THIS *IMPRESSIVE* DISPLAY OF HUMILITY AND FAIRNESS AS CEREBUS RETURNED TO THE BUSINESS AT HAND...

YOU SEEM TO HAVE A *REMARKABLE* CONTROL OVER DIFFICULT SITUATIONS...

AND THERE ARE TIMES WHEN THE SITUATION IS MORE DIFFICULT THAN IT APPEARS...

NOW...

...I BELIEVE YOU HAVE SOME JEWELRY TO SHOW ME...

AS YOU CAN *PLAINLY SEE*, THESE ARE SOME OF THE FINEST AND MOST *DELICATE* EXAMPLES OF THE JEWELLER'S CRAFT...

I WOULD ASK THAT YOU EXAMINE EACH LINK·· THERE ARE VIRTUALLY NO FLAWS! OF COURSE RESS HAS ALWAYS BEEN NOTED FOR...

STRANGE.

STRANGE?

WHAT IS STRANGE?

NOTHING! NOTHING! uh·· CEREBUS WISHES TO KNOW SOMETHING ABOUT THIS OWL...

AH, THE OWL! YOU HAVE THE EYE OF A *CONNOISSEUR!* A CLASSIC PIECE SCULPTED WITH INFINITE CARE AND ADORNED BY THE FINEST...

DID YOU CUT YOURSELF SHAVING, MY FRIEND?

WHY·· *NO!* WHAT ON EARTH WOULD MAKE YOU THINK THAT I HAD...?

THERE'S...

...*BLOOD* ON YOUR NECK...

BLOOD? NOW WHERE COULD I HAVE...

OH, NO! IS··IS IT... COULD IT BE THE P...P...P...

HIGHLY UNLIKELY... THE SUDDEN ERUPTION OF BLOOD IS ONLY *ONE* OF THE SYMPTOMS ...

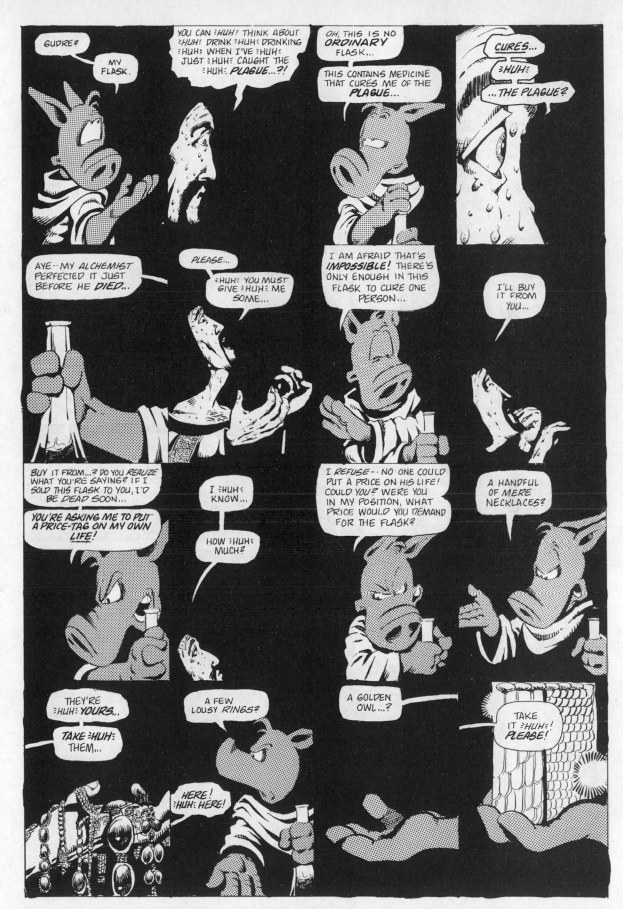

403

SOME HOURS LATER...

UNCUT DIAMONDS... MY SILK HANDKERCHIEF...

PLEASE! IT'S ALL I HAVE...

WHAT ZERBUTZ SAY TO FOP-WHO-SMELL-LIKE-FLOWERS?

I DO NOT KNOW -- BUT VHATEFER IT VAS, IT SEEMS TO BE VORKING!

BUT SURELY A LIFE MEANS MORE THAN A PILE OF BAUBLES! WOULD YOU THINK ME UNREASONABLE IF I ASKED FOR YOUR GUARDS' HELMETS AS WELL?

YOU HEARD HIM -- HAVE YOUR MEN SURRENDER THEIR HELMETS...

YOU HAVE BOUGHT OUR SERVICES -- NOT OUR ARMOUR! WHAT COULD YOU DO ABOUT IT IF WE WERE TO REFUSE?

I-COULD-BREATH-ON-YOU-

CLANK CLANG

VERY WELL -- PERHAPS THESE FEW TRINKETS WILL CONSOLE THE SURVIVORS STILL LEFT AFTER I HAVE PASSED FROM THIS MORTAL COIL...

YOU BETTER GO BEFORE I CHANGE MY MIND!

CERTAINLY! OH THANK YOU, THANK YOU!

ZERBUTZ! OFER HERE!

WHAT DO YOU WANT, *GRAUS*?

GRAUS UND WARRIORS VANT KNOW ZUMTHING...

HOW YOU GET LOOT FROM MERCHANT ...?

MERCHANT SHOW CEREBUS JEWELS! CEREBUS WANT...

MERCHANT SAY "COST MUCH MONEY"

CEREBUS SHOW MERCHANT BLOOD CEREBUS SAY "STICK IT IN YOUR EAR PANSY- BREATH"

CEREBUS SAY "THIS BLOOD COULD BE *YOURS,* EH?"

MERCHANT CLUTCH CHEST-- GASP! WHIMPER! CEREBUS SAY "GIVE·ME·LOOT!"

PANSY- BREATH WHINE "I HAVE MANY WARRIORS --THEY PROTECT ME!"

CLUTCH CHEST-- GASP, WHIMPER, WHINE!

JA! JA!

GRAUS SEE! GRAUS REMEMBER!

CEREBUS SAY "PANSY BREATH, YOU SEE YOUR WARRIOR OVER THERE?

PANSY- BREATH SAY "Y- YES,"...

CEREBUS SAY "GIVE ME LOOT, *NOW*..."

"OR CEREBUS WILL STUFF HIM UP YOUR RIGHT NOSTRIL"

NOSTRIL RIGHT NOSTRIL

RIGHT NOSTRIL!

JA! JA!

GRAUS REMEMBER NOW!!

CEREBUS SURVEYED THE CROWD GATHERING AROUND HIM, HANGING ON EVERY WORD OF HIS TALE OF BRAVADO AND DARING...

HE HAD ORIGINALLY THOUGHT GUDRE A GENIUS FOR HIS ABILITY TO UNITE THESE BARBARIANS...

PERHAPS IT WAS NOT AS DIFFICULT AS IT APPEARED AT FIRST GLANCE ...AND PERHAPS IN THE NEAR FUTURE...

THEN, CEREBUS SAY "YOU SEE FLASK?"

"UH-HUH", SAY PANSY BREATH.

"CEREBUS ALWAYS WONDER HOW MANY POINTY-HEAD WARRIORS WOULD *FIT* IN ONE."..

AND THEY *GIVE* YOU HELMETS...

GRAUS SEE! GRAUS REMEMBER!

THERE MIGHT BE ROOM FOR ANOTHER "GOTT OF THUNTER" IN THIS ARMY...

SHE-DEVIL IN THE SHADOWS

NOW THAT THEY WERE **IN** TOGITH CEREBUS WAS NOT QUITE SO HAPPY THAT GRAUS HAD ACCOMPANIED HIM...HE **HAD**, OF COURSE, SAVED CEREBUS THE TROUBLE OF HAVING TO CARRY SOME HUNDRED POUNDS OF FINE JEWELRY. BUT, BEDAZZLED BY THE MYRIAD ATTRACTIONS OF A BIG CITY, GRAUS HAD QUICKLY BECOME MORE TROUBLE THAN HE WAS WORTH...

AWAITING WORD FROM THE DUKE OF AGERDEN ON THE TRADE VALUE OF THE ASSORTED TRINKETS AND BAUBLES, CEREBUS HAD BEEN FORCED TO INVEST SEVERAL HOURS IN SEARCH OF HIS IMPULSIVE COMPANION!

HI, THERE... REMEMBER ME?

ZERBUTZ! PERCE ISS TELLINK FORTUNE OFF GRAUS!

DARE CEREBUS INQUIRE AS TO THE STATE OF OUR **FOOD** AND **LODGINGS** MONEY...?

ISS GONE, BUT NOT WORRY ...GRAUS FINT BREAT CRUSTS IN GARBAGE WAGON UND ALLEY- WAY NEARBY VITH MUCH STRAW

CEREBUS HEAVES A SIGH -- HE HADN'T REALLY EXPECTED ANY OF THE MONEY TO BE LEFT... WELL, WITH ANY LUCK THEIR BUSINESS WOULD BE FINISHED SOON AND THEY...

PERHAPS, *GRAUS* -- YOUR FRIEND WOULD LIKE *HIS* FORTUNE TOLD...?

CEREBUS DOES NOT *APPROVE* OF YOUR LIVELIHOOD...

TAKING IN --? I MAKE *FIVE GOLD PIECES* IN A GOOD NIGHT ...

WHAT DO YOU EXPECT ME TO DO?

STARCH EVERY *LOIN-CLOTH* IN *BOREALA*...?

FORTUNE-TELLING? IT IS AN HONEST WAY TO MAKE A LIVING... WHAT DON'T YOU...

YOU DON'T MEAN TO TELL *CEREBUS* THAT GRAUS SPENT THREE HOURS DOWN HERE HAVING HIS... *FORTUNE* TOLD?

HUH! HUH! HUH!

WELL? WHAT ABOUT IT, YOU SHORT, GRAY PRUDE? I HAVE TO PAY MY RENT DON'T I?

YOU-FIND-SOMETHING-*FUNNY*-ABOUT THAT?

THERE ARE *OTHER* WAYS FOR A YOUNG GIRL TO PAY HER RENT ...

TAKING IN *LAUNDRY* FOR EXAMPLE ...

NO! NO!

GRAUS VAS uh LAUGHINK AT FUNNY CURTAINS

MEANWHILE, HUNDREDS OF MILES TO THE NORTH, LORD GORCE (LORD JULIUS' CHOICE TO RAISE AND LEAD AN ARMY AGAINST CEREBUS AND THE T'GITANS) CONFERS WITH COMMANDER SARTE, HEAD OF SEAF'S MILITARY GOVERNMENT...

I UNDERSTAND THAT *LORD JULIUS* HAS PUT YOU IN CHARGE OF RAISING AN ARMY TO DEFEAT THE BARBARIANS WHO HAVE CAPTURED *FLUROC*...

AS USUAL, COMMANDER

YOUR SOURCES ARE *WELL-INFORMED*...

IN POINT OF *FACT*, THAT IS PRECISELY WHY I HAVE *COME* HERE! YOUR LONG-STANDING FRIENDSHIP WITH LORD JU... RATHER, WITH *PALNU*... RAISED HOPES IN ME THAT I MIGHT FIND YOUR GOVERNMENT TO BE ...*SYMPATHETIC?*

QUITE SO... INDEED...

I AM ALSO GIVEN TO UNDER-STAND THAT YOU ARE A MAN OF SOME *AMBITION?*

I SUPPOSE WE ARE *ALL* AMBITIOUS...

...IN OUR OWN WAY COMMANDER...

QUITE SO! INDEED! OF COURSE, SINCE I AM A MILITARY MAN, I FIND IT...*ODD* THAT LORD JULIUS WOULD CHOOSE ANOTHER MAN TO LEAD *HIS* ARMY...

LORD JULIUS HAS *TOLD* ME THAT HE IS QUITE BUSY.. MAKING CERTAIN...

...*TRAVEL PLANS*...

I SEE!

AND WOULD I BE MISTAKEN IN ASSUMING THAT YOU FIND *LORD JULIUS'* TRAVEL PLANS A TRIFLE ··ah···

...*PREMATURE?*

SIR?

WHAT I MEAN IS; DOES IT NOT STRIKE A LOYAL... AND *AMBITIOUS*... MAN LIKE YOURSELF *UNUSUAL* AND *DANGEROUS* FOR YOUR COUNTRY TO BE WITHOUT A LEADER AT THIS CRITICAL TIME?

ONCE I HAVE DEFEATED THE T'GITANS, I INTEND TO *RETURN* TO PALNU...

WHEN WORD OF MY ACHIEVMENT HAS SPREAD THE PEOPLE WILL BE ASKED TO CHOOSE THEIR NEW GRANDLORD FROM THE...

...*AVAILABLE* CANDIDATES...

I SEE. AND YOU WILL, OF *COURSE*, BE ONE OF THESE CANDIDATES?

MUCH WILL DEPEND ON THE WILL OF THE PEOPLE.... OF COURSE THE TIMING OF THE ELECTION MAY PLAY A PART IN THEIR CHOICE

I INTEND TO HOLD IT THE DAY AFTER MY TRIUMPHANT *VICTORY PARADE*...

I THINK YOU WILL FIND THE ARMIES OF SEAF MUCH TO YOUR LIKING..., YOU MAY DO WITH THEM AS YOU SEE FIT ...AND IF *I* SHOULD EVER NEED A FEW SMALL.... *FAVOURS?*

THE COMMANDER OF SEAF IS *ALWAYS* WELCOME IN PALNU

...AND IN THE OFFICE OF THE *GRANDLORD*...

I AM SO GLAD WE'VE HAD THIS OPPORTUNITY TO *CHAT*, LORD GORCE

YOU KNOW YOUR WAY OUT?

LORD GORCE?

HE'S GIVEN ME FULL CONTROL OF AN ARMY HARKER...

...AND THERE WILL BE NO OPPOSITION FROM SEAF WHEN THE PEOPLE PROCLAIM ME AS GRANDLORD...

EXCELLENT, SIR...!

EVERY SOLDIER WHO SWEARS EXCLUSIVE LOYALTY TO ME IS TO BE GIVEN DOUBLE HIS FIRST MONTH'S PAY... ALL WHO WOULD REMAIN LOYAL TO COMMANDER SARTE ARE TO BE EXECUTED... OH, AND HARKER...

SIR?

I THINK IT WOULD BE BEST TO SAY NOTHING UNTIL THEY ARE TWENTY MILES INSIDE OUR BORDER

IT WILL MAKE THEIR DECISION A LITTLE EASIER...

YES, SIR... WHERE DO WE GO NOW?

IANAG...

PRINCE SHOMBER HAS BEEN EAGER TO MOVE INTO OUR HOME- LAND RECENTLY. ANYTIME HE HAS TO GO FIVE YEARS WITHOUT AN EXPANSION OF HIS BORDER, HE BREAKS OUT IN HIVES...

I'LL OFFER HIM CI'NUFINN PROVINCE IN EXCHANGE FOR SOME OF HIS LIGHT CAVALRY...

CI'NUFINN PROVINCE! BUT, SIR, THE PEOPLE WOULD NEVER STAND FOR SUCH A...

YOU'RE NOT LISTENING, HARKER -- I SAID I WOULD OFFER HIM CI'NUFINN PROVINCE...

I NEVER SAID ANYTHING ABOUT GIVING HIM CI'NUFINN PROVINCE ...

"YOU STAY HERE...CEREBUS IS GOING INSIDE; TALK TO DUKE OF AGERDEN, FIND OUT HOW MANY TROOPS WE GET FOR JEWELRY! AS SOON AS CEREBUS GET LETTER PROMISING TROOPS, WE GO BACK TO FORTUNE LADY'S! GET OUR STUFF AND GO HOME. BUT, UNTIL-THEN-YOU-STAY-HERE! IF CEREBUS COME OUT AND YOU ARE GONE, CEREBUS MAKE GRAUS-BURGERS OUT OF YOU! IF YOU UNDERSTAND, BLINK TWICE, AND THEN CEREBUS WILL LET GO OF YOUR TONGUE..."

BUT TO BE *HONEST* WITH YOU, THERE'S REALLY TOO MUCH JEWELRY AROUND RIGHT NOW...IF YOU WANTED CASH--BUT *PIKEMEN AND CAVALRY?* THEY'RE TOO MUCH IN DEMAND TO TRADE FOR JEWELRY

EVERYONE...I MEAN *EVERY-ONE*--SEEMS TO BE HAVING A WAR RIGHT NOW...

CEREBUS LIKED YOU BETTER WHEN YOU WERE SELLING PORNOGRAPHIC PRAYER BOOKS IN THE "DOG AND DUCK"

HOW MANY TIMES DO I HAVE TO *TELL* YOU--I'M *LEGITIMATE* NOW! I'M A CERTIFIED DUKE OF THE HOUSE OF AGERDEN

I'LL HAVE YOU KNOW THAT I HAVE *ALSO* BEEN NAMED *CHAIR-MAN* OF THE ROYAL COMMITEE ON SCULPTURE

WONDERFUL...

TWICE A WEEK THAT FLITTY PRINCE OF YOURS DROPS BY TO OGLE ALL OF THESE *LIMP-WRISTED* STATUES...

THAT *STILL* DOESN'T EXPLAIN WHY CEREBUS CAN'T HAVE TWO BANDS OF PIKE AND SOME HEAVY CAVALRY...

I TELL YOU *WHAT*--IT'S AGAINST MY BETTER JUDGEMENT, BUT SUPPOSE FOR OLD TIMES' SAKE, I WERE TO *GIVE* YOU YOUR MERCENARIES--*FREE*... AND SUPPOSE I WERE TO ASK FOR A SMALL...TOKEN PAYMENT...

GO ON...

SAY--FOR THE SAKE ARGUMENT--THIS SMALL, EYE-PLEASING *OWL*...

I GET IT *NOW!*

THE OWL'S WORTH A *FORTUNE*, RIGHT?

LOOK! IF YOU'RE GOING TO GO ALL *CYNICAL* ON ME...

OF *COURSE* IT IS!

IS IT WORTH A FORTUNE OR ISN'T IT?

BUT IF YOU *KNOW* WHAT IT'S *WORTH* THEN THERE'S NO FUN IN CHEATING YOU...

OH.

SORRY.

QUITE ALL RIGHT...

ACTUALLY, THE OWL ITSELF IS WORTH ALMOST *NOTHING* -- BUT WITH ITS *TWIN*...!

WHAT WOULD YOU SAY TO TWO BANDS OF THE *FINEST HAND-PICKED* PIKEMEN SOUTH OF THE FELD RIVER

AND THE HEAVY CAVALRY YOU ASKED FOR..?

THAT WOULD DEPEND ON HOW MANY PEOPLE CEREBUS HAS TO *KILL* TO GET THIS *"TWIN OWL"*

"KILL"?

GOOD HEAVENS -- NOTHING AS DRASTIC AS ALL *THAT* -- I JUST HAPPEN TO KNOW THE COLLECTOR WHO *HAS* THE OTHER OWL...

I WAS HOPING THAT, AS A GESTURE OF GOOD FAITH -- YOU WOULD BE WILLING TO ..... *ACQUIRE* IT FOR ME...

...SAVE ME THE TROUBLE AS IT WERE,...

AND WHAT IS CEREBUS SUPPOSED TO *SAY* TO THIS *"COLLECTOR"*

SAY? WHY, YOU DON'T *SAY* ANYTHING! NO ONE'S SEEN HIM IN THREE WEEKS...

SO YOU WANT CEREBUS TO JUST WALK IN AND *STEAL* THE OWL?

ACQUIRE!

ACQUIRE THE OWL -- *PLEASE!* BE CAREFUL OF WHAT YOU SAY! I'M A...

...*LEGITIMATE DUKE.* YES -- THERE'S A *RUMOUR* GOING AROUND...

WELL -- CEREBUS ONLY HOPES THESE PIKEMEN ARE ALL YOU SAY THEY ARE...

THERE'S A DEATH PENALTY IN TOGITH FOR *"ACQUIRING"*...

THE BRUGEL ARMS TAVERN...CEREBUS WOULD NEED A HALF-HOUR OR SO ALONE IN HORTNE'S ROOMS! IT WOULD REQUIRE SOME KIND OF STORY THAT WOULD FRIGHTEN THE OWNER -- MAKE HIM LET CEREBUS INTO THE CORRECT ROOM BUT DISSUADE HIM FROM FOLLOWING THE EARTH-PIG...

A TAVERN OWNER. HMMM. THE BEST BET WAS SOME KIND OF THREAT TO HIS BUSINESS! AN INFESTATION OF **ONLIU MAN-EATING TERMITES**, MAYBE. "YOU GO TO BED ONE NIGHT AND BY THE NEXT MORNING YOUR TAVERN IS REDUCED TO SAWDUST...AND THERE THEY ARE! MILLIONS OF THEM! PERCHED AT THE FOOT OF YOUR BED, LICKING THEIR LITTLE CHOPS..."

"SMEARING YOUR TOES WITH THEIR HIDEOUS KILLER TERMITE BARBECUE SAUCE"

BLESS THE LIVING TARIM!

YOU'RE HERE!

YOU'VE GOT TO DO SOMETHING! THREE WEEKS! THREE WEEKS! ALL OF THE PEOPLE WHO'VE GONE DOWN THERE -- TH-THEY'VE NOT COME BACK UP AGAIN...!

DOWN THERE? TO THE CELLAR YOU MEAN?

AYE! THE CELLAR!! FIVE SOULS LOST!!

WHAT'S DOWN THERE? I MEAN ORDINARILY...

IT'S -- IT'S MASTER HORTNE'S APARTMENT!

YOU HAVEN'T SEEN ANY **TERMITES** AROUND, HAVE YOU?

WHAT?

NOTHING.

414

POOR MASTER HORTNE-- THREE WEEKS! HE'S PROBABLY BEEN DEAD ALL THIS TIME... KILLED BY *THAT...THAT...*

HAS ANYONE SEEN THE... WHATEVER IT IS?

NO -- BUT YOU CAN HEAR IT WHEN SOMEONE GOES DOWN -- SILENCE AND THEN THE SCREAMS-- *HORRIBLE* BLOOD-CHILLING SCREAMS ...

I DON'T HAVE TO TELL YOU WHAT IT'S DONE TO MY BUSINESS! NO ON WILL COME IN FOR A DRINK... EXCEPT WHEN THE WORD SPREADS THAT SOMEONE ELSE IS VENTURING DOWN THERE

THEN THE PLACE IS PACKED WITH PEOPLE BETTING ON THE TIME IT WILL TAKE FOR THE SCREAMING TO START...

AN HOUR LATER, ARMED WITH A SWORD THE EARTH-PIG DESCENDS INTO THE *STYGIAN* GLOOM...

TWO BITS HE DOESN'T MAKE IT TO THE BOTTOM OF THE STAIRS...

THREE-TO-ONE? ANY TAKERS?

YOU'RE COVERED ...

BUT NOT BEFORE BETTING A GOLD COIN AT TWENTY-TO-ONE ODDS THAT HE WILL RETURN *SAFELY*...

EACH SOUND SEEMS MAGNIFIED OUT OF ALL PROPORTION...

... AS THE EARTH-PIG STRAINS TO ANTICIPATE THE ATTACK OF HIS UNSEEN FOE

THERE IS A SMELL OF DEATH IN THE AIR -- SHARP AND *PERSISTENT*...

HE HEARS A SOUND FROM SOMEWHERE TO HIS LEFT...

HE *PAUSES*...

...AS A FIGURE STEPS FROM THE SHADOWS *SNARLING*...

SOPHIA! WHAT ARE...?

GEET-A

THE FIRST STROKE, DELIVERED WITH IMMENSE POWER AND PRECISION, ELIMINATES ANY DOUBT OF **MISTAKEN IDENTITY**...

THE SECOND DRIVES THE EARTH-PIG BACK A FEW FEET AS HE BEGINS TO PLAN HIS ATTACK...

THE THIRD STROKE CATCHES HIM OFF-BALANCE AND HE BARELY MANAGES TO DEFLECT IT...

THE FOURTH STROKE MISSES ONLY BY ACCIDENT, AS HE IS CAUGHT WITH HIS SWORD ARM DOWN...

...RED SOPHIA SIMPLY WASN'T THAT **SKILLED**...

THE FIFTH GRAZES HIS SHOULDER AND, AS HIS FINGERS GO NUMB, THE SWORD CLATTERS TO THE FLOOR...

...IT IS THEN THAT HE NOTICES THE DOOR A FEW FEET AWAY...

...AND WONDERS, ABSENTLY, IF HE WILL LIVE TO REACH IT...

CEREBUS CROUCHES LOW AND LEAPS FORWARD AS THE SWORD HUMS ANGRILY ABOVE HIM...

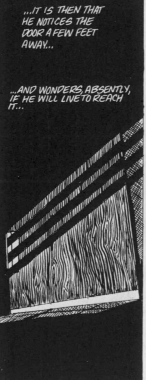

NOW LITTLE MORE THAN A FOOT AND A HALF FROM HIS GOAL, HE PRESSES AGAINST THE DAMP STONE FLOOR...

...AND THE RETURN STROKE MISSES, AS WELL...

RISING TO A CROUCHING POSITION, CEREBUS BEGINS TO REACH FOR HIS FALLEN WEAPON...

AS HE HAD EXPECTED...

...SOPHIA'S LOOK-ALIKE IS THERE BEFORE HIM, SWORD POISED TO ADMINISTER THE DEATH-BLOW...

BUT, CEREBUS IS ALREADY SCRAMBLING FOR THE DOOR...

TOO LATE, SHE REALIZES HER MISTAKE! SHE TURNS, ENRAGED, THE SWORD RAISED ONCE MORE...

EVEN AS CEREBUS BURSTS THROUGH THE DOORWAY TO SAFETY...

...PRAYING ALL THE WHILE THAT THERE IS A...

...LOCK ON THIS SIDE OF IT...

SWAM

CLAK

WELL, WELL, WELL, IF IT ISN'T CEREBUS, THE WORLD-RENOWNED AARDVARK...

DON'T JUST STAND THERE GETTING EMOTIONALLY INVOLVED WITH MY *DOOR*...

COME IN! COME IN!

HENROT!* CEREBUS SHOULD HAVE GUESSED...

SO THAT *IS* RED SOPHIA OUT THERE THEN?

RED SOPHIA? MY *GOODNESS*-- NO! NO! NO!

* RED SOPHIA'S FATHER. SEE CEREBUS #3 "SONG OF RED SOPHIA"

MOVE *ALONG*, GRISELDA! YOU'LL HAVE TO FORGIVE THEM...

...WE DON'T GET MUCH *COMPANY* DOWN HERE...

NO--THAT ISN'T *SOPHIA*-- I HAVEN'T SEEN HER IN OVER A YEAR...

YOU SEE, I MISSED HER *TERRIBLY*...

NEXT TIME, AIM BETWEEN THE *EYES*...

I'M GOING TO *IGNORE* THAT...

"I ANGUISHED FOR MONTHS--WHEN SUDDENLY IT OCCURRED TO ME -- I WAS A **MAGICIAN**! WHAT WAS TO PREVENT ME FROM _MAKING_ MYSELF A RED SOPHIA?! THIS TIME, SHE WOULDN'T JUST BE A DAUGHTER, -- THIS TIME SHE WOULD BE A _POSSESSION_! THE VERY THOUGHT! NO BACKTALK! NO..."HEY, BEARD-O -- HOW LONG DO I HAVE TO WAIT 'TIL YOU CROAK -- HUH? HOW LONG?"

"I COULD ELIMINATE ALL OF THE FLAWS --THE MISTAKES OF NATURE! AND _AUGMENT_ THE ≡ahem≡ MORE _POSITIVE_ QUALITIES ..."

YOU WANTED THEM TO HANG TO HER _KNEES_...

PRECISELY...

I MEAN _NO_! DON'T BE SUCH A WISEASS AARDVARK...

...SO I ORDERED MY APPENTICES AWAY--THIS WAS **BLACK ART** I WAS CONTEMPLATING! I NEEDED EVERY OUNCE OF MAGIC I COULD SUMMON TO CREATE A NEW SOPHIA FROM THE TRACES LEFT IN THIS HER NEW HOME IN TOGITH

SHE WAS A PERFECT DOUBLE. AND THAT WAS THE TOUGH PART-- CHANGING _ONLY_ ASPECTS OF HER! THERE WERE PARTS OF HER BRAIN THAT HAD TO BE BUILT FROM SCRATCH

...OBEDIENCE, TIDINESS, THRIFT....

AND SO IT WENT FOR TWO WEEKS UNTIL I HAD COMPLETED IT --A PERFECT VERSION OF SOPHIA

I DECIDED FAIRLY EARLY TO SWITCH TO FINE SILK INSTEAD OF CHAINMAIL

I'M NOT AS PARTIAL TO **SCAR TISSUE** AS I ONCE WAS...

I HAD HOPED THAT IT MIGHT IMPROVE HER DISPOSITION A WEE BIT, AS WELL

AFTER HER ALL-NIGHT BINGES, I'D FIND DISTURBING ...THINGS IN HER ROOM...

THINGS? WHAT KIND OF THINGS?

IT TOOK ONLY A FEW DAYS FOR ME TO REALIZE SHE WAS **FAR** FROM PERFECT! HER LANGUAGE WAS THE FIRST SIGN-- INSTEAD OF "BEARD-O" IT WAS "OLD TOAD-HUMPER" OR "FOUL DUNG HEAP"--THAT WAS WHEN I NAMED HER **GEET-A**, AN OLD BOREALAN WORD MEANING "SHE-OF-THE-FOUL-MOUTH-AND-DYNAMITE-KNOCKERS"

SHE STARTED COMING HOME LATER AND LATER, SINGING BAWDY BALLADS AND MAKING RUDE NOISES WITH VARIOUS PARTS OF HER **ANATOMY**...THE TOGITH CHAMBER OF COMMERCE REVOKED MY "GOOD NEIGHBOR AWARD."... THE MAGICIANS GUILD CANCELLED THEIR FATHER AND DAUGHTER BANQUET BECAUSE THEY WERE AFRAID WE MIGHT COME...

SEVERED HEADS, INTERNAL ORGANS, GOLD FILLINGS, RINGS WITH FINGERS STILL IN THEM-- SHE SAID A GIRL-FRIEND GAVE THEM TO HER, BUT I WASN'T FOOLED FOR A MINUTE...

IN SHORT SHE WAS EVERYTHING SOPHIA WAS AND MORE--AND **STILL** I WASN'T SATISFIED! I MEDITATED UNTIL I CAME UP WITH THE REASON...

WHICH WAS?

I HAD NEVER LIKED **RED SOPHIA** IN THE FIRST PLACE

I COULD SEE ONLY TWO SOLUTIONS...

I COULD SEND HER OUT TO CONQUER THE SEPRAN EMPIRE AND **MOVE** WHILE SHE WAS GONE...

OR YOU COULD MAKE HER YOUR **PERSONAL** WATCHDOG

SHOO!

I WAS AFRAID SHE WOULD DEFEAT THE EMPEROR'S LEGIONS AND RETURN BEFORE I GOT EVERYTHING **PACKED**...

ACTUALLY, IT WAS A VERY SIMPLE PROCESS--I JUST WAITED UNTIL SHE CAME HOME DRUNK AND CONJURED A CHAIN CONNECTING HER LEFT ANKLE TO THE FAR WALL...AS I SUSPECTED SHE HAD LET HER NATURAL IMMUNITY TO SORCERY LAPSE WHILE INEBRIATED...

SHE ERECTED HER DEFENSES AGAIN IN THE BLINKING OF AN EYE, BUT IT WAS ALREADY TOO LATE

SHE'LL NEVER BE CAUGHT WITH HER GUARD DOWN AGAIN...

BUT...

ALL SHE CAN DO IS VENT HER ANGER ON MY OCCASIONAL VISITORS...

SHE REALLY IS A WONDERFULLY *VICIOUS* WATCHDOG, TOO

BUT I GUESS YOU ALREADY FOUND THAT OUT, DIDN'T YOU?

BUT-- THAT MEANS YOU CAN'T LEAVE-- YOU'RE PRACTICALLY HER PRISONER...!

PRISONER?

YOU'VE GOT TO BE KIDDING! SO FAR, SHE'S HACKED UP TWO BILL COLLECTORS, TWO ENCYCLOPEDIA SALESMEN AND MY *EX-WIFE*...

THIS IS THE LONGEST PERIOD OF UNINTERRUPTED WORK I'VE MANAGED SINCE I WAS *SIXTEEN*...

ACTUALLY, THOUGH, IT DOES MEAN THAT *YOU'RE* A PRISONER...

I'LL TELL YOU *WHAT!* I'LL JUST WHIP YOU UP A QUICK SLEEPING BAG AND A TOOTHBRUSH...

THANKS ANYWAY...

BUT CEREBUS PLANS TO GET OUT OF HERE WHILE HE STILL HAS SOME HIS SANITY INTACT

ALL THAT CEREBUS WILL NEED IS A SHIELD OF INVISIBILITY

OR FOR YOU TO PUT GEET-A TO SLEEP FOR A FEW MINUTES...

I'M AFRAID GEET-A'S DEFENSES ARE TOO GOOD... MY MAGIC CAN'T HELP YOU AT ALL...

OH DEAR, YOU'RE NOT GETTING ANGRY ARE YOU?...

OF COURSE CEREBUS IS ANGRY!! WHAT ARE YOU GOING TO DO ABOUT IT?

DO?

WHY I'M NOT GOING TO DO ANYTHING...

CAN'T SAY THE SAME FOR MY PET GERBIES, THOUGH -- THEY FEED ON VIOLENT EMOTIONS...

ESPECIALLY ANGER...

DON'T TENSE UP...

JUST KEEP RELAXED... BREATHE IN AND BREATHE OUT-- RELAAAX...

THIS ISN'T EASY...

YOU'RE DOING FINE...

ANOTHER FIVE MINUTES AND THEY COULD START TO LOOSEN THEIR GRIP...

CEREBUS JUST HAD A THOUGHT...

IT MUST HAVE BEEN A GOOD ONE -- THREE OF THE GERBIES JUST LET GO...

THESE GERBIES... THEY'RE NOT TECHNICALLY MAGICAL ARE THEY?...

AS I SAID THEY'RE PETS-- MAGICIANS BREED THEM AS ORGANIC CONTROLS -- THEY KEEP US FROM GETTING TOO EMOTIONAL...

YOU CAN'T AFFORD ANY FEELINGS TO INTRUDE ON A DELICATE INCANTATION -- IT UPSETS THINGS TOO MUCH -- BLEW UP MY FIRST APPRENTICE THAT WAY...

eh-- WOULD YOU MIND JUST GETTING CRANKY FOR A FEW MORE MINUTES--? I HAVEN'T FED THEM LATELY

ACTUALLY, CEREBUS CAN DO BETTER THAN A FEW MINUTES OF CRANKINESS...

PERMIT CEREBUS TO *DEMONSTRATE* ...

TARIM...

I ALMOST FORGOT

YOU WOULDN'T HAPPEN TO HAVE A GOLDEN OWL AROUND HERE WOULD YOU?

I MAY HAVE AT ONE TIME! I USE A LOT OF GOLD IN MY *SPELLS!* IF I *DID,* IT WAS MELTED DOWN AGES AGO...

WHY? WAS IT *IMPORTANT?*

ACTUALLY, IT *IS* ...

I DON'T SUPPOSE YOU COULD WHIP ONE UP FOR OLD TIMES' SAKE?

SURE. HOW'S THIS?

MMMM NO...

IT HAS TO LOOK LIKE THE *OTHER* ONE.

MORE LIKE THIS...

...YOU *KNOW?*

HO. HO. HO.

SMALL JOKE. I THINK I REMEMBER THE OWL YOU'RE THINKING OF ...

LIKE *SO?*

HMM... WELL *DONE!*

HOW LONG WILL IT HOLD ITS SHAPE?

EXACTLY SIX MONTHS

THAT SHOULD BE LONG ENOUGH.,.

GEET-A?

CEREBUS WOULD LIKE TO LEAVE NOW

UNH?

SO WHY DON'T YOU TAKE THAT PITIFUL EXCUSE FOR A BODY ...

AND RELOCATE IT TEMPORARILY?-- CEREBUS DOESN'T WANT TO HAVE TO FIGHT YOU...

THE SMELL IS BAD ENOUGH FROM OVER HERE...

RRRR

TALK ABOUT DEVASTATING REJOINDERS-- DID YOU MAKE IT UP YOURSELF...

OR WAS YOUR SPEECH THERAPIST PART WOLF?

okay Henrot-- let them...

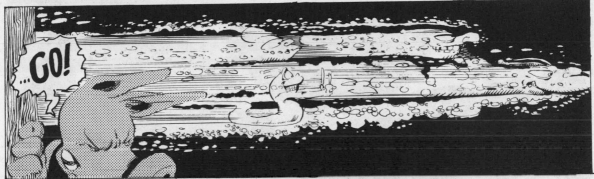

...GO!

DON'T GET UP, GEET-A -- CEREBUS CAN FIND THE DOOR ON HIS OWN...

MGMFGG SGBTSHA GABG!!

YOU'RE QUITE WELCOME...

CEREBUS HAS JUST COME TO RETRIEVE OUR PACKS ...CEREBUS CAN'T STAY...

WHAT A *SHAME*--I WAS JUST ABOUT TO POUR SOME *WINE*...

OF COURSE A FEW EXTRA MINUTES ISN'T GOING TO MAKE MUCH *DIFFERENCE*...

YOU'RE *WELCOME*...

CEREBUS DIDN'T SAY 'THANK YOU.'

YES--I *NOTICED*...

GRAUS-- CEREBUS ASKED ME TO GIVE YOU THE LETTER FOR GUDRE

HE'S GOING TO STAY WITH *ME* FOR A WHILE...

ZERBUTZ NOT DIS-A-PROOF OFF PERCE'S LIFE-LEE-HOOT NOW, EH? *HUH HUH HUH*...

BE CAREFUL YOU NOT HURT ZERBUTZ--ISS NOT SUCH BIG WARRIOR AS GRAUS

HUH HUH HUH

DON'T WORRY, GRAUS-- I'M GOING TO TAKE GOOD CARE OF CEREBUS...

VERY GOOD CARE...

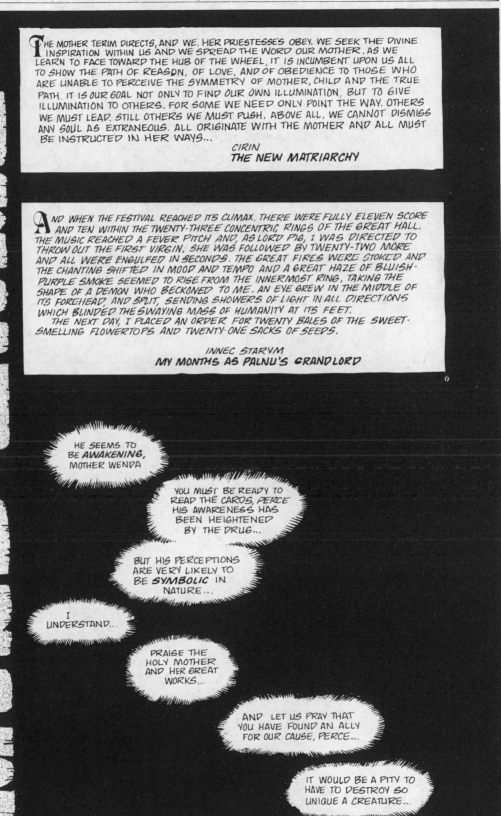

THE MOTHER TERIM DIRECTS, AND WE, HER PRIESTESSES OBEY. WE SEEK THE DIVINE INSPIRATION WITHIN US AND WE SPREAD THE WORD OUR MOTHER, AS WE LEARN TO FACE TOWARD THE HUB OF THE WHEEL, IT IS INCUMBENT UPON US ALL TO SHOW THE PATH OF REASON, OF LOVE, AND OF OBEDIENCE TO THOSE WHO ARE UNABLE TO PERCEIVE THE SYMMETRY OF MOTHER, CHILD AND THE TRUE PATH. IT IS OUR GOAL NOT ONLY TO FIND OUR OWN ILLUMINATION, BUT TO GIVE ILLUMINATION TO OTHERS. FOR SOME WE NEED ONLY POINT THE WAY. OTHERS WE MUST LEAD. STILL OTHERS WE MUST PUSH. ABOVE ALL, WE CANNOT DISMISS ANY SOUL AS EXTRANEOUS. ALL ORIGINATE WITH THE MOTHER AND ALL MUST BE INSTRUCTED IN HER WAYS...

CIRIN
THE NEW MATRIARCHY

AND WHEN THE FESTIVAL REACHED ITS CLIMAX, THERE WERE FULLY ELEVEN SCORE AND TEN WITHIN THE TWENTY-THREE CONCENTRIC RINGS OF THE GREAT HALL. THE MUSIC REACHED A FEVER PITCH AND, AS LORD PIG, I WAS DIRECTED TO THROW OUT THE FIRST VIRGIN; SHE WAS FOLLOWED BY TWENTY-TWO MORE AND ALL WERE ENGULFED IN SECONDS. THE GREAT FIRES WERE STOKED AND THE CHANTING SHIFTED IN MOOD AND TEMPO AND A GREAT HAZE OF BLUISH-PURPLE SMOKE SEEMED TO RISE FROM THE INNERMOST RING, TAKING THE SHAPE OF A DEMON WHO BECKONED TO ME. AN EYE GREW IN THE MIDDLE OF ITS FOREHEAD, AND SPLIT, SENDING SHOWERS OF LIGHT IN ALL DIRECTIONS WHICH BLINDED THE SWAYING MASS OF HUMANITY AT ITS FEET.
THE NEXT DAY, I PLACED AN ORDER FOR TWENTY BALES OF THE SWEET-SMELLING FLOWERTOPS AND TWENTY-ONE SACKS OF SEEDS.

INNEC STARYM
MY MONTHS AS PALNU'S GRANDLORD

HE SEEMS TO BE *AWAKENING*, MOTHER WENDA

YOU MUST BE READY TO READ THE CARDS, *PERCE* HIS AWARENESS HAS BEEN HEIGHTENED BY THE DRUG...

BUT HIS PERCEPTIONS ARE VERY LIKELY TO BE *SYMBOLIC* IN NATURE...

I UNDERSTAND...

PRAISE THE HOLY MOTHER AND HER GREAT WORKS...

AND LET US PRAY THAT YOU HAVE FOUND AN ALLY FOR OUR CAUSE, PERCE...

IT WOULD BE A PITY TO HAVE TO DESTROY SO UNIQUE A CREATURE...

MIND GAME

429

EXCUSE ME...

AH, CEREBUS-- WE WERE GETTING WORRIED ...

SO CEREBUS WAS HEARING.

WHAT DID THE VOICE SAY TO YOU?

IT ADVISED CEREBUS TO TRY *REAL ESTATE* AS A HEDGE AGAINST INFLATION. *NOW*-- DO YOU *MIND* EXPLAINING WHAT IS GOING ON HERE?

WHY-- YOU'VE BEEN SELECTED FOR INITIATION INTO THE SACRED ORDER OF THE DIVINE MOTHER

WHICH MEANS?

YOU'VE BEEN GIVEN A RARE OPPORTUNITY TO SEEK OUT A REVELATION IN THE SEVENTH SPHERE --A SIGN FROM OUR *DIVINE MOTHER* ...

A SIGN THAT WILL SHOW THE WAY OF *ILLUMINATION* FOR ALL...

AND IF THE DIVINE MOTHER SHOULD HAPPEN TO JUDGE CEREBUS UNSUITABLE AS A *MESSENGER*?

WE'LL BE FORCED TO KILL YOU, OF COURSE.

CEREBUS DOESN'T MEAN TO RUSH YOU ...

IT WASN'T IN *"THE NEW MATRIARCHY"* SO IT HAS TO BE IN *"DUALISM AS FALLACY"*

I'M READING AS FAST AS I CAN...

AND THIS PASSAGE IS GOING TO *IMPRESS* THEM...?

CEREBUS?

I WISH HE WOULDN'T STOP BREATHING... IT'S A LITTLE *UNNERVING* ...

THEY'LL *LOVE* IT! TRUST ME-- IT'S THE REVELATION THAT THE INNER CIRCLE HAS BEEN WAITING FOR...

BY THE WAY-- WHAT DO YOU GET OUT OF THIS DEAL?

ARE YOU JOKING? THIS LOOKS LIKE MORE FUN THAN THE LAST FIVE PARTIES I ATTENDED ...

WHAT AN *EXCITING* LIFE YOU WILL HAVE --A LIFE OF PURPOSE AND WORTH

CEREBUS?

THEY WANT TO LOCK CEREBUS AWAY IN A CONVENT...

DON'T KNOCK IT, STEADY EMPLOYMENT IS HARD TO COME BY IN THIS DAY AND AGE ...

YOU *KNEW* THIS WAS GOING TO HAPPEN?

SAY, FELLA-- I JUST SAVED YOUR LIFE...

WHATEVER BECAME OF OLD- FASHIONED GRATITUDE?

GRATITUDE?

YOU GET CEREBUS LOCKED AWAY IN A CONVENT TO SPEND THE REST OF HIS LIFE IN A STATE CLOSELY RESEMBLING A COMA ...

WHILE A BUNCH OF RELIGIOUS FANATICS DERIVE ORAL GRATIFICATION FROM HIS FEET...

...AND YOU EXPECT *GRATITUDE?*

WELL IT'S NOT AS IF I DON'T HAVE ANYTHING *BETTER* TO DO, I HAVE MY OWN QUASI- RELIGIOUS MOVEMENT TO WORRY ABOUT...

CEREBUS DOESN'T...

uh-- YOUR *OWN* MOVEMENT?

I THOUGHT YOU'D RECOGNIZE ME··I'M *SUENTEUS PO*...

FOUNDER OF ILLUSIONISM...?

CEREBUS THOUGHT YOU WERE DEAD..

QUITE *UNDERSTANDABLE*. MOST PEOPLE ONE HUNDRED AND EIGHTY TWO YEARS OLD *ARE* DEAD...

433

435

YOU MUST LISTEN CAREFULLY, WENDA! CEREBUS HASN'T MUCH TIME...

I'M LISTENING ...

THERE IS SOME SINISTER ILLUSIONIST PLOT AFOOT... THEIR MOST *INFLUENTIAL* MEMBERS ARE ALL GATHERED IN THE SEVENTH SPHERE...

CEREBUS' LOYALTY LIES WITH THE ALL-KNOWING *MOTHER!* IT IS FOR THIS REASON THAT CEREBUS IS WILLING TO RISK *ALL* TO DISCOVER THEIR PLAN...

ONCE CEREBUS ENTERS THE FIELD OF THEIR INFLUENCE HE IS LIKELY TO BE *OVER-WHELMED* BY SELF-INDULGENCE

THE ILLUSIONISTS ARE *MASTERS* OF HEDONISM -- ONE FALSE STEP AND CEREBUS COULD BE HAVING TOO MUCH *FUN* TO RESIST...!

IN SHORT...

THIS MAY BE THE LAST TIME THAT YOU SEE CEREBUS AS HE IS NOW...

GRIM... REVERENT ...

...RESPONSIBLE ...

CEREBUS IS NOW GOING TO PERMIT HIMSELF TO SINK TO THE VERY *DEPTHS* OF *DEPRAVITY*... TO EXPERIENCE FAITH-SAPPING *PLEASURE* AND *DECADENCE*... IT IS WITH SOMBER VISAGE THAT CEREBUS GOES...

THE HOLY MOTHER WILLING, THAT GRIMNESS WILL SEE CEREBUS THROUGH...

PRAY FOR CEREBUS, WENDA...

I WILL, CEREBUS-- YOU *KNOW* I WILL!

PO?!

438

439

WHEN CEREBUS GIVES YOU THE SIGNAL, YOUR FOLLOWERS ARE TO BREAK THE WINDOW...

WENDA! CEREBUS HAS MANAGED TO ESCAPE THEIR CLUTCHES... THEY PLAN A HORRIBLE FATE FOR TOGITH!

OH-NO!

IF THEY HAVE THEIR WAY, INSIDE OF A FORTNIGHT, TOGITH WILL BE STRIPPED OF ITS CIVILIZED VENEER--REDUCED TO A STATE OF BARBARISM BARELY A STEP REMOVED FROM THE BEASTS OF THE FIELD...

BUT, I THOUGHT MEN WERE ALREADY RUNNING TOGITH...

THEN DRAG ALL THE CLOTH INTO THE STREET...

AND BURN IT--BE VERY CAREFUL TO NOT INHALE--EVEN THE SMALLEST PARTICLE OF GINSHU COULD TURN YOU INTO AN UP-STANDING CITIZEN...

NO! NO! IT'S MUCH WORSE THAN THAT--IT'S A PLOT TO BRING A NEW DARK AGE UPON THE CITY!

BUT HOW?...

CLOTHING! THEY'RE GOING TO DESTROY CLOTHING!

AN OPEN SPACE WILL MINIMIZE THE RISK...

...SO BE SURE YOU BURN THE CLOTH IN THE STREET AND NOT IN THE WINDOW...

THAT'S HORRIBLE! WE MUST TAKE ACTION BEFORE IT'S...

...CLOTHING?!

ARE YOU GETTING ALL THIS, PO?

WHAT'S THAT? I'M SORRY I WASN'T LISTENING...

I DON'T GET IT.

DO CEREBUS A FAVOUR AND PUT THE PIPE AWAY UNTIL THE JOB IS DONE, OKAY?

JUST GET YOUR FOLLOWERS INTO POSITION AND TELL THEM TO BURN THE CLOTH IN THE STREET...

OH YEAH! FUMES OR SOMETHING RIGHT? I'LL GET THEM THERE--DON'T WORRY...

WHAT IS A HUMAN BEING WITHOUT HIS *CLOTHES?* LITTLE MORE THAN AN *ANIMAL!* AND THAT'S THE WAY THE *ILLUSIONISTS* WANT *EVERYONE* TO BE ...

AH -- I BEGIN TO SEE!

IT'S A TWO-STAGE PLAN. FIRST, THEY DESTROY ALL THE RAW MATERIALS BY BURNING CLOTH, WRECKING LOOMS, SNAPPING NEEDLES, TANGLING THREAD, LAYING SIEGE TO LARGE TEXTILE MILLS, ASSASSINATING SHEEP...

HOW *GHASTLY!*

AND THAT'S ONLY THE BEGINNING! ONCE THEY'VE MADE IT IMPOSSIBLE TO *REPLACE* YOUR CLOTHING, THEN THE SQUADS OF WARDROBE MARAUDERS GO TO WORK -- BREAKING INTO HOMES AND PUTTING EVERY LAST BUTTON AND BOOTLACE TO THE TORCH...

MAY THE HOLY MOTHER HAVE MERCY ON US ...

BEFORE LONG, THEY'LL BE SWARMING INTO THE STREETS, RIPPING THE CLOTHES OFF OF *PASSERS-BY* AND THROWING EVERY STITCH ONTO HUGE BONFIRES! NO ONE -- *NO ONE* -- WILL BE SAFE!!

THEY MUST BE STOPPED! BY THE SACRED BOOKS OF CIRIN -- *THEY-MUST-BE-STOPPED!*

441

442

OH, WOW -- THEY FORGOT THE TORCH -- I *TOLD* YOU GUYS -- I *SAID*, "REMEMBER TO BRING THE TORCH"...

SAY, CEREBUS -- IS IT OKAY IF THEY JUST RIP THE CLOTH TO SHREDS?

NO... WAIT... IT'S OKAY... SHEA BROUGHT A BOX OF MATCHES...

GOOD MAN, SHEA -- FIVE MORE LIKE YOU AND WE COULD TAKE OVER THE WORLD...

WENDA...

THERE ARE ALMOST TWO DOZEN ILLUSIONISTS OUT THERE WREAKING *HAVOC*...

ARE YOU SURE YOUR SISTERS WILL BE ABLE TO HANDLE THEM?

OH OF COURSE, I JUST WISH THEY WERE *STURDIER* ENEMIES -- LIKE THE HARD-LINE *TARIMITES*...

ILLUSIONISTS TEND TO BLOW OVER IN A STIFF WIND...

THAT'S WHAT SURPRISES ME -- THE ILLUSIONISTS ARE HARDLY *EQUIPPED* FOR A MULTI-LEVEL *REVOLUTION!* I WONDER HOW PO MANAGED TO CONVINCE THEM THEY *WERE?*

YOU HAVE NO IDEA HOW EASY SOME GROUPS ARE TO *MANIPULATE*...

WHAT?

NOTHING.

CEREBUS WAS JUST THINKING OUT LOUD

AS I EXPECTED -- NO RESISTANCE AT ALL TO OUR ATTACK...
WOMEN ARE ATTACKING YOU? REALLY? WHAT ARE YOU COMPLAINING ABOUT?
OH. I SEE. CLUBS AND PIPES AND THINGS?
HMM.
DID THEY SAY WHAT THEY WERE ANGRY ABOUT?
WENDA!
NOT EVEN A HINT, EH?
I JUST HEARD PO'S VOICE! -- THE FABRIC SHOP IS ONLY A DIVERSION...
WELL, I GUESS THEY JUST WANT A FIGHT -- AND IF THEY WANT A FIGHT -- WE'LL GIVE THEM A FIGHT...
A WHAT?
HOW ARE WE DOING IN THE FIGHT, BY THE WAY?
A DIVERSION!
THE ILLUSIONISTS ARE ATTACKING IN FULL FORCE AT THE TOGITH-WESTERN TEXTILE MILL...
ASIDE FROM SHEA SETTING FIRE TO A COUPLE OF THEM, HOW ARE WE DOING?
I MUST LEAD OUR FORCES THERE, THEN!
TWO DOWN -- CEREBUS IS HOME FREE
YES, WENDA! YOU MUST LEAD YOUR TROOPS FOR THE GREATER GLORY OF OUR SACRED...
GULP

UH-HUH.......UH-HUH.... UH-HUH......-- SOUNDS LIKE IT'S TIME FOR A STRATEGIC RETREAT

I'M AFRAID MY LADS ARE IN A BIT OF TROUBLE, CEREBUS...

HMM, *TRIED* THAT ALREADY DID YOU...?

NOT THAT THEY CAN'T HANDLE A MASS OF FRAGILE WOMEN...

SO WHICH ALTERNATE PLAN *ARE* YOU USING?

IT'S JUST...

D-DID YOU JUST DROP SOMETHING DOWN--CEREBUS' *THROAT?*...

"WHINING AND BEGGING FOR MERCY." I SEE.

OH, AYE!--JUST IN CASE YOU HAD ANY PLANS TO *LEAVE* WHILE I'M GONE

IT'S A SLEEPING POTION-- IT TAKES EFFECT IN SECONDS... SEE YOU IN A FEW HOURS...

WENDA! WAIT!! CEREBUS HAS TO,...T,..OBEXFPRL

445

BUT THAT WAS *IMPOSSIBLE* ....HE HAD ESCAPED FROM WENDA AND PERCE *OBVIOUSLY* --BUT WHY WOULD HE HAVE FLED *NORTH*?!

HE WAS SUPPOSED TO BE IN FLUROC NO LATER THAN *CONCORDANCE EVE* FOR THE ASSAULT ON PALNU ...

ONLY TEN DAYS OR SO REMAINED UNTIL THE FESTIVAL OF SPRING'S ARRIVAL ...

HE WOULD NEED A HORSE. A HARD THREE DAYS' RIDE WOULD TAKE HIM TO THE CONQUERED CITY

LEAVING TIME ENOUGH FOR DRILLING HIS TROOPS BEFORE THE MARCH SOUTH TO PALNU ...

NOW CEREBUS KNOWS WHAT IS *AMISS!*

...THE STREETS! THEY'RE *DESERTED!*

MAYHAP SOME PHILANTHROPIST FOOTED THE BILL FOR A MASSIVE *EXTERMINATION* PROGRAM?

NAY-- TOO SENSIBLE FOR THESE ...

EH?...

FIX --I SAY, *FIX YOUR ANTENNA!* YOU'ALL GOT A DANGEROUS CASE OF THE *DROOPS* THERE, SON...

DANGLE, THAT IS...

KNOK! KNOK!

CEREBUS DOESN'T BELIEVE THIS...

YES?

WHO?

CONGRATULATIONS CITIZEN...

"CAPTAIN COCKROACH!"

WELL, PARBOIL MY HINDQUARTERS IF IT *ISN'T*...

CEREBUS JUST HAS A COUPLE OF QUESTIONS AND THEN HE HAS A WAR TO CATCH--QUESTION ONE:...

...HSIFFY?

DEROGATORY REFERENCE TO PERSONNEL INDIGENOUS TO THE HSIFAN KHANATE

"...SEEMS TO FAIRLY *UNHINGE* THE LITTLE BUGGERS USED IN A *SOCIAL* CONTEXT

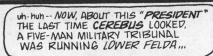

uh-huh-- NOW, ABOUT THIS "*PRESIDENT*" THE LAST TIME *CEREBUS* LOOKED, A FIVE-MAN MILITARY TRIBUNAL WAS RUNNING *LOWER FELDA*...

TRIBUNAL? HEH-HEH! DON'T BE *NAIVE*, SON...

PRESIDENT WEISSHAUPT IS THE *MAN OF THE MOMENT*...THE PEOPLE'S *CHOICE*, THAT IS!

HE'S A REAL HUMANITARIAN *TOO*-- PLANS TO ERADICATE THE *HSIFFIES* FOR THE GREATER GOOD OF *MANKIND*...

uh-huh

AND WHAT DOES THIS *DEMI-GOD* GET OUT OF THE DEAL?

THE JOY OF BEING THE FATHER OF HIS *COUNTRY*, SON...

"LIKE FREEDOM-LOVING MEN *EVERYWHERE*, PRESIDENT WEISSHAUPT DEDICATES HIS LIFE TO CORRECTING *INJUSTICE*."

"WHERE ELSE BUT LOWER FELDA COULD A MAN OF HUMBLE BIRTH, RAISE HIMSELF IN *THIRTY YEARS* TO THE EXALTED POST OF *COMMANDER*-IN-CHIEF...

"WHERE HE OCCUPIES HIS TIME PRODUCING THE FINEST EXAMPLES OF PURE-BRED MANHOOD FOR THE TASK OF WIPING OUT HSIFANS *PERMANENTLY*."

WE'RE GOING TO SEE HIM NOW IF Y'ALL...

TEN MINUTES.

AND THEN CEREBUS WILL *HAVE* TO LEAVE...

451

WATCH YOUR STEP! THESE -- I *SAY* -- THESE STAIRS ARE ABOUT AS SHAKY AS A LONG-TAILED CAT IN A ROOMFUL OF *ROCKING CHAIRS*

UNSAFE, THAT IS...

THE OVAL HIDEOUT IS DOWN H'YAR, SON! THIS IS WHERE THE *PRESIDENT* PLANS WHAT HE'S GOING TO DO TO THE COUNTRY...

WE HAVE TO WAIT *HERE*

CAPTAIN COCKROACH IS *ALWAYS* THE FIRST TO ENTER THE *OVAL HIDEOUT*...

IT MIGHT BE A FEW *MINUTES,* YET...

THE OH-AY-EF IS A LITTLE SEE-EL-YOU-EM-ESS-WHY...

IF Y'ALL CATCH MY *DRIFT*...

MR. PRESIDENT...

CAPTAIN COCKROACH REPORTING, *SIR!*

AT EASE, *CAPTAIN*...

I'VE BROUGHT A FOREIGNER OF *INDETERMINATE* ORIGIN TO MEET YOU, SIR

MMM. I CERTAINLY HOPE HE'S *CLEANER* THAN THE LAST ONE...

MOMENTS LATER...

OH, YES SIR, MR. PRESIDENT...

RIGHT AWAY, SIR...

LISTEN FOR SOME REASON HE WANTS TO SEE YOU ALONE INSIDE THERE ARE A FEW THINGS YOU HAVE TO KEEP FROM DOING NO MATTER WHAT HAPPENS IN THERE ONE: DON'T UNDER ANY

MOVE YOUR HANDS OR LOSE THEM, COOTIE.

YOU SEE?! YOU SEE?!

YOU CAN'T SAY THINGS LIKE THAT TO THE PRESIDENT!

IF HE WANTS TO TOUCH YOU, YOU'RE GOING TO HAVE TO LET HIM! YOU UNDERSTAND?!

YOU-MUST-NOT-BREAK -THE-PRESIDENT!!

CAPTAIN? IS HE COMING IN OR NOT...?

OH, YESSIR, MR. PRESIDENT! TWO SHAKES OF A LAMB'S TAIL, SIR!

DON'T TOUCH ANYTHING

CALL HIM MR. PRESIDENT

DON'T SIT UNTIL HE DOES

APPROACH THE DESK FROM THE LEFT IF HE'S BEHIND IT...

DON'T MENTION HIS FAMILY...

DON'T SAY ANYTHING UNTIL HE SPEAKS TO YOU...

DON'T EAT THE FRUIT

AND WHATEVER YOU DO, DON'T STARE AT HIS ANKLE!!

WHA...? IS HE A CRIPPLE OR SOMETHING?

oh my...

...GOD.

453

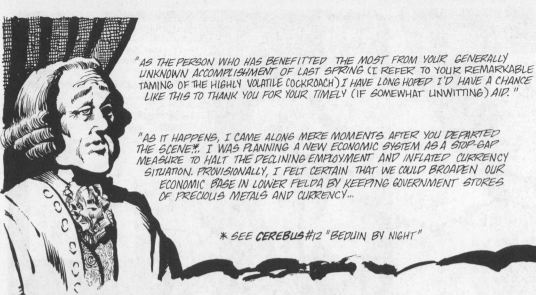

"AS THE PERSON WHO HAS BENEFITTED THE MOST FROM YOUR GENERALLY UNKNOWN ACCOMPLISHMENT OF LAST SPRING (I REFER TO YOUR REMARKABLE TAMING OF THE HIGHLY VOLATILE COCKROACH) I HAVE LONG HOPED I'D HAVE A CHANCE LIKE THIS TO THANK YOU FOR YOUR TIMELY (IF SOMEWHAT UNWITTING) AID."

"AS IT HAPPENS, I CAME ALONG MERE MOMENTS AFTER YOU DEPARTED THE SCENE.* I WAS PLANNING A NEW ECONOMIC SYSTEM AS A STOP-GAP MEASURE TO HALT THE DECLINING EMPLOYMENT AND INFLATED CURRENCY SITUATION. PROVISIONALLY, I FELT CERTAIN THAT WE COULD BROADEN OUR ECONOMIC BASE IN LOWER FELDA BY KEEPING GOVERNMENT STORES OF PRECIOUS METALS AND CURRENCY..."

* SEE *CEREBUS* #12 "BEDUIN BY NIGHT"

"BUT WHEN I SAW THE COCKROACH UNCONSCIOUS THERE, EVERYTHING JUST SEEMED TO JELL INTO A DEFINITE PLAN...WHICH AT THAT TIME CONSISTED OF A FEW LIMITED OBJECTIVES..."

I SAY THERE, OLD FELLOW...

THAT WOULDN'T HAPPEN TO BE THE COCKROACH IN THE PURPLE SUIT WOULD IT?

WHY, NOW THAT YOU MENTION IT, I BELIEVE THAT'S WHAT HE SAID... ACCENT ON THE "OACH" I BELIEVE ...RECALL, THAT IS ...

I'LL GIVE YOU TWO GOLD COINS, IF YOU'LL CARRY HIM TO MY HOUSE ...

IF Y'ALL WAIT 'TIL HE WAKES UP YOU COULD PROBABLY CONVINCE HIM TO WALK THERE FOR FREE ...

MM. ACTUALLY, I PREFER HIM THIS WAY FOR THE TIME BEING ...

NEVER...I SAY... NEVER LET IT BE SAID THAT ELROD OF MELVINBONE TURNED DOWN A HIGH-PAYING JOB...

"HE TOLD ME ALL ABOUT YOUR SET-TO WITH THE GENDARMES..."

"AND WHEN THE COCKROACH TALKED TO ME LATER HE FILLED IN MOST OF THE BLANKS..."

"WHEN WE ARRIVED HERE, I HAD ELROD REMOVED TO A GUEST ROOM WHERE HE STAYED FOR THE SIX MONTHS I NEEDED..."

"I THEN HAD THE COCKROACH BROUGHT DOWNSTAIRS, STILL UNCONSCIOUS..."

"I HAD HEARD ENOUGH ABOUT HIM TO FEEL I COULD PERSUADE HIM TO DIRECT HIS ENERGIES INTO MORE USEFUL DISCIPLINES"

"...AND MAKING ME RICH BEYOND MY WILDEST DREAMS SEEMED AS GOOD A PLACE AS ANY TO START..."

"HE AWOKE ABOUT AN HOUR LATER..."

"I TOLD HIM HE WAS IMMERSED IN A MIRACLE SOLUTION OF 'ALUCASE' WHICH MADE HIS MUSCLES LARGER EVERY TIME HE USED THEM. I EXPLAINED THAT PROF. REISENSHEIN HAD DIED BEFORE HE COULD REVEAL THE FORMULA AND THAT HE (THE COCKROACH) WAS THE ONLY TEST CASE."

"I ADDED THAT IT SEEMED TO ME, AS PRESIDENT OF THE UNITED FELDWAR STATES, THAT SOMEONE WITH THAT KIND OF ADVANTAGE WHO DIDN'T MAKE USE OF IT WAS OBVIOUSLY A NO-GOOD ROTTEN STINKING SCUM OF A HSIFAN TRAITOR...

"HE PLEDGED UNDYING FEALTY..."

"BUT, THE SOLUTION WAS A FAKE-- HOW DID YOU BUILD HIS MUSCLES?

"I HAD HIM MOVE MY COLLECTION OF MARBLE STATUES FROM THE BASEMENT TO THE ATTIC..."

"IT'S ACTUALLY NOT DIFFICULT TO BUILD A PHYSICALLY SUPERIOR HUMAN SPECIMEN..."

"THE TOUGH PART IS FINDING SOMEONE GULLIBLE ENOUGH TO WORK AT IT FOR SIX MONTHS..."

"ELROD WAS MOST IMPRESSED, HE PROMISED TO WORK GRATIS IF HE COULD BE THE SUBJECT OF THE NEXT EXPERIMENT."

"CEREBUS DOESN'T UNDERSTAND WHY YOU WOULD NEED ELROD."

"I PLAN TO RUN LOWER FELDA IN A FEW YEARS"

"AND I FIRMLY BELIEVE THAT IF YOU CAN'T FOOL ALL OF THE PEOPLE ALL OF THE TIME, YOU SHOULD START BREEDING THEM FOR STUPIDITY..."

"I RELEASED THE FIRST OF MY 'MESSAGES' DETAILING PROFESSOR REISENSHEIN'S NEW INVENTION, ANNOUNCING THAT THE COCKROACH WAS THE SUBJECT OF THE FIRST TEST AND NOTIFYING THE POPULACE THAT AS PRESIDENT I WAS CONFERRING UPON HIM THE HONORARY TITLE OF "CAPTAIN" IN THE ARMY OF LOWER FELDA..."

"THE NEXT WEEK I ANNOUNCED THAT PROFESSOR REISENSHEIN HAD BEEN KILLED BY HSIFAN SPIES, THAT CAPT. COCKROACH WAS GOING TO THE PEOPLE FOR CONTRIBUTIONS TO HELP REDISCOVER THE FORMULA FOR "ALUCASE."

"I ALSO ANNOUNCED THAT EACH CONTRIBUTION OF SIX SILVER PIECES WOULD ENTITLE THE BUYER TO A WAR BOND WORTH TWELVE SILVER PIECES AT ANY SHOP IN BEDUIN..."

BUSINESS WAS (QUITE UNDERSTANDABLY) FAIRLY BRISK...

"THE TRIBUNAL DECLARED OPEN SEASON ON ANY CITIZEN VENTURING INTO THE STREETS IN AN ATTEMPT TO STOP THE FLOW OF THEIR CURRENCY INTO MY POCKETS!"

BUT THEY'RE STILL HELPLESS...

SINGLE-HANDEDLY I'VE MANAGED TO PUT INTO EFFECT THE BIGGEST HALF-PRICE SALE IN BEDUIN'S HISTORY...

AND YOU ENGRAVE ALL THIS ONTO PRINTING PLATES EVERY WEEK?!

NO...I USE MOVABLE TYPE -- INDIVIDUAL LETTERS CAST IN LEAD MOLDS, IT'S AN INVENTION OF MY OWN. THE TRIBUNAL IS GOING CRAZY TRYING TO FIGURE OUT HOW I DO IT...

YOU CONNED THE COCKROACH INTO BUILDING *HIMSELF* INTO A WALKING MUSCLE EXHIBIT...

...BUT HOW DID YOU MANAGE TO MAKE HIM A FOOT TALLER?

HAND-MADE BOOTS WITH A FORM-FITTING SPACE TO HOLD HIS FOOT IN A *VERTICAL* POSITION...

WITH THE AMOUNT OF MONEY I'M TAKING IN, I THOUGHT THE *LEAST* I COULD DO WAS MAKE SURE EVERYONE GETS A GOOD LOOK AT THE BIG LUG...

NOW...

HOW DOES ALL THIS TIE IN WITH WIPING OUT THE *HSIFANS?*

THE WILL OF THE PEOPLE... THE TRIBUNAL IS BEGINNING TO LEARN THAT THE AVERAGE BEDUINITE IS *COMPLETELY* BORED BY THE DIFFERENCES BETWEEN *CIRINISM, KEVILLISM* AND ALL THE OTHER HALF-BAKED RELIGIOUS "ISM'S"

NO MATTER *WHICH* ONE YOU CHOOSE, YOU'RE GOING TO BE OUT OF STEP WITH ALMOST *EVERYONE* ELSE...

BUT IT *ISN'T* HARD TO GET A CONSENSUS ABOUT *HSIFANS* -- THEY'RE YELLOW-SKINNED, THEIR EYES LOOK FUNNY AND *THEY'RE NOMADS,* FOR TARIM'S SAKE

AND WHAT'S MORE, NO ONE IN LOWER FELDA EVER *SEES* ONE...

ALL *I'VE* DONE IS PUT ON PAPER WHAT YOU CAN HEAR ON ANY STREET CORNER IN THIS CITY -- THE *HSIFANS* ARE SNEAKY, BAD-SMELLING, GIBBERISH-SPOUTING LITTLE WEASEL-EYED DEMONS WHO THINK THEY'RE TOO GOOD FOR US DECENT CIVILIZED FOLK AND IF WE DON'T ELIMINATE THEM *NOW,* IT'S ONLY A MATTER OF TIME BEFORE THEY PITCH TENTS IN OUR LIVING ROOMS

BUT THE TRIBUNAL HAS A *"HANDS OFF"* POLICY TOWARDS THE HSIFAN *DON'T* THEY?

FOR THE MOMENT.

A FEW WEEKS AGO, I CALLED FOR BEDUIN'S ADULT MALES TO ENTER THE ARMY *VOLUNTARILY* SO WE CAN PREPARE FOR A MASSIVE CAMPAIGN AGAINST THE *HSIFAN* KHANATE...

REGISTRATION *TRIPLED* OVERNIGHT...

SO IF THE *TRIBUNAL* DOESN'T DECLARE WAR ON THE *HSIFANS*

THEY'LL BE FACING AN UNPARALLELED *INSURRECTION* IN THE RANKS...

EXACTLY...

WELL, *CEREBUS* SAID HE WOULD STAY FOR TEN MINUTES, AND HE CERTAINLY GOT HIS *MONEY'S* WORTH...

HAVE FUN,

WITHOUT THE PROPER DOCUMENTS YOU'LL NEVER GET PAST THE *GENDARMES*...

AND EVEN IF YOU *DO*, THE CITY WAS SEALED A MONTH AGO IN AN EFFORT TO CATCH *CAPTAIN CRETINOUS*...

AND EVEN IF YOU DEFEAT THE GUARDS *AT* THE GATE, IT TAKES THREE MEN TO WORK THE WINCH THAT RAISES AND LOWERS THE...

CEREBUS *GETS* THE IDEA...

HOW *DOES* ONE GET OUT OF BEDUIN?

MMMM. YOU KNOW, THERE ARE ONLY FIVE BOTTLES OF *CHATEAU DONTE '21* LEFT -- AND I HAVE *THREE* OF THEM...

RUMOURS THAT THE HOUSE NEVER AGAIN ACHIEVED THIS LEVEL OF POTENCY, CLARITY AND SWEETNESS ARE UNFORTUNATELY (AS YOU'LL SEE) ALL TOO *TRUE*...

AS TO GETTING OUT OF BEDUIN, YOU NEED PAPERS FROM THE *TRIBUNAL*, VERY DIFFICULT TO OBTAIN...

MM. FORGOT THE GLASSES...

OR YOU COULD FIND SOMEONE WITH THE BEST FORGERIES MONEY CAN BUY...

I USUALLY CHARGE FIFTY GOLD PIECES FOR FORGED PAPERS...

BUT I SUPPOSE IN A CASE LIKE THIS I COULD JUST *GIVE* YOU THE PAPERS, COULDN'T I?

HOW'S YOUR WINE?

MM?

EGSLUNT...

ABSULULEY

...EGSLUNT

'ISAWFULLY DECEN' UV YOU...

Y'KNOW?

OH, PIFFLE... IT'S THE VERY LEAST I CAN DO FOR SOMEONE RESPONSIBLE FOR MAKING ME A MILLIONARE SEVERAL TIMES OVER...

PRESDET GAVE CERBUS PAPERS ...

PAPERSAY CERBUS IS FINE FINE FINE!

IT JUST MAKES ME WONDER ABOUT THE YOUTH OF TODAY -- HOW CAN YOU GET ANYTHING WHEN YOU'RE DRUNK OUT OF YOUR ...

HSIFFY-SNEAK-ATTACK, BUNKY!

LOOK OUT!

SPANG!

BUNKY, OLD CHUM -- DO CEREBUS' EYES LOOK A BIT STRANGE?

I MEAN, NOT THAT I'M BEING CRITICAL OR ANYTHING

NOT TO WORRY, SON -- HE'S JUST A LITTLE UNKDRAY -- IPSYTAY, THAT IS ...

DRUNG?

DRUNG?!

DON' KIDGERSELF! CERBUSIS FINE FINE FINE

A BRASS DISC?

NOW WHO WOULD THROW A BRASS DISC AT THE IDOL OF ALL LOWER FELDA?

WHAT'S MORE IMPORTANT ...

DOES HE HAVE ANY MORE?

THE ALLEY ACROSS THE STREET ...

HURRY!

HE -- I SAY -- HE SOUNDS SOBER, CAPTAIN!

MAYBE WE SHOULD DO WHAT HE SAYS ...

YOU TWO HAVE BEEN *PLAYING* "BEAT THE HSIFFIES" FOR A WHILE...

WELL, YOU'RE NOW FACING THE *REAL* THING...

FORTUNATELY FOR YOU, CEREBUS HAS HAD SOME EXPERIENCE WITH HSIFAN SOPAI ASSASSINS...

DON'T TAKE THIS THE WRONG WAY, *SON*, BUT...uh...

...A FEW MINUTES AGO YOU WEREN'T QUITE SO...eh...*COHERENT*...

LUCID, THAT IS...

THE LAST THING CEREBUS REMEMBERS IS HAVING SOME WINE IN THE *PRESIDENT'S* OFFICE...

CEREBUS WAS DRUGGED A FEW DAYS AGO... THE WINE PROBABLY MIXED WITH THE RESIDUE IN HIS SYSTEM

JUST BE GRATEFUL HE'S OKAY NOW...

YOU DON'T GET TWO CHANCES WITH A SOPAI ASSASSIN VERY *OFTEN*...

FIRST THINGS FIRST: YOU ESCAPE *FROM*, NOT FIGHT *WITH* SOPAI... KEEP LARGE SOLID OBJECTS BETWEEN YOU AND THEM AT ALL TIMES...

THOSE BRASS DISCS ARE CALLED *YAN-SU*.

...AND THEY CAN TAKE YOUR HEAD OFF WHEN THROWN BY AN *EXPERT*

THERE'S ONE THING YOU SHOULD *NEVER* DO WHEN FACING A *SOPAI*...

AND WHAT'S THAT, SON?

UMMM...

CERBUS HASN' THE FOGGIES'

RILLY.

461

I THINK...

I SAY-- I THINK HE'S SUFFERED A *RELAPSE* ...

NOPE NOPE CERBUS HASN'GOT A CLUE ...

YEAH?

WELL, THAT SUITS *CAPTAIN COCKROACH* JUST *FINE*...

I NEVER *DID* MUCH CARE FOR *RUNNING* FROM A SCRAP...

WHAT...uh *DO YOU* THINK WE OUGHT TO DO?

THAT *DEPENDS* SON -- DEPENDS ON WHAT CEREBUS WAS ABOUT TO TELL US NOT TO *DO*...

IF HE WAS ABOUT TO SAY "YOU *NEVER* STAY IN ONE PLACE WHEN FACING A *SOPAI* " ...

..."THEN I THINK WE SHOULD GRAB HIM AND MAKE A RUN FOR IT...

DOO-DAH DOO-DAH ≡HIC≡

THAT SOUNDS GOOD TO ME! SHOW THE RAT-EYED LITTLE *HSIFFY SCUM* HE CAN'T TRAP *US*...

ON THE *OTHER* HAND...

IF HE WAS ABOUT TO SAY "NEVER LEAVE YOUR PLACE OF CONCEALMENT", THEN I THINK WE SHOULD STAY HERE...

THE WAY I FIGURE IT, THE WORST THAT CAN HAPPEN IF WE TRY *RUNNING* IS THAT WE GET OUR BRAINS BASHED OUT ...

UNFORTUNATELY...

THAT'S -- I SAY -- THAT'S *ALSO* THE WORST THAT CAN HAPPEN IF WE *STAY PUT*...

YEAH?

WELL, YOU FORGET, BUNKY OLD CHUM, THAT *CAPTAIN COCKROACH* IS A PROTOTYPE OF THE *SUPERMEN OF THE FUTURE!*

YOU CAN WAIT HERE WITH THAT *WINO BUNNY* 'TIL YOU GROW SOME EYEBALLS, BUT *CAPTAIN COCKROACH*

SPTWANG

...WILL BE RIGHT HERE BESIDE YOU TO MAKE SURE YOU'RE *SAFE*...

THANKS.

NO THANKS NEEDED. IT'S MY *JOB*.

AS CEREBUS WAS *SAYING* -- IF WE STAND *HERE*, HE'S JUST GOING TO OUTFLANK US...

MOVE FARTHER DOWN THE ALLEY -- IF WE STAY CLOSE TO THE WALL, WE SHOULD BE ABLE TO SEE HIM COMING ...

WHY DO YOU SUPPOSE HE'S ATTACKING *US?* ...

NO DOUBT HIRED BY THE *TRIBUNAL*... IF IT MAKES YOU FEEL ANY BETTER HE PROBABLY COST THEM A FORTUNE...

WHAT DO YOU SUPPOSE THE ODDS ARE ON US *GETTING* THAT *HSIFFY WEASEL?*

PERHAPS CEREBUS ISN'T MAKING HIMSELF *UNDERSTOOD*...

THE ODDS ARE ABOUT TWELVE-TO-ONE...

MM. I CAN LIVE WITH THAT.

THAT *ONE* OF US GETS OUT OF HERE *ALIVE*.

OH.

YOU MEAN, WE MIGHT GET ...*KILLED?*

THAT'S *IMPOSSIBLE* SON -- WE'RE *HEROES*...

ACTUALLY, THAT'S WHAT CEREBUS WAS BASING HIS ODDS ON -- *TWELVE-TO-ONE* THE ASSASSIN IS ONLY HUNTING YOU TWO *HEROES*...

COME TO THINK OF IT, YOU'RE PROBABLY SKINNY ENOUGH TO BE A DIFFICULT *TARGET*...

BUT, I'M AFRAID *CHUNKY* HERE IS GOING TO BE TWO HUNDRED AND TWENTY POUNDS OF COLD CUTS IN A MINUTE OR SO...

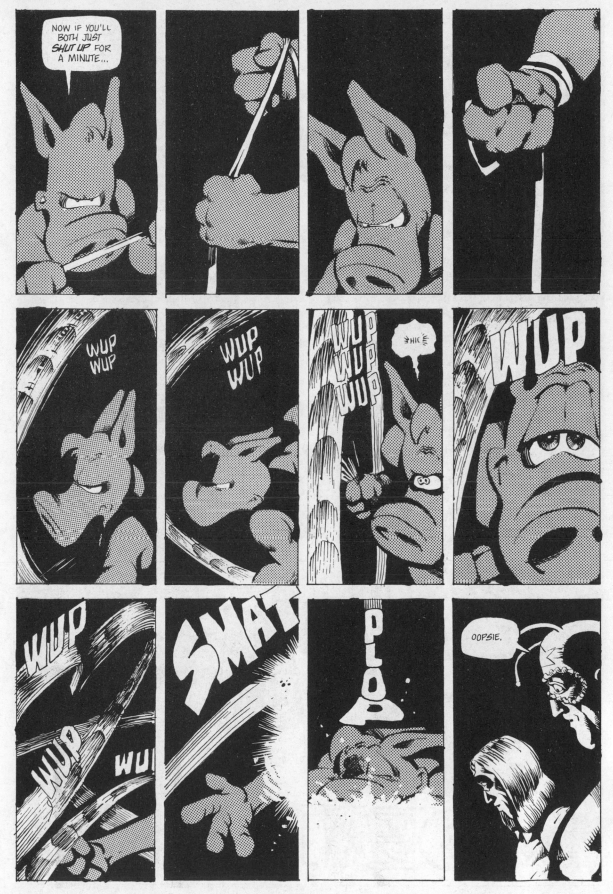

465

the DEATH of ELROD

SYNOPSIS: CEREBUS LIES SPRAWLED IN THE SNOW, AS *CAPTAIN COCKROACH* AND *BUNKY* COME TO THE CONCLUSION THAT IT IS DEFINITELY ADVISABLE THAT THEY PREPARE TO IMMEDIATELY TAKE THE NEXT STEP, BEFORE IT'S TOO LATE TO CHANGE THEIR MINDS...

AS DANGER LOOMS *NEARBY*...

...BUNKY (AKA ELROD) SUGGESTS A BOLD PLAN...

HOWZABOUT YOU TURN YOUR-SELF IN IF THEY PROMISE NOT TO HURT ME?

YOU'RE PANICKING FOR NO REASON, OLD *CHUM* -- WE HAVE TO AID OUR LITTLE GRAY WOUNDED *WINO*...

YOU DARE TO FACE THE WRATH OF *CAPTAIN COCKROACH*, eh? I ADOPTED THAT BOY WHEN HIS PARENTS WERE KILLED BY RED CLAW *ACROBATS* ... *

I TAUGHT HIM HOW TO HANG *TOUGH* -- HOW TO BREAK A MAN'S NECK WITH JUST HIS BARE HANDS AND A *CROW-BAR!* AND *NOW* -- "THANKS" TO *YOU* -- I HAVE TO FIND ANOTHER ADOLESCENT WITH AN UNHEALTHY NEED FOR CLOSE MALE COMPANIONSHIP *AND* -START -ALL-OVER-AGAIN-FROM-SCRA-

CRAK

-UNGG!

HAAI...

...YHO!

* LIVES IN A WORLD ALL HIS OWN, *FOLKS* ...

OOOLPH!

HAAI...

YHO!

GOOMPH!

HAAI

THIS ... IS ... YOUR LAST ?PANT? CHANCE

... GIVE ... UP ... ? HSIFFY?

uh?

WELL, DEEP-FRY MY CORNBREAD ...

I -- I SAY -- I CAN *BREATHE* AGAIN..

BUNKY?

IS IT REALLY YOU...?

REALLY AND *TRULY*?

BUNKY? BUNKY IS FACE DOWN IN THE SNOW, SON -- I'VE -- I SAY, I'VE TRADED IN MY RUGGED GOOD LOOKS AND SENSITIVE DEMEANOR FOR A NEAR MONOPOLY IN THE *MUSCLE MARKET*...

I NEED A *NEW* NAME THAT FITS MY NEW *IMAGE* -- SOMETHING WITH PANACHE -- LIKE *DEADALBINO!*

DEADALBINO?

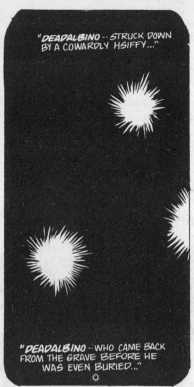

"*DEADALBINO* -- STRUCK DOWN BY A COWARDLY HSIFFY..."

"*DEADALBINO* -- WHO CAME BACK FROM THE GRAVE BEFORE HE WAS EVEN BURIED..."

"*DEADALBINO!* WHO FOUND HIMSELF WANDERING AWAY FROM THE SCENE OF HIS OWN MURDER"

"*DEADALBINO!* WHO FOUND THAT HE WAS NO LONGER QUITE ALL THERE (PHYSICALLY, THAT IS)..."

"*DEADALBINO!* WHO, DESPITE THE TRAUMA OF BEING DEAD..."

"RETURNED TO SAVE THE LIFE OF HIS IDOL, GUARDIAN AND KEEPER..."

DESIST!

UNHAND THAT *BUG*, SUH!

YOU'RE -- I SAY -- YOU'RE DAMAGING MY *MEAL TICKET!*

"DEADALBINO! WHO DISCOVERED HE HAD THE ABILITY TO MAKE HUMAN BEINGS SUBLET THEIR BODIES..."

DON'T PLAY DUMB WITH ME, SON -- I WANT TO KNOW WHY YOU'RE TRYING TO DISLOCATE THIS MAN'S BODY -- IT'S --

JUST, I MIGHT ADD, IN TIME TO SAVE YOU FROM GETTING A CUSTOM-DENTED SCALP...

WHA... I SAY... WHA..?!

JUST THINK, SON, WHAT TWO MUSCULAR TYPES LIKE US COULD EARN! -- WHY, TAG-TEAM WRESTLING ALONE...

HUNH!

ALL I CAN SAY IS, IF I FOUND MYSELF IN THE BODY OF A HSIFAN, I'D DO THE ONLY HONORABLE THING...

...I'D KILL MYSELF!

YOU'VE GOT A POINT THERE, SON, BUT MAYBE I SHOULD FIND OUT IF THE PRESIDENT WANTS ME TO CHOP ANY FIREWOOD WITH MY BARE HANDS OR SOMETHING...

...BEFORE I GO FALLING ON ANY SWORDS

WELL, LET'S GO ASK HIM...

WAITAMINNIT, SON -- WE'VE GOT SOME STUFF HERE THAT SIMPLY -- I SAY -- SIMPLY HAS TO COME WITH US...

MY BODY, FOR ONE...

WHY? YOU'RE NOT USING IT...

SENTIMENTAL ATTACHMENT -- I WAS IN THAT BODY ALMOST CONSTANTLY SINCE THE DAY I WAS BORN...

WE'LL MAKE A DEAL, SON -- I'LL CARRY MY TALL, THIN AND WHITE EX-SELF...

AND Y'ALL CAN CARRY PUNCH, THE WONDER BUNNY, HERE!

471

AMAZING! AND YOU HAVE NO IDEA HOW IT *HAPPENED* ...

NOT-- I SAY-- NOT EVEN A *CLUE* ...

AHEM!

LOOKS LIKE CEREBUS IS COMING AROUND ...

WELL, I SUPPOSE WE SHOULD FILL YOU IN ON WHAT YOU MISSED

THEN WE'LL HAVE TO WORK ON A WAY TO MAKE USE OF THIS...

CEREBUS IS NOT *LISTENING* ...

BUT SO MUCH HAS *HAPPENED*-- SURELY YOU'D LIKE TO KNOW WHY YOU'RE STILL *ALIVE?* ...

WATCH MY LIPS, MR. PRESIDENT

CEREBUS- IS- NOT- LISTENING

CEREBUS IS GOING TO GET UP, WALK OUT THAT DOOR AND ESCAPE FROM THIS STUPID CITY

LOOK -- THERE'S *CAPTAIN COCKROACH* STANDING NEXT TO A SOPAI ASSASSIN -- DOES CEREBUS WANT AN *EXPLANATION?* NO!

CEREBUS HAS HAD IT UP TO *HERE* WITH LONG-WINDED EXPLANATIONS -- EVERY TIME HE LISTENS TO ONE HE ENDS UP *SNOUT-DEEP* IN SOMEONE *ELSE'S* MESS...

YOU CAN FILL THIS ROOM WITH SOPAI ASSASSINS, SEVEN- FOOT COOTIES, GREEN BEARS AND DANCING *BOREALANS* IF YOU WANT TO

CEREBUS IS *LEAVING...*

WELL, Y'ALL BE SURE TO WRITE IF YOU GET WORK, SON...

NGGHHH!

HEH HEH HEH...

THE SOPAI ASSASSIN HAS ELROD'S VOICE.

A NICE TRY

YOU ALMOST *HAD* CEREBUS THERE ...

BUT IT'S NOT GOING TO WORK!! ASK CEREBUS WHY IT'S NOT GOING TO WORK ...

WHY IS IT NOT GOING TO WORK?

BECAUSE 'CEREBUS HAS A *WAR* WAITING FOR HIM...

THAT'S RIGHT -- A WAR! CEREBUS IS ALLIED WITH A WELL-ORGANIZED AND HEAVILY-ARMED BAND OF T'GITANS! ON CONCORDANCE EVE WE'RE GOING TO MARCH ON THE CITY OF PALNU AND SMASH IT INTO *SUBMISSION*...

WITH THAT ANCIENT CITY AS A BASE AND USING ITS WEALTH AS PAY FOR THE FINEST MERCENARIES, WE'RE GOING TO PROVE THAT THESE DAMNED SOUTHLAND SOLDIERS WILL FALL LIKE MATCH-STICKS WHEN FACED WITH A REAL ARMY

AN ARMY THAT DOESN'T WHINE IF YOU DON'T STOP EVERY FEW MILES FOR HOT CHOCOLATE AND MARSHMALLOWS...

BEDUIN IS RIPE FOR THE TAKING -- AND CEREBUS ISN'T TALKING ABOUT IDIOTIC PAMPHLETS AND SIDE-SHOW STRONGMEN -- WHEN *WE* TAKE BEDUIN, IT WILL BE BY FORCE-OF-ARMS...

YOU SOUTHLANDERS TALK AND TALK AND TALK! SAY WHAT YOU WILL ABOUT T'GITANS -- THEY SMELL BAD, THEY HAVE NO TABLE MANNERS -- BUT, BY TARIM AT LEAST THEY DON'T SPEND EVERY WAKING MINUTE FILLING THE AIR AROUND THEM WITH *BLOODY* <u>WORDS!</u>

SO, YOU TAKE YOUR PHILOSOPHERS AND YOUR MAGISTRATES AND YOUR PRIESTS AND YOUR CLERKS AND YOUR MERCHANTS AND YOU PILE THEM SIX DEEP AROUND THE CITY WALLS BECAUSE WHEN WE *DO* ATTACK THAT'S ABOUT ALL THEY'RE GOING TO BE GOOD FOR...

IT'S NOT THAT *CEREBUS* HAS ANYTHING AGAINST WEAK-WILLED, OVER-EDUCATED, SNIVELLING CITY-DWELLERS *PERSONALLY*, IT'S JUST THAT...

uh...

WHAT ARE YOU DOING?

MILITARY REPORTS FOR THE LAST MONTH

AH!

"PALNU ATTACKED ON CONCORDANCE EVE BY T'GITANS AND MERCENARY LIGHT CAVALRY AND PIKE..."

"ATTACKERS REPELLED AND HUNTED DOWN BY LORD GORCE'S TROOPS"

"NO SURVIVORS"

CONCORDANCE EVE WAS SOME WEEKS AGO...

IT WOULD APPEAR THAT YOU WERE DRUGGED A LITTLE MORE THOROUGHLY THAN YOU FIRST *THOUGHT*...

OH YEAH?

YOU THINK THAT COMES AS A *SURPRISE* TO CEREBUS?

YOU THINK CEREBUS DIDN'T *KNOW* THAT?

HUH?

YOU'RE NOT AS SMART AS YOU *THINK* YOU ARE, SOUTHLANDER...

THIS IS JUST A MINOR SETBACK! *NO* PROBLEM...

IT'LL TAKE MORE THAN JUST ONE *BATTLE* TO...

OKAY OKAY

HOW *DID* THE SOPAI ASSASSIN GET ELROD'S VOICE?

NOW THAT WE'RE ALL UP-TO-DATE ON OUR *PRESENT* SITUATION...

I THINK WE SHOULD EXAMINE *OUR* STRENGTHS AND WEAKNESSES AND DETERMINE HOW WE CAN BEST UTILIZE THEM IN THE NEAR FUTURE...

AS WELL AS DETERMINING A LONG-RANGE FORECAST OF OUR *OBJECTIVES*...

MR. PRESIDENT, I THINK THE *FIRST* ORDER OF BUSINESS SHOULD BE THE *EXECUTION* OF ANY HSIFFIES PRESENT IN THIS ROOM...

AS A SECURITY PRECAUTION...

ACTUALLY, MR. PRESIDENT-- THE *BEE-YOU-GEE* IS JUST A LITTLE *AITCH-YOU-ARE-TEE* ABOUT ME *BEE-EE-AY* TEEING HIM TO A *PEE-YOU-EL-PEE*...

THAT'S A LIE!

YOU-- I SAY-- YOU DON'T EVEN KNOW WHAT I *SAID*, SON...

IT DOESN'T *MATTER* WHAT YOU *SAID*-- YOU *LIE ALL* THE TIME!!

OH, YEAH?!

TARIM.

FOR YOUR INFORMATION I JUST TOLD THE PRESIDENT THAT YOU'RE FEELING SORRY FOR YOURSELF BECAUSE A HSIFFY BEAT YOU UP--*PULVERIZED* YOU THAT IS...

BEAT ME UP?!

FOR *YOUR* INFORMATION, I WAS JUST ABOUT TO WHUP HIM WHEN YOU *BUTTED IN*...!

WHAT--I SAY--WHAT WERE YOU GOING TO DO? BREAK HIS *FOOT* WITH YOUR *SKULL*?

EASY-- I SAY *EASY* SON...

...YOU LOOK LIKE YOU CAME IN *THIRD* IN A *HATCHET* FIGHT...

THANKS, BUNKY OLD CHUM -- WHERE'S THAT *HSIFFY CREEP?*

DISAPPEARED, EH? COULDN'T *TAKE* IT, EH?

HEHEH HEH HEH ≥KOFF≤ ≥KOFF≤

S'GOOD THING

I WAS STARTING TO GET *PEEVED*

CAPTAIN?

YES, MR. PRESIDENT

YOU KNOW THE *DRAPERIES* IN THE UPSTAIRS STUDY?

OH, YES*SIR* MR. PRESIDENT!

BE A GOOD CHAP AND GO WATCH THEM FOR AWHILE

...MAKE SURE THEY DON'T *EAT* THE *HOUSE PLANTS* ...

OH, YESSIR MR. PRESIDENT, SIR...

I'LL GET RIGHT ON IT, *SIR*...

RIGHT AWAY

YUP.

NO HSIFFY DRAPES ARE GOING TO EAT THE HOUSE PLANTS WHILE *I'M* IN CHARGE

NOSIREE MR. PRESIDENT, SIR...

CALL IT A CRAZY HUNCH, BUT CEREBUS DOESN'T BELIEVE YOU'RE *REALLY* CONCERNED ABOUT THE DRAPES EATING YOUR HOUSE-PLANTS...

A MORE SENSIBLE STORY WOULD ONLY HAVE MADE HIS HEAD HURT...

EH-- DO YOU REALIZE ELROD JUST NOW TOOK OVER *YOUR* BODY AS WELL?

HMM. I RATHER *THOUGHT* NOT ...

CAN YOU SEE *NOW* WHY THE *BIG BUG* IS NO LONGER A NECESSARY PART OF MY TEAM?

I NOW HAVE SOMEONE ON MY SIDE WHO IS CAPABLE OF ASSUMING *ANYONE'S* BODY AT WILL...

HAHAHA

IT NEVER CEASES TO AMAZE ME THAT THE LOWER CLASSES ARE AS FASCINATED BY MONEY AS THEY ARE...

MONEY OF ALL THINGS!

HAHA HAHA

I'M SORRY, I DON'T *MEAN* TO SOUND SO....

SO...

...SO MUCH LIKE AN ARISTOCRATIC *SNOB* WITH NO APPRECIATION FOR ANYTHING BESIDES HIS OWN OVER-INFLATED *EGO?*

TOUCHÉ

MM. YES!

HE COULD TAKE OVER ANY BANKER'S BODY AND JUST EMPTY HIS VAULT DOWN TO THE LAST *HALF-PIECE*...

BUT *REALLY* -- AN OPPORTUNITY LIKE THIS *SHOULDN'T* BE WASTED ON SOMETHING AS *MUNDANE* AS ACCUMULATING MERE CURRENCY

THERE *ARE* MORE IMPORTANT THINGS, YOU KNOW...

UH-HUH? LIKE *WHAT?*

POWER,

POWER?

POWER IS BETTER THAN *MONEY*...?

MOST *ASSUREDLY*...

POWER ALSO *IS* MONEY!

LIKE THE TREASURY I'M GOING TO CONTROL AFTER ELROD TAKES OVER THE BODY OF THE EXECUTIVE GENERAL OF THE MILITARY TRIBUNAL...

AHA! CEREBUS UNDERSTANDS *NOW!*

IT WOULD BEAT SENDING FRICK AND FRACK OUT TO SELL *WAR BONDS*, WOULDN'T IT?

AND IT WOULD GET THE *TRIBUNAL* OFF OF MY BACK, *PERMANENTLY* ...

BUT THE TRIBUNAL IS MADE UP OF *FIVE* MEN...

WHAT'S TO KEEP THEM FROM *OUT-VOTING* WHOMEVER ELROD TAKES OVER?

NOW YOU'RE LETTING PETTY *DETAILS* BOG YOU DOWN...

THAT'S WHY *I'M* WEALTHY AND THE PRESIDENT OF THE UNITED FELDWAR STATES...

...AND ALL *YOU'LL* EVER BE IS *POOR* AND A SWORD-FOR-HIRE...

WE FIRST GET ELROD TO TAKE OVER THE BODY OF EXECUTIVE COMMANDER LAFORT, WHO WILL ADMIT TO HIS ROLE IN THE SEPRAN LAMP-OIL PAYOFF SCANDAL...

AND *RESIGN* ...

BUT THAT LEAVES FOUR MEMBERS WHO...

THREE.

THREE?

AS SOON AS LAFORT IS CARTED OFF TO PRISON, SECOND GENERAL DESHEN WILL BE SO MOVED BY THIS SHOW OF HONESTY...

...THAT HE WILL ADMIT TO HIS PART IN THE *KEVILLIST REBELLION* FIVE YEARS AGO...

AND RESIGN AS WELL?

PRECISELY.

BUT, THAT STILL LEAVES THREE MEMBERS...

WHAT *THEN?*

THEY'RE ALL *SCANDAL-FREE* AREN'T THEY?

AS FAR AS *I* KNOW THEY ARE...

GENERAL MINON, *HOWEVER,* HAS FORMER EXECUTIVE COMMANDER SERET UNDER HIS THUMB...

IF MINON PROPOSED A MOTION RECOMMENDING THAT *SERET* COMMIT SUICIDE, SERET WOULD *SECOND* IT...

SO?

SO ELROD THEN TAKES OVER MINON'S BODY. ANYTHING HE PROPOSES WILL PASS WITH SERET'S WILLING ACQUIESCENCE

GENERAL CHEEN WILL BE THE ONLY DISSENTING MEMBER

AND I'LL RULE LOWER FELDA...

NEAT. *VERY* NEAT.

I KNOW. *AMAZING* AREN'T I?

WAIT -- I SAY -- WAIT JUST A FLEA-FLICKIN' *MINUTE* HERE. ALL I'VE HEARD IS "ELROD'LL DO THIS" AND "ELROD'LL DO THAT"...

DOESN'T -- I SAY -- DOESN'T ANYONE WANT TO HEAR WHAT *DEAD ALBINO* HAS TO *SAY?*

NOT *ESPECIALLY.*

WHY, NOW THAT YOU *MENTION* IT, WE NEED A PLAN TO GET US PAST THE TWO AGENDA SECRETARIES

AFTER ALL, YOU CAN'T TAKE OVER BOTH BODIES AT *ONE TIME!*

IT WOULD BE A GREAT HELP IF YOU COULD FIGURE SOMETHING OUT...

UH...

WELL -- UM -- UH -- GET US PAST THE ADENDUM SECRETARIES? -- I-- YEAH... I CAN SEE HOW THAT WOULD UH...

HMM.

I'D SURE -- I SAY -- I'D SURE *LIKE* TO BE USEFUL.

USEFUL, EH?

IF YOU WEREN'T SO LUMPY, YOU MIGHT MAKE A HALF-DECENT *SOFA...*

CEREBUS JUST HAD A THOUGHT-- SUPPOSE ...

SUPPOSE WE MARCH RIGHT IN AND TELL THEM THAT YOU ARE PRESIDENT WEISSHAUPT...

THAT WOULD CERTAINLY GET US IN TO SEE THE TRIBUNAL IN A HURRY, BUT, I DON'T ...

CEREBUS ISN'T FINISHED...

YOU BRING ELROD'S CORPSE WITH YOU -- AS PROOF THAT YOU'VE SEEN THE ERROR OF YOUR WAYS

YOU KILLED HIM, SEE?

I'M WITH YOU SO FAR...

"PLEASE-- I CAN TELL YOU WHERE TO FIND CAPTAIN COCKROACH AS WELL"

"I'M AN OLD MAN-- I DON'T WANT TO DIE IN PRISON"

"I'M A TRAITOR, BUT I ASK FOR CLEMENCY"

HAHA! TWO BIRDS WITH ONE CONFESSION...

I LIKE IT! I LIKE IT!

AFTER LAFORT AND DESHEN MAKE THEIR RESIGNATION SPEECHES

"MINON" ANNOUNCES THAT HE IS APPOINTING YOU HIS OFFICIAL ADVISOR...

"A RARE DISPLAY OF REHABILITATION BLAH BLAH BLAH EVERYONE DESERVES A SECOND CHANCE BLAH BLAHBLAH

WONDERFUL!

ELROD AND I, SIDE-BY-SIDE ON THE TRIBUNAL, RUNNING LOWER FELDA...

YOU KNOW, I THINK I MAY HAVE BEEN TOO HASTY IN JUDGING YOU-- YOU MIGHT NOT DIE BROKE AFTER ALL

IN FACT, I THINK YOU MIGHT EVEN BE CABINET MATERIAL

HOW WOULD YOU LIKE TO BE THE FIRST SECRETARY OF THE INTERIOR FOR THE GOVERNMENT OF THE UNITED FELDWAR STATES

THAT ALL DEPENDS. WHAT DOES THE SECRETARY OF THE INTERIOR DO...?

DRINK, GAMBLE AND SUPERVISE PUBLIC EXECUTIONS OF ANYONE WHO SPEAKS OUT AGAINST MY ADMINISTRATION ...

MR. PRESIDENT

I HUMBLY ACCEPT THIS GREAT HONOUR

AND I DO HUMBLY SWEAR THAT I WILL, TO THE BEST OF MY ABILITY, REMAIN FALLING-DOWN DRUNK AT LEAST NINETY PERCENT OF THE TIME

NINETY-FIVE PERCENT.

NINETY-FIVE PERCENT.

THEN, BY THE POWER VESTED IN ME BY MY OWN OVER-INFLATED EGO, I NOW DECLARE THIS BRIDGE OFFICIALLY OPEN

DRINK?

MY FRIENDS-- IT IS MY SAD DUTY ON THIS OCCASION, AS YOUR EXECUTIVE COMMANDER FOR ME...TO TAKE,...THIS,,,OPPORTUNITY... TO EXPRESS MY... DEEPEST REGRET... THAT I MUST TAKE.,, FULL...RESPONSIBILITY FOR THE ACTIONS ...OF MY BROTHER,,,,IN THE ,,,,,,RECENT... SEPRAN LAMP-OIL,.,. PAYOFF...SCANDAL... NOT ONLY DID I,... TELL MY BROTHER THAT SUCH ACTIONS AS HE TOOK...AT THAT TIME ,,,WAS *NOT* IN THE NATIONAL INTEREST BUT...THAT IN FACT THERE EXISTED A REAL POSSIBILITY THAT BOTH HE... AND I ,,,WOULD BE CAUGHT WITH OUR HANDS ,,,IN THE COOKIE JAR...UP TO OUR RESPECTIVE ,,,ELBOWS...

AMAZING!

NO EXPRESSION, NO COHERENCE AND SYNTAX YOU COULD SPEND A LIFETIME UNRAVELLING...

HE'S SO MUCH LIKE THE ORIGINAL IT'S ALMOST *SCARY...*

MY FELLOW LOWER FELDANS...

I WOULD LIKE TO ADD A FEW WORDS TO WHAT MY..."COLLEAGUE" HAS *ALREADY* STATED...

I AM *NOT* A CROOK...

I *AM*, HOWEVER, A SLEAZY NO-ACCOUNT OPPORTUNIST AND A *BOUGHT-AND-PAID-FOR* POLITICAL HACK...

I MAY NOT HAVE *STARTED* THAT KEVILLIST REBELLION FIVE YEARS AGO...

BUT IF I *DIDN'T,* IT WAS ONE OF ONLY A HANDFUL OF MAJOR SCANDALS I *DIDN'T* TAKE PART IN AT THAT TIME...

YOU HAVEN'T SEEN *ANYTHING* YET...

WE'VE BEEN WORKING ON HIS "DESHEN"

IT IS,,, FOR THIS REASON,,, THAT I INTEND...FOR REASONS PREVIOUSLY STATED TO RESIGN...EFFECTIVE IMMEDIATELY THIS ...POSITION

I ASK ,,,NOW,,,THAT THE GUARDS COME ,,,AND TAKE,..,ME ...AWAY,,,

NO, NO! MORE *SCOWL!*

ANGER! GIVE ME ANGER AND BITTER-NESS ...

ANGER, BITTERNESS AND *PARANOIA!*

GOOD! GOOD!

I WOULD ASK NOW THAT THE GUARDS COME AND TAKE ME AWAY, AS WELL

AS FAR AS *I'M* CONCERNED ...

HANGING'S TOO *GOOD* FOR ME!

I THINK HE'S *READY*...

I THINK YOU'RE *RIGHT*...

AND SO...

I DON'T WANT YOU TO TAKE THIS THE WRONG WAY, BUT I THINK IT WOULD BE BETTER IF YOU LET *ME* DO THE TALKING...

CEREBUS DOESN'T MIND. TALKING TO BUREAUCRATS MAKES HIM *NAUSEOUS*

ELROD ISN'T TOO *HEAVY*, I HOPE...

NOT IN THE LEAST...

HE'S GETTING STIFF ENOUGH THAT IT'S LIKE CARRYING A PLASTER STATUE...

MOST ESTEEMED AGENDA SECRETARY NERAK...

I AM *PRESIDENT WEISSHAUPT*, TRAITOR, ROGUE AND UNWORTHY SON OF OUR MOTHER-LAND...

I HAVE BROUGHT THE CORPSE OF BUNKY THE ALBINO AS A GESTURE OF MY SINCERE REGRET...

I WISH TO APPEAR BEFORE THE TRIBUNAL TO SUBMIT MYSELF TO THEIR JUDGEMENT...

THIS...

...THIS COMES AS QUITE A *SURPRISE*, WEISS-HAUPT...

YOU REALIZE, OF COURSE, THAT THE TRIBUNAL IS NOT LIKELY TO VIEW YOUR CASE WITH ANY MEASURE OF... *COMPASSION*...?

I FEEL, *SIR*, THAT MY SINCERITY-- AND MY INTENTION TO SURRENDER CAPTAIN COCKROACH TO THEM-- WILL *CONVINCE* THE TRIBUNAL OF MY NEWFOUND PATRIOTISM

PSST.

PSST. CEREBUS.

WHAT IN BLAZES ARE YOU DOING IN *THERE?*

I JUST THOUGHT I'D SEE IF IT STILL FELT THE SAME

VERY WELL. EXECUTIVE COMMANDER LAFORT WILL BE NOTIFIED OF YOUR REQUEST.

GUARD. TAKE THIS NOTE *INSIDE*...

WELL, GET OUT OF THERE *NOW!* YOU'RE GOING TO RUIN OUR WHOLE PLAN...

I CAN'T!

YOU *WHAT!?!*

I'M STUCK.

SO!

AS I *SUSPECTED!* THIS IS SOME MANNER OF *IDIOTIC TRICK!!*

GUARD! ARREST THEM ALL!

I'M ≥GASP≥ I'M ≥GASP≥ STILL HERE

WHERE DO WE ≥GASP≥ GO NOW?

WELL-- OFFHAND, I'D SAY *YOU* WERE GOING TO PRISON...

WHILE CEREBUS IS... UNH! ...GOING TO... UNH! SQUEEZE BETWEEN THESE RAILS

AND USE YOUR FORGED PAPERS ...

...TO PASS THROUGH THE *EAST GATE* ONE BLOCK THAT WAY...

BUT-- BUT-- YOU *CAN'T!*

YOU CAN'T LEAVE ME HERE!

I COULDN'T POSSIBLY BEAT FOUR ARMED GUARDS *SINGLE-HANDED!*

THIS IS *TRUE...*

CEREBUS COULD...

BUT, LIKE YOU *SAID...*

CEREBUS WILL NEVER BE ANYTHING MORE THAN A SWORD-FOR-HIRE

WHILE *YOU* ON THE OTHER HAND...

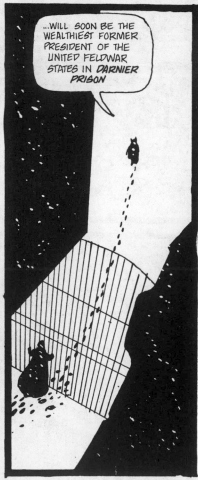

...WILL SOON BE THE WEALTHIEST FORMER PRESIDENT OF THE UNITED FELDWAR STATES IN *DARNIER PRISON*

486

BEDUIN LAY MANY MILES BEHIND THE EARTH-PIG...THE SWELLING AROUND THE GASH IN HIS LEG HAD SUBSIDED *SOMEWHAT* AND THE CRUST OF ICE ON HIS CRUDELY-WRAPPED BANDAGE HAD EFFECTIVELY *NUMBED* THE PAIN...

IT HAD BEEN A FINAL *INSULT* FROM THE CITY...

...A NAIL JUTTING TOO FAR OUT OF A WAGON WHEEL SPOKE CATCHING CEREBUS JUST BELOW THE KNEE

EACH STEP BRINGS HIM THAT MUCH CLOSER TO COLLAPSE...ALREADY THE LEG HAD FOLDED UNDER HIM TWICE

HE NEEDED SOMEPLACE DRY AND WARM TO REST HIS LEG AND SOME ALCOHOL TO CLEAN THE WOUND *THOROUGHLY*...

The BEGUILING

AT LAST, CEREBUS SEES A HOUSE IN THE DISTANCE, ALMOST COMPLETELY OBSCURED BY THE FALLING SNOW...

CEREBUS REFUSED TO ACKNOWLEDGE EVEN TO HIMSELF THAT THE INITIAL WOUND HAD BEEN A MERE SCRATCH --AND HAD WORSENED ONLY *AFTER* HE HAD JUMPED INTO THE MOVING WAGON AND UNLEASHED A MIGHTY KICK AT THE SURPRISED DRIVER...

THE EARTH-PIG MUTTERS GRIMLY ABOUT CIVILIANS WHO GO AROUND WITH CHAIN-MAIL UNDER THEIR CLOTHES...

489

491

MADAME DuFORT SO DISTRUSTS OUTSIDERS DOESN'T SHE? HER EVERY WAKING MOMENT IS DEVOTED TO SHELTERING US...

FOR JANETTE AND KATRINA WHO ARE SO MUCH LESS *MATURE* ...THERE IS A GREAT NEED FOR SUCH CLOSE SUPERVISION. I, HOWEVER, AM NOT LIKE *THEM*...

FOR EXAMPLE... IT DOES NOT FRIGHTEN ME TO BE ALONE WITH ONE SUCH AS YOU, M'SIEU, YOU PROBABLY FIND THIS ATTITUDE RE-FRESHING -- SO MANY GIRLS FIND IT DIFFICULT TO RELAX AROUND A MEMBER OF THE OPPOSITE...

AROUND MEN I MEAN.

I THINK STIMULATING WITH MEN CAN BE QUITE CONVERSATIONAL AT TIMES.

HA HA HA...

SILLY ME-- THAT'S NOT WHAT I MEANT TO SAY AT ALL...

CEREBUS COULD HAVE SWORN HE HEARD SOMEONE MENTION *WHISKEY*.

...BUT, THEN WE ARE ADULTS ARE WE NOT, WE TWO? ... WE CAN SPEAK OF .... "*STIMULATING*" ...

BEING WORDLY WE TWO, IT DOESN'T... *DISTURB* US.

I FEEL WE HAVE AN UNDERSTANDING ABOUT SPEAKING YOU AND I

WE MIGHT EVEN SPEAK OF...*BODILY FUNCTIONS* WERE WE SO DISPOSED

RIGHT RIGHT

NOW HOW ABOUT THE ...

THERESA! A SOLDIER APPROACHES! ...

I AM *SORRY*, M'SIEU

I'M AFRAID THE SECURITY OF THE SCHOOL COMES FIRST...

HEY! WAIT!

WHAT ARE YOU GOING TO DO?

KNIT HIM TO *DEATH*?!

YOU...

HEY!!

OF ALL THE IDIOTIC

492

I DON' WANNA HURT YOU, OL' LADY...

BUT...

MY SOJERS REST HE' OKAY?

I'M AFRAID YOU MISUNDERSTAND, M'SIEU...

MY-SOJERS-REST-HE'

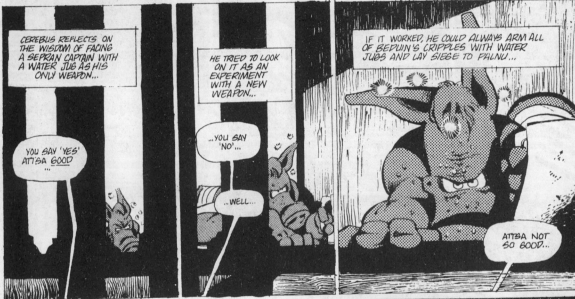

CEREBUS REFLECTS ON THE WISDOM OF FACING A SEPRAN CAPTAIN WITH A WATER JUG AS HIS ONLY WEAPON...

YOU SAY 'YES' ATT'SA GOOD'...

HE TRIED TO LOOK ON IT AS AN EXPERIMENT WITH A NEW WEAPON...

...YOU SAY 'NO'...

...WELL...

IF IT WORKED, HE COULD ALWAYS ARM ALL OF BEDUIN'S CRIPPLES WITH WATER JUGS AND LAY SIEGE TO PALNU...

ATT'SA NOT SO GOOD...

I SEE WE ARE NOT COMMUNICATING AT ALL, M'SIEU

MORE'S THE PITY...

I DO NOT, HOWEVER, INTEND TO ALLOW SOLDIERS INTO MY SCHOOL

KATRINA?

ONE...

TWO...

494

BUT CEREBUS CAN GUARANTEE YOU THAT EVERY INCH OF COUNTRYSIDE AROUND HERE IS FROZEN *SOLID*...

THEY WON'T LOSE A SINGLE MAN...

AND YOU BELIEVE THAT THIS SHOULD *WORRY US?*

WELL THAT DEPENDS

HOW WORRIED ARE YOU GOING TO BE BY SIXTEEN THOUSAND SEPRANS MARCHING PAST YOUR SCHOOL?

THAT'S A *CONSERVATIVE* GUESS ON CEREBUS' PART...

IT DEPENDS ON WHETHER THE SEPRANS ARE UNDER-ESTIMATING THE CIRINISTS' MILITARY STRENGTH

MA DIEU.

I MUST SUMMON MY GIRLS-- WE WILL NEED A *PLAN!*

SURE SURE

MAYBE YOU CAN CROCHET SIXTEEN THOUSAND PUP TENTS AND LEAVE THEM ON YOUR FRONT STEP AS A PEACE OFFERING...

I WILL NOT GIVE UP SO EASILY, M'SIEU.

AS HE LISTENS TO THE SOUND OF MADAME DuFORT'S FOOTSTEPS FADING, CEREBUS GLARES BALEFULLY AT HIS LEFT LEG...

...OR BALANCE SIXTEEN THOUSAND FLATIRONS OVER YOUR WINDOWS AND DOORS TO KNOCK THEM OUT IF THEY TRY TO BREAK IN.

LATER...

WELL.

IT IS A GOOD THING WE HAVE HAD THIS MUCH WARNING, NO?

THEY ARE. *ONLY* SOLDIERS.

SURELY WE CAN THINK OF SOMETHING TO FOOL THEM.

LOOK! CEREBUS CAN TELL YOU THE ONLY *PLAUSIBLE* COURSE OF ACTION...

YOU JUST HAVE TO *LEAVE*.-TRY AND REACH ONE OF THE LARGER TOWNS

WHERE YOU'LL BE SAFE...

CEREBUS ISN'T ABLE TO TRAVEL OR HE WOULD GO WITH YOU

IT DOESN'T MAKE ANY SENSE TO FACE FOUR SEPRAN LEGIONS IF YOU DON'T *HAVE* TO...

WHAT ABOUT A QUARANTINE, M'SIEU?

SURELY EVEN SEPRAN SOLDIERS WOULD AVOID A PLAGUE-RIDDEN...

THE SEPRAN LEGIONS TRAVEL WITH THEIR OWN PHYSICIANS

HANG A QUARANTINE SIGN ON THE DOOR AND YOU'LL BE HIP-DEEP IN TONGUE DEPRESSORS ...

THERE'S NOTHING A SEPRAN PHYSICIAN LIKES *BETTER* THAN SOME HORRIBLY DEFORMED PLAGUE VICTIM TO POKE AND JAB AND PLUCK AT...

SO UNLESS YOU KNOW OF A GOOD WAY TO DEFORM YOUR GIRLS CEREBUS IS AFRAID YOUR PLAN WON'T WORK...

MADAME?

I BELIEVE I HAVE AN IDEA.

AFTER JANETTE RELATES HER IDEA...

NO.

M'SIEU... ...WILL YOU NOT RECONSIDER?

HER IDEA IS A GOOD ONE. IF WE DO AS YOU SAY AND LEAVE YOU WILL FALL INTO THE HANDS OF THE SEPRANS...

THIS WAY YOU WILL BE SAFE ··AND SO WILL OUR SCHOOL...

M'SIEU?

CEREBUS... ...IS... THINKING ...ABOUT IT!!

AND SO...

"JOINA DA ARMY" SHE SAY. "ITA BE AGOOD FO' Y'U! Y'U MEK ALOTSA MONEY,"

"Y'U BE ABLE TO BUY AY'U OWN AFARM IN ATHREE YEARS, ANH?"

" I'M ANOT WANT TO BE COLT," I SAY.

"WHASSAMATTA FO' Y'U," SHE SAY ·· "LOWER FELDA, SHE'S AWARM AS ATOAST!"

"THREE YEARS ABE UP BEFORE Y'U KNOW IT,"

WHEN I'M AGET HOME ...

IN ATHREE YEARS

I'MA KILLA HER.

em...

eh...

'ALO!

I'M AWELCOME ME TO Y'U COUNTRY...

I'M ANEED A PLACE TO STAY...

MY FRIEN' TOO AS AWELL

I'M SORRY, M'SIEU

ONE OF MY GIRLS HAS THE PLAGUE

YOU AND YOUR FRIEND WOULD NOT WANT TO STAY HERE

NOW IF YOU WILL EXCUSE ME.

PLAGUE, ANH?

I'M ASHOO NOT WAN' TO GET ATHE PLAGUE

BUT MAYB' THERE ISA NO PLAGUE

ANH?

MAYB' Y'U SAY TO Y'USELF "'EY! THIS ISSA BIG A DUMB SEPRAN HE'"

" I'M ATELL AHIM A COCK AN' A BULL STORY"

" I'M A TELL HIM ABOUT A PLAGUE"

WAL...

MAYB' THISA BIG A DUMB SEPRAN WILL SEE THIS A GORL FOR HIMASELF, ANH?

IF YOU... INSIST, M'SIEU...

I WILL ASK THAT YOU NOT MAKE TOO MUCH NOISE ...

DONNA WORRY

IN HERE.

I WILL ASK YOU AGAIN TO BE VERY QUIET.

501

SERGEAN'? YOU INNA HE'?

EH! MY FREN'-- FINALL' HE GET THROUGH DA SNOW. TIBERIUS!!

I'M ASHOW MY FREN'--HOKAY?

VERY WELL, BUT THEN YOU'LL BOTH *HAVE* TO LEAVE...

DONNA WORRY! I'M A LIKEA MY NOSE TO STAY *THIS* ASIZE...

'EY TIBERIUS!

Y'U WANNA TO SEE DA *UGLIEST* LITTLA GORL...

INNA DA WHOLE AWIDE A WORL'?

HEE HEE

UGL' HUH?

SHOO! SHOO!

I'M A NO KID Y'U

Y'U BE LUCK' NOT ATO LOSE AY'U *LUNCH*.

HEE HEE THISSA SOUND A PRETT' GOOD, SERGEAN'

JUST ONE A LOOK

ANNA THEN WE LEAVE

THANK YOU, M'SIEU

EH? WASSA *THIS*?

TARIM!

502

504

YOUR WEAPON DOES NOT **SOUND** LIKE IT IS IN PERFECT WORKING ORDER KATRINA...

I WOULD SUGGEST YOU CLEAN AND OIL IT **IMMEDIATELY** ...

YES MADAME.

JANETTE.

YOUR AIM WAS OFF BY **FIVE INCHES**-- IT IS NOTHING THAT A FEW HOURS OF PRACTICE WOULD NOT **CORRECT.**

YES MADAME...

THERESA. I WANT YOU TO SEE IF IT IS STILL **SNOWING.**

IF IT **ISN'T**, THERE WILL BE FOOTPRINTS OUTSIDE

TAKE THE BROOM AND ELIMINATE ANY TRACE OF OUR VISITORS' PASSING

STAY ALERT-- OTHER SOLDIERS ARE APT TO BE NEARBY...

IF YOU SEE ANY, RETURN IMMEDIATELY

YES MADAME

YES MADAME

AND HAVE TWO MORE BEDS MOVED IN HERE ...

JANETTE-- M'SIEU CEREBUS WILL NEED TWO M...

PARDON, MADAME?

THE COMING OF SPRING AT MADAME DUFORT'S SCHOOL -- THE THREAT OF SEPRAN SOLDIERS (SEE *CEREBUS* Nº 23) VANISHES WITH THE SNOW AND ICE AS THE SURROUNDING LAND THAWS INTO MUD AND MARSH...AH, *SPRING* -- WHEN A YOUNG MAN'S FANCY TURNS TO THOUGHTS OF LOVE AND A CERTAIN AARDVARK'S THOUGHTS REMAIN FIXED ON GETTING *OUT* OF MADAME DUFORT'S SCHOOL IN THE VERY NEAR FUTURE...

SWAMP SOUNDS

FOR THE MOMENT, THE EARTH-PIG IS FIGHTING A LOSING BATTLE WITH *BOREDOM*...

REALLY, THERESA...YOU SHOULD BUTTON UP YOUR DRESS... WHAT WOULD *MADAME* SAY?...

OH, JANETTE-- DON'T BE SO BLOODY DAMN *TIRESOME*....

I DON'T GIVE A BLOODY *DAMN* WHAT MADAME WOULD SAY ...

THE*RES*A!

YOUR *LANGUAGE!*

YOU *SEE,* CEREBUS MY LOVE -- THEY'RE ALL SO...SO...*PROVINCIAL!*

IT REALLY IS JUST *TOO BLOODY DAMN* BORING AROUND HERE....

FOR PITY'S SAKE, *THERESA!* ...

QUIT SHOWING OFF AND BUTTON YOUR *DRESS*

I BET A QUARTER OF A BOTTLE OF *WHISKEY...*

YOU DON'T WANT ME TO BUTTON MY DRESS, *DO* YOU, CEREBUS...

MY OWN TRUE LOVE ...

MM?

CEREBUS CAN'T REMEMBER THE RULES TO THIS *MORONIC* GAME...

I'LL EXPLAIN IT *ONCE MORE* -- THE BEST HAND IS MAGICIAN AND THREE PRIESTESSES, THEN MAGICIAN AND TWO PRIESTESSES THEN TWO PRIESTESSES AND TWO KINGS, THEN TWO KINGS AND TWO QUEENS, THEN A QUEEN AND THREE KINGS THEN A KING AND THREE QUEENS... PRIESTS ARE WILD AND THERE'S TWO DRAWS -- IF YOU HAVE TWO QUEENS OR TWO FIVES YOU SAY *"GIMPSEE DOODLE"* AND EACH PLAYER HAS TO PAY YOU TWICE WHAT THEY BET ON THE INITIAL WAGER UNLESS YOU'VE *ALREADY* DRAWN A NEW CARD AND THEN YOU ONLY GET TWICE THE INITIAL WAGER FROM THE PLAYER ON YOUR LEFT, UNLESS HE HAS TWO KINGS AND THEN HE SAYS *"OOPEE DOOP"* AND YOU HAVE TO PAY *HIM* THE AMOUNT YOU OTHERWISE WOULD HAVE WON, SEE?

THERE IS *NOTHING* CEREBUS HATES MORE THAN *'CUTE'* CARD GAMES.

*AC*TUALLY, I'M RATHER *SURPRISED* THAT YOU'RE NOT MORE *FAMILIAR* WITH THE GAME...

FROM WHAT *I'VE* HEARD THE ARISTOCRACY IN ESHNOSPUR IS ABSOLUTELY *OBSESSED* WITH IT...

CEREBUS BETS A COPPER PIECE...

THE LAST TIME CEREBUS WAS IN *ESHNOSPUR* THE ONLY GAME THE ARISTOCRACY WAS PLAYING WAS CALLED "*POISON YOUR IN-LAWS*"

ONE CARD.

YOU WERE THERE DURING THE *REBELLION?* OH, HOW *GRAND!* AND DID YOU SEE THE 'LION OF THE COAST' HIMSELF...

PRINCE RASHAZAR?

ONE CARD KATRINA DARLING...

RASHAZAR? AYE. CEREBUS SAW HIM ESCAPE FROM THE CITY...

AH, OF COURSE -- ASTRIDE HIS BLACK CHARGER, STRIKING DOWN BLACKGUARDS AND VILLAINS AS HE WENT...

BLACK CHARGER?

CEREBUS DIDN'T SEE ANY BLACK CHARGER -- UNLESS RASHAZAR HAD IT HIDDEN UNDER HIS DRESS...

TWO COPPER BITS

≡DRESS?≡

AYE -- HE WAS DISGUISED AS A *SLAVE GIRL*...

...HE GAVE CEREBUS FIVE GOLD COINS AND BEGGED ME NOT TO TELL ANYONE WHO HE WAS... OH, BY THE WAY...

"GIMPSEE DOODLE."...

TWO KINGS AND TWO QUEENS...

PASS THE BOTTLE...

DOUBLE THE INITIAL WAGER -- A HALF BOTTLE OF WHISKEY

HMM.

THAT'S ALL OF YOUR MONEY, JEWELRY AND LIQUOR CEREBUS HAS WON...

QUITE ALL RIGHT.

THIS GAME WAS GETTING AWFULLY BLOODY DAMN *BORING* ANYWAY...

MM.

510

M'SIEUZ

MM?

YOU DIDN'T *REALLY* USE A WOMAN FOR A SHIELD...

DID YOU?

NO... CEREBUS WAS JUST MAKING A POINT ABOUT THE "CODE OF HONOUR"

I THINK I UNDERSTAND, M'SIEU...

I HAVE TO GO, NOW.

AND CEREBUS DIDN'T HAVE THE NERVE TO TELL YOU ABOUT THE TIME HE USED ONE FOR A *BATTERING RAM*...

MOMENTS LATER...

TARIM.

SLOHSCHLUKSLLOKSHOLUCKSCHHLOPPGOPPSLOSHLOPPSLO

THERE IT IS AGAIN...

HE HAD HEARD THE SAME SOUNDS SINCE HIS ARRIVAL WEEKS BEFORE...

...SOMETIMES LASTING FOR HOURS...

...SOMETIMES ONLY FOR MINUTES.

HIS FIRST GUESS HAD BEEN THAT MADAME AND THE GIRLS WERE CAUSING IT...

MADAME WAS A GOOD ENOUGH LIAR TO FOOL HIM-- BUT THE GIRLS...

IF THEY *HAD* HAD A HAND IN IT, THEY WOULD HAVE OFFERED A STORY-- HOWEVER IMPLAUSIBLE...

"THAT? OH-- THAT'S ESTARCION MUD-WRESTLING--AN INTEGRAL PART OF OUR CURRICULUM"

"DIDN'T WE TELL YOU? THAT'S MADAME'S PET HIPPO--THERESA TAKES HIM OUT WHEN HE HAS TO TINKLE."

SCHLUPSHLOOMPGLUSHUMGLUMPSHUMPSHOOPSHOOLKSHOOMKSKLIKSLOOMSHLONKSHOM

WHATEVER IT WAS, IT WAS BIG, AND PROBABLY SORCEROUS IN ORIGIN...

"AND THAT" THOUGHT THE EARTH-PIG "COULD MEAN *TROUBLE*...

AFTER A TIME, THE SOUND FADES. CEREBUS, LOST IN THOUGHT, CONTINUES TO STARE OUT THE WINDOW AT THE DRIVING RAIN...

M'SIEU-- I'VE COME TO CHECK THE WOUND ON YOUR...

HMM.

WHEN I GAVE YOU THAT CRUTCH, I DIDN'T INTEND FOR YOU TO WEAR IT OUT...

CEREBUS WAS JUST...

RESTING HERE

THINKING.

SO? WHAT'S THE VERDICT?

I BELIEVE YOU WILL BE OUR GUEST FOR ANOTHER WEEK OR SO...

WHAT?

IT'S BEEN FOUR WEEKS ALREADY

BE THAT AS IT MAY, M'SIEU...

IT WAS NOT I WHO ABSENT-MINDEDLY HIT MY FOOT ON THE FLOOR TO SIGNAL THAT MY SUPPER WAS A FEW MINUTES LATE

PERHAPS IF YOU COULD THINK OF A WAY TO INDICATE YOUR IMPATIENCE THAT WAS LESS...ah...

...DESTRUCTIVE?

CEREBUS' FIRST IDEA WAS TO SET FIRE TO THE HALLWAY...

AH!

YOU WERE ON THE RIGHT TRACK, THEN...

WHEN YOU GET TO THE POINT WHERE YOU CHOOSE TO SIMPLY WAIT A FEW EXTRA MINUTES...

YOU WILL HAVE MADE REAL PROGRESS

NON?

FOR NOW, HOWEVER, YOU WILL HAVE ANOTHER WEEK OR SO...

TO MORE FULLY DEVELOP YOUR NEW-FOUND PATIENCE...

CEREBUS HAS HEARD THE SOUNDS AGAIN ...

I SEE. AND DO YOU STILL BELIEVE THE GIRLS AND I ARE *RESPONSIBLE?*

YOU MAY FIND THIS HARD TO BELIEVE MADAME...

BUT CEREBUS IS *NOW* CONVINCED THAT SOME MANNER OF SORCERER OR WIZARD HAS TAKEN AN INTEREST IN YOUR GIRLS...

AND HAS SENT SOMEONE...

OR *SOMETHING*

HERE TO GET THEM

PARDON ME FOR INTERRUPTING, M'SIEU, BUT THIS STORY IS RATHER *FAMILIAR*...

THE LAST SOLDIER WHO STAYED HERE CLAIMED THERE WERE *WOOD TROLLS* IN OUR WALLS ...

HE SUGGESTED THAT I ALLOW THE GIRLS TO SLEEP WITH *HIM* IN HERE ...

JUST SO THAT HE COULD "KEEP A CLOSE WATCH ON THEM" OF *COURSE*

MADAME.

CEREBUS IS BEING QUITE *SERIOUS!*

HE WAS BEING QUITE SERIOUS AS WELL, M'SIEU

I SUPPOSE I SHOULD HEAR YOU OUT, THOUGH

WHAT ARE YOU *RECOMMENDING* THAT I DO?

KEEP YOUR GIRLS INDOORS --INSIST THAT THEY NOT GO OUTSIDE AT ALL...

TELL THEM TO STAY TOGETHER AS MUCH AS *POSSIBLE*

AND ABOVE ALL THEY SHOULD NOT INVESTIGATE ANY STRANGE *SOUNDS* ...

THE GIRLS HAVE A *NUMBER* OF LESSONS TO DO, M'SIEU

I DOUBT THEY WILL HAVE TIME TO INVESTIGATE ANYTHING ...

GOOD NIGHT, M'SIEU

SLEEP WELL.

NOT FOR THE FIRST TIME, CEREBUS WISHES HE COULD READ THE THOUGHTS LURKING BEHIND MADAME DUFORT'S ENIGMATIC HALF-SMILE...

THE NEXT DAY, CEREBUS IS UNABLE TO SHAKE THE FEELING OF IMPENDING *DISASTER*...

WOULD YOU NOT *AGREE* M'SIEU...?

WHAT'S THAT? CEREBUS WASN'T *LISTENING*

I WAS *SAVING*, M'SIEU

TWO CARDS

THAT YOU ARE A TRIFLE *EXTREME* IN YOUR BELIEFS ABOUT CHIVALRY AND HEROISM, NON?

LISTENING TO *YOU* ONE WOULD BE LED TO BELIEVE THAT YOU DON'T THINK SUCH THINGS AS HEROISM EXIST...

THAT'S *PROBABLY* BECAUSE CEREBUS DOESN'T BELIEVE SUCH THINGS AS HEROISM EXIST...

NOW *REALLY*, M'SIEU ...

KING ANDROS' DEFENCE OF THE MOUNTAIN PASS?

THE DUKE OF AKSHUN AND THE RESCUE OF HIS BROTHER FROM THE ONLIU?

NEED I GO ON?

ANCIENT HISTORY *THERESA*

NO VERIFICATION POSSIBLE

LEGENDS AND FABLES FOR THE IMPRESSIONABLE

NAME CEREBUS ONE EXAMPLE OF A HERO STILL LIVING TODAY ...

AS A MATTER OF *FACT*, M'SIEU I CAN NAME *TWO*

ONE IS *KATRINA'S* UNCLE -- HER SISTER HAS TOLD US ALL ABOUT HIS MOST RECENT FEAT WHEN SHE CAME HERE

SO YOU CAN HARDLY CALL IT A LEGEND OR A FABLE

NOW, THERESA, I'M SURE M'SIEU CEREBUS...

OH *PIFFLE* KATRINA...

IT'S TIME SOMEONE LET HIM KNOW HE'S NOT AS SMART AS HE THINKS HE IS...

CEREBUS IS LISTENING...

HE DESCENDED INTO THE BOWELS OF THE EARTH UNDER HIS CITY, UNARMED,

THE LEGIONS OF HELL *DESCENDED*

BUT WITH IRON THEWS AND *SLEDGE HAMMER* BLOWS, HE MADE SHORT WORK OF THEM...

IN SEARCH OF THE FOE WHO SOUGHT TO SPOIL HIS PEOPLE'S CELEBRATION OF A MAJOR FESTIVAL...

AND THEN, ACROSS A BRIDGE OF AGED AND CRUMBLING STONES

HE SAW. HIS *FOE!*

THEY LOCKED IN MORTAL COMBAT, POUNDING EACH OTHER WITH BLOWS THAT WOULD HAVE CRUSHED LESSER MEN...

AN ACT OF TRUE HEROISM

AT LAST, HOWEVER, PURITY AND NOBILITY WON THE DAY...

THAT'S RIGHT, M'SIEU -- THE GRANDLORD OF PALNU! -- AND WE HEARD THE WHOLE STORY FROM HIS NIECE ONLY *DAYS* AFTER IT *HAPPENED...*

WHAT DO YOU SAY TO *THAT?*

CEREBUS DOESN'T KNOW QUITE WHAT TO SAY...

AND THAT IS ONLY THE *FIRST* EXAMPLE, M'SIEU ...

AND HIS BRONZE MUSCLES STREAMING WITH SWEAT, HE WATCHED HIS FOE DIS-APPEAR INTO THE GAPING MAW OF HELL... THE FESTIVAL HAD BEEN SAVED...

ALL IN A DAY'S WORK FOR LORD JULIUS...

THE OTHER WAS TOLD TO US **ALL** BY THE LAST SOLDIER TO STAY HERE -- THE SWASHBUCKLING ALBINO BRIGAND **ELROD OF MELVINBONE** WHO STRODE INTO SERREA JUST TWO SUMMERS AGO

AND WITH NAUGHT TO AID HIM SAVE HIS RUNE-CARVED BLACK BLADE **SEERSUCKER**...

-- THE MINUTES WORE INTO HOURS AND HE FOUGHT ON -- UNTIL AT LAST ALL OF HIS FOES LAY DEAD OR HAD ESCAPED...

BATTLED THE CREAM OF THE EMPEROR'S CITY GUARDS SINGLE-HANDEDLY...

AT TIMES, AS MANY AS A DOZEN SWORDS WERE RAISED AGAINST HIM...

FULLY FIVE SCORE SOLDIERS HAD TASTED THE BLACK METAL OF **SEERSUCKER**...

AND DO YOU KNOW THE REASON THIS MOST FEARLESS WARRIOR RISKED HIS LIFE?

IT WAS TO SAVE THE LIFE OF A SMALL CHILD IN A RABBIT COSTUME...

CEREBUS COULDN'T IMAGINE...

AGAIN, M'SIEU

AN ACT OF TRUE **HEROISM**

FOR WHAT ELSE **COULD** YOU CALL IT?

ACTUALLY, CEREBUS CAN THINK OF **SEVERAL** CHOICE DESCRIPTIONS...

THERESA!

JANETTE

KATRINA

'HEROISM' ISN'T ONE OF THEM, THOUGH

WE MUST GO, M'SIEU

TOMORROW WE WILL TALK ABOUT SOME OTHER HEROES, NON?

CEREBUS CAN HARDLY WAIT
...

SLEEP.

SLEEP OF **DREAMS.**
DREAMS OF THINGS
IN THE **BLACKNESS.**
REACHING,
GRASPING.

SOUNDS.

LOUDER THAN BEFORE.
SOFT- WET AND GROWING
AS THE BLACKNESS

...CLOSES AROUND
THE EARTH- PIG.

SCHLUCKSCHUMSLUKSHU

A SENSATION OF PULLING.
MUSCLES THAT DON'T
RESPOND, THE BLACKNESS
LIKE BANDS OF IRON
WRAPPING TIGHTLY...

PULLING.

TOWARDS **WHAT?** TIGHTER
NOW, CHOKING AND CLENCHING

SHLUCKSHTUPSHU

PULLING.

DOWN.

TOWARDS THE SOUND, SOFT-
WET AND LOUDER STILL...

PULLING THE EARTH- PIG
TOWARDS THE SOUND...

INSIDE. THE
SOUND, **INSIDE**

517

INSIDE. THE SOUND INSIDE... THE WORDS ARE A HALF-REMEMBERED REALITY IN THIS WHITE DAZZLE WORLD OF SOUND IN WHICH THE EARTH-PIG FINDS HIMSELF TUMBLING END OVER END... THE SOUND INSIDE

CEREBUS STRUGGLES TO GRASP THE SIGNIFICANCE OF THE WORDS EVEN AS HIS DESCENT SLOWS AND HE FINDS HIMSELF FLOATING INSIDE THE SOUND THE SOUND INSIDE INSIDE THE SOUND INSIDE INSIDE

UNTIL FINALLY CEREBUS...

WAKES UP...

...TO FIND...

UNTIL A VERY SHORT TIME AGO, I WAS ONE OF A SELECT GROUP OF ALCHEMISTS STUDYING IN *RACHINNE*

MY WORK HAD BEEN *ADEQUATE* IF UNSPECTACULAR WHEN I MADE A *REMARKABLE* DISCOVERY...

QUITE BY ACCIDENT...

STUDYING THE *CHILDREN'S FABLES* WRITTEN BY SUENTEUS PO ALMOST A HUNDRED YEARS AGO...

I DISCOVERED THAT THEY WERE IN FACT *ALLEGORIES* FOR VERY COMPLEX SPELLS AND INCANTATIONS...

YOU'RE JOKING.

NOT AT ALL...

...WHY, IF I COULD FIGURE OUT WHAT THE *PUMPKIN* IN THE LAST PARAGRAPH OF "*BLINKY BOAR AND THE STRAWBERRY PATCH*" REPRESENTED, I COULD MAKE *GOLD* OUT OF *PIG MANURE*...

I DID MANAGE TO DECIPHER "*OLD GOOBER BEAR AND THE NASTY HEDGEHOG*." IT WAS THE LOST FORMULA FOR THE CREATION OF THE MYTHIC *APOCALYPSE BEAST*

ARMED WITH PO'S BOOK AND MY OWN PRIN-STAKING RESEARCH, I ADDRESSED A PANEL OF MY PEERS...

I HAD COMPLETED ONLY THE FIRST FEW SENTENCES OF MY SPEECH WHEN THE SOUND OF THEIR COLLECTIVE LAUGHTER DROWNED OUT ALL OF MY ATTEMPTS TO CONTINUE...

THE NEXT DAY I LEFT VOWING TO RETURN WHEN I HAD CONJURED AND HARNESSED THE BEAST

I CAME HERE AND BEGAN MY SCHOOL·· I NEEDED ADOLESCENTS AS A FOCUS FOR THE SPELL...

I HAND-PICKED THREE HEALTHY YOUNG MEN, SCREENING THEM CAREFULLY FOR MENTAL AND PHYSICAL ABILITIES...

I HAD INTENTIONALLY SELECTED BOYS FROM WEALTHY FAMILIES, HAVING NO FUNDS OF MY OWN TO FEED AND HOUSE THREE STUDENTS. THE POSSIBILITY OF WAR WITH UPPER FELDA, HOWEVER, HAD DIMMED THEIR INTEREST IN SCHOLASTIC PURSUITS...

...SO I TRIED A SECOND GROUP...

...AND A THIRD...

...AND A FOURTH.

THINGS WENT FROM BAD TO **WORSE**...

FINALLY I DID MANAGE TO FIND A BOY WHO, WITH MY ASSISTANCE, COULD MENTALLY INFLUENCE THE ENERGY GENERATED BY HIS WILL...

UNFORTUNATELY, HE WAS SOMETHING OF A **PRACTICAL JOKER**...

AND I HAD TO REFUND THE TUITION PAID BY THE PARENTS OF THE OTHER TWO BOYS...

SO AFTER I GOT RID OF THE BOY, AND PAID OFF THE PARENTS, I WAS BACK WHERE I STARTED...

AND **BROKE.**

CLEARLY WHAT I NEEDED WAS THREE BOYS TO FURNISH THE ENERGY FOR THE BEAST

IT WAS THEN THAT I WAS STRUCK BY AN **INSPIRATION...**

WAS THERE ANY REASON THE **BEAST** COULDN'T BE A **WOMAN...?**

--ITS ENERGY FURNISHED BY ADOLESCENT **GIRLS...?**

AND SO I BEGAN MADAME DUFORT'S SCHOOL FOR GIFTED DEBUTANTES. IT WAS THE PERFECT SOLUTION-- THE DAUGHTERS OF WEALTHY FAMILIES WERE WELL-MANNERED, USED TO FOLLOWING ORDERS AND EAGER FOR AN EDUCATION. I CONTACTED SEVERAL...

CEREBUS GETS THE IDEA..

WEREN'T THEY A LITTLE SUSPICIOUS OF YOUR BRAND OF TEACHING...?

NOT AT ALL -- I JUST TOLD THEM THAT THEY WERE PRACTICING THE ESHNOSOPURIAN COURTING CHANT

EVER SINCE THAT RIDICULOUS FIVE-DAY REBELLION

THEY'RE SIMPLY MAD FOR ANYTHING FROM THAT DISMAL COASTAL CITY...

CEREBUS NOTICED THAT--

IF YOU DON'T MIND, CEREBUS' LEG HAS HAD ENOUGH EXCERCISE FOR ONE NIGHT

MAKE YOURSELF COMFORTABLE

ANYWAY-- WITH THE OCCASIONAL WAYWARD SOLDIER FOR COMPANY, THE GIRLS PROGRESSED AT AN **ASTONISHING** RATE...

UNTIL NOW THEY ARE IN A FULL TRANCE-LIKE STATE, HOLDING THE ENERGIES BALANCED IN THE CENTER OF THE CIRCLE

ENERGIES NOW AT MY COMMAND

SPRINGTIME IN LOWER FELDA AND THE RAINS CONTINUE **UNABATED**...

...HIS LEG HEALED, CEREBUS HAS CHOSEN TO ACCOMPANY PROFESSOR CHARLES X. CLAREMONT ON HIS MISSION OF **REVENGE**...

...HIS CURIOSITY ABOUT THE APOCALYPSE BEAST WOMAN-THING AND PROFESSOR CHARLES X'S PLAN COMPELS HIM TO TAKE THE LONGER ROUTE TO THE EIGHT BAGS OF GOLD HE HAD HIDDEN BENEATH THE FLOORBOARDS OF A SMALL FARMHOUSE NEAR FLUROC...*

'AS FOR THE PROFESSOR, HE WELCOMES THE OPPORTUNITY TO EXPLAIN HIS GENIUS MORE FULLY...

* SEE CEREBUS #17

THE LINE OF ENERGY IS MY PSYCHIC LINK WITH KATRINA, THERESA AND JANETTE...AS LONG AS IT IS MAINTAINED, THEY WILL REMAIN IN A STATE OF SUSPENDED MOTION...

HOW LONG CAN YOU MAINTAIN IT?

FIVE TO TEN YEARS WITH NO LOSS OF STRENGTH OR CONTROL ...

AND THE GIRLS ARE NOT HARMED BY ALL THIS?

QUITE THE **CONTRARY**... THEY'RE ENJOYING FIVE TO TEN YEARS OF DREAMLESS RELAXED **SLEEP**...

CEREBUS STILL DOESN'T UNDERSTAND WHAT YOU **WANT** THIS BEAST TO **DO**...

THIS WOMAN, THIS THING

THERE HAVE BEEN SEVERAL IN THIS *HEMISPHERE* ALONE

THE LAST ONE TO ACHIEVE MASTERY WAS PRINCE GISSE. IN A FIT OF *DEPRESSION*, HE DECIDED ON THE WORD "ME"

HE WON THE *OUTSTANDING ACHIEVEMENT AWARD* FROM THE UNSHIB MORTICIANS' GUILD FIVE YEARS IN A ROW

SOUNDS LIKE A LOT OF SENSELESS *VIOLENCE* TO CEREBUS...

IT COULD BE *WORSE* YOU KNOW -- SUPPOSE A *POLITICIAN* HAD ACHIEVED MASTERY?

HE'D LIKELY DECIDE ON A WORD LIKE "POVERTY,"...

OR "UNEMPLOYMENT"

IT'S ONE OF THE MORE PLAUSIBLE SOLUTIONS TO *URBAN OVER-CROWDING* YOU'D HAVE TO ADMIT...

SO WHAT WORD DID *YOU* DECIDE ON...?

"FEAR"

I FIGURED I COULD ELIMINATE A LARGE SEGMENT OF THE POPULATION RIGHT AWAY AND GET THE REST WHEN PANIC STARTS TO SPREAD...

THEN WHY ARE YOU GOING OUT OF YOUR WAY TO GET REVENGE ON YOUR FORMER PEERS?

IT'S SORT OF A *TRADITION* AMONG THOSE WHO'VE ACHIEVED MASTERY OF THE BEAST...

AN UNCALLED FOR ACT OF SMALL-MINDED AND ACRIMONIUS VENGEANCE...

JUST TO GET THE WHOLE-SALE SLAUGHTER OF INNOCENTS OFF ON THE RIGHT FOOT...

IF YOU DON'T MIND CEREBUS OFFERING AN OPINION -- IT'S HARD TO FIGURE WHAT YOU *GET* OUT OF THIS DEAL...

PRECIOUS! ONE MOMENT, DEAR!

...BESIDES A CHANCE TO WATCH HUMAN BEINGS REDUCED TO SMOLDERING ASHES BY YOUR WALKING *EGGPLANT*...

A NICE, BIG HOUSE TO LIVE IN...

WHAT?

THERE'S NO REAL REASON TO MAKE THE *WHOLE* JOURNEY WITHOUT A REST STOP. BESIDES IF I'M GOING TO WREAK HAVOC ON THE COUNTRYSIDE, I'M GOING TO NEED A PLACE TO UNWIND AT NIGHT...

THE CASTLE, HUH?

WHAT IF SOMEONE LIVES THERE?

WE'LL GO IN *WITHOUT* WOMAN-THING-- IF WE COME ACROSS SOMEONE, WE'LL TELL HIM THERE'S A HORRIBLE MONSTER THAT CHASED US RIGHT UP TO HIS FRONT GATE...

HE'LL TAKE ONE LOOK AT HER-- BECOME PARALYZED WITH *FEAR* AND...

FFFT!

INCINERATED EX-CASTLE OWNER...

PRECISELY!

AND SO...

HOW MUCH FARTHER IS IT?

WE'RE ALMOST HALFWAY... THINK OF ALL THE EXCITEMENT WHEN STORIES ABOUT WOMAN-THING START BECOMING WIDE-SPREAD...

ANGRY MOBS OF FRIGHTENED VILLAGERS WITH TORCHES AND PITCHFORKS SCREAMING FOR MY BLOOD...

...LED BY LOCAL PRIESTS WITH WOODEN STAKES AND GARLIC-FLAVORED HOLY WATER...

OH HOW I LOVE BEING *EVIL!*

WE'LL HIDE WOMAN-THING JUST INSIDE THE GATE WHILE WE CHECK OUT THE GROUND FLOOR FOR THE SOON-TO-BE-LATE OWNER...

AND FOR ANY ODD BOTTLES OF ALE WE MIGHT FIND ...

A DRINK -- NOT A BAD THOUGHT, BUT FIRST THINGS *FIRST*...

PRECIOUS? OVER THIS WAY -- WE HAVE TO HIDE YOU, *DEAR*...

MAGNIFICENT -- A DEFINITE RELIC OF THE *BLACK TOWER* PERIOD! MOST SATISFACTORY FOR MY *PURPOSES*...

WE'LL BRING HIM BACK THIS WAY WITH US DISTRACTING HIM UNTIL HE'S BARELY A FOOT AWAY FROM WOMAN-THING

AND I'LL INSTRUCT HER TO GRAB HIM BY THE *THROAT*...

IF THAT DOESN'T MAKE HIM JUMP OUT OF HIS SKIN, *NOTHING* WILL...

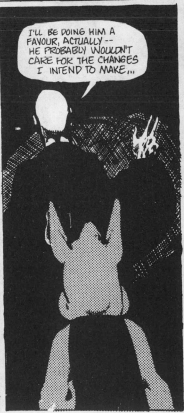

I'LL BE DOING HIM A FAVOUR, ACTUALLY -- HE PROBABLY WOULDN'T CARE FOR THE CHANGES I INTEND TO MAKE...

WONDERFUL

GREAT *WORKMANSHIP*

I'M *IMPRESSED.*

I REALLY AM...

532

MWRRR

I'VE GOT A PATRON WHO WOULD GIVE YOU THE KEYS TO HIS MISTRESS' CHASTITY BELT FOR A PIECE OF WORK LIKE THIS...

LOVES ALL THIS NEW *WEIRD* STUFF...

NOT INTO IT M'SELF...

HE'S *IMPRESSED*, CLAREMONT

MAYBE YOU SHOULD *SETTLE* FOR THAT.

THIS IS THE *APOCALYPSE BEAST*

NOT SOME CLEVER PIECE OF CLOCK-WORK...

IF HE DOESN'T KNOW ENOUGH TO BE *TERRIFIED*, THEN I SHALL HAVE TO *TEACH* HIM!

IT MUST HAVE TAKEN YOU *YEARS* TO LOCATE...

MY BUTLER WILL PREPARE TWO ROOMS...

AND YOU CAN LET ME KNOW HOW MUCH YOU WANT FOR THE --uh

THING.

I'D KILL MYSELF BEFORE I'D SELL WOMAN-THING...

OHO! A *COLLECTOR!*

SORRY, FRIEND-- I HAD YOU *PEGGED* AS AN *IMPORTER* OR A *DEALER*...

WELL, EVEN *BETTER*...

WE CAN TALK ABOUT OUR *COLLECTIONS*...

I'LL GET SOME *WINE*...

WHY DON'T YOU JUST ACCEPT HIS OFFER AND STAY HERE AS HIS *GUEST?*

NO!

THERE HAS TO BE *SOME WAY* TO FRIGHTEN HIM...

THINK!

THINK.

THINK.

BACK AGAIN...

I BROUGHT MY THREE LATEST CANVASSES, IN CASE YOU'RE INTO IT...

THINK.

THINK.

THIS IS MY FIFTH VERSION OF THIS PAINTING... IT'S LIKE... AN ALLEGORY, RIGHT? THE MONSTER REPRESENTS THE TEMPTATION OF EVIL THOUGHTS...

THE GIRL REPRESENTS THE BASIC WICKEDNESS OF HUMANITY...

AND HER BREASTS FALLING OUT OF HER DRESS REPRESENT THE DILEMMA FACING THE INDIVIDUAL

I SOLD THE FIRST FOUR VERSIONS TO A MONASTERY...

IN THIS PAINTING, THE GIRL CHAINED TO A WALL REPRESENTS THE REPRESSED NATURE OF THE ORTHODOX TARIMITE'S MIND

HERE THE BREASTS REPRESENT THE INNER CONFLICT BETWEEN LUST AND ABSTINENCE

CONSEQUENTLY, THEY ARE A GOOD DEAL LARGER THAN THE BREASTS IN THE OTHER PAINTING...

I'VE SOLD AROUND FIFTY OF THESE...

I HAVE IT!

I'VE COME UP WITH A PLAN... I'M GOING TO HAVE WOMAN-THING PICK HIM UP AND HOLD HIM OVER THE EDGE OF THE CLIFF BY ONE HAND...

THE MOMENT HE PANICS, HE'LL BE QUICK-FRIED...

ASK HIM WHERE HE KEEPS THE REST OF THE LIQUOR, FIRST...

THIS ONE IS FOR A TREASURY EXECUTIVE IN PALNU. HERE THE BREASTS REPRESENT THE CONFLICT BETWEEN SHORT-TERM PROFIT GOUGING AND NEST-EGG MERCANTILE BANKING...

UNFORTUNATELY, I DIDN'T LEAVE ROOM FOR THE GIRL'S HEAD...

HE TOLD ME TO NOT WORRY ABOUT IT.

DON'T *HURT* HIM, PRECIOUS...

NOT *YET* ANYWAY...

YOU CAN'T BEAT BREASTS WHEN IT COMES TO UNIVERSAL SYMBOLS...

I DID BOWLS OF FRUIT FOR YEARS -- YOU EVER TRY USING RIPE BREAD-FRUIT TO ILLUSTRATE MAN'S INABILITY TO REACH HARMONY WITH HIS ENVIRONMENT...?

IT DOESN'T *WORK* -- BUT *BREASTS!* BREASTS *WORK!* THE FIRST THING PEOPLE ASK IS "WHAT IS THIS? BREASTS?"

YOU *SEE?* BREASTS OPEN UP A *DIALOGUE!* THERE IS A NEED TO COMMUNICATE ABOUT BREASTS...

THEIR FIRST QUESTION IS "*WHAT IS THIS*"

FORTUNATELY FOR MY BANK ACCOUNT, THEIR SECOND QUESTION IS GENERALLY "CAN YOU DO ONE OF THOSE FOR *ME?*"

BREASTS ARE EVEN MORE POPULAR THAN *MONSTERS!* BEYOND A SHADOW OF A DOUBT ANY ARTIST WHO IS NOT PUTTING BREASTS IN HIS PAINTINGS IS CUTTING HIMSELF OFF FROM EIGHTY PERCENT OF THE ART-CONSUMING PUBLIC...

I THINK IT'S ONLY FAIR TO TELL YOU THAT WOMAN-THING IS ABOUT TO...

...UH?

DOWN, PRECIOUS!

PUT HIM, *DOWN!*

THE MONSTER IN THAT PAINTING YOU'RE HOLDING...

WHAT ABOUT IT?

WHERE DID YOU GET THE IDEA FOR IT?

WHO? *HIM*?

THAT'S *FILBERT*...

...MY TWELVE-FOOT GREEN ART OBJECT...

HE'S UPSTAIRS WITH THE REST OF MY REFERENCE COLLECTION...

WHEN I BOUGHT THE PLACE, THEY THREW HIM IN ALONG WITH A SHOWER CURTAIN AND A BENT SAUCE-PAN...

THEN I SUGGEST WE ALL GO *UPSTAIRS*.

OH, SURE!

I WANT TO GET YOUR OPINION ON MY SEPRAN BEADWORK...

BRING HIM WITH YOU, *PRECIOUS*

IT REALLY IS VERY NICE OF YOU--DROPPING BY LIKE THIS...

I'VE BEEN SPENDING MORE TIME WITH MY COLLECTION LATELY TRYING TO GET AN IDEA FOR ANOTHER THEME FOR MY NEXT PAINTING

SOMETHING MORE THAN BREASTS OR MONSTERS...

NOT THAT I HAVE ANYTHING *AGAINST* BREASTS YOU UNDERSTAND...

I JUST FIGURE IT'S TIME FOR ME TO SET MY SIGHTS A LITTLE HIGHER...

...SO TO SPEAK.

HE HAS NO *CONCEPTION* OF HOW UTTERLY *STUPID* HE IS...

HE LOOKS ON THIS... "*FILBERT*"...AS JUST ONE MORE PIECE IN HIS FOOLISH COLLECTION...

IT'S THE DOUBLE DOORS AT THE TOP OF THE STAIRS...

YOU THINK IT'S SOMETHING *ELSE*?

IF THAT PAINTING IS AN ACCURATE COPY, THERE IS ONLY *ONE* THING "*FILBERT*" *COULD* BE...

...LORD ROTH-SUMP'S ORIGINAL APOCALYPSE BEAST!

536

CEREBUS THOUGHT THESE BEASTS WERE SOMETHING OF A *RARITY*...

EITHER THEY'RE HAVING A SUDDEN *POPULATION EXPLOSION* OR...

RARE? OF COURSE THEY'RE RARE!

THIS HAS NEVER HAPPENED BEFORE IN RECORDED HISTORY...

WERE I TO BE ABLE TO BRING LIFE TO THE *SECOND* BEAST AS WELL...

NO! I DARE NOT EVEN HOPE!

THE DOORS SWING OPEN...

CLAREMONT ENTERS SLOWLY, BLINKING IN THE DIM LIGHT... GRADUALLY, THE ROOM COMES INTO FOCUS - CLUTTERED WITH *DEBRIS*...

AS IF OF ITS OWN VOLITION, A THIN BAND OF ENERGY LEAPS FROM HIS RIGHT HAND INTO THE ROOM...

A SMALL MASS OF CRUDELY SHAPED STONE IS SUDDENLY OUTLINED IN LIGHT

TWO CREASES OF WHITE FORM ON THE SURFACE OF THE MASS...

...AND IT BEGINS TO LURCH TOWARD THE INTRUDERS...

CEREBUS?

I SEEM TO BE IN NEED OF SOME *PROTECTION*...

IMMEDIATELY!

UH...

UNH?!

PROTECTION?

CEREBUS THOUGHT YOU KNEW HOW TO HANDLE THOSE THINGS...

DON'T BE RIDICULOUS --THIS ISN'T *ROTH- SUMP'S* BEAST...

IT'S A SORCEROUS *"WATCHDOG"--* UNDOUBTEDLY LEFT BY HIS LORDSHIP TO *DEFEND* THE BEAST...

IF IT MANAGES TO TOUCH ME, THE RESULTING CATACLYSM COULD REDUCE THIS CASTLE TO RUBBLE ...

I'M AFRAID I DON'T HAVE TIME FOR A MORE *ELABORATE* EXPLANATION

NOW, IF YOU DON'T WANT TO GET CRUSHED BY A...

RIGHT.

BUT, IF CEREBUS EVER FINDS OUT YOU JUST MADE ALL THAT UP...

"ONE SHARP BLOW BETWEEN THE EYES..."

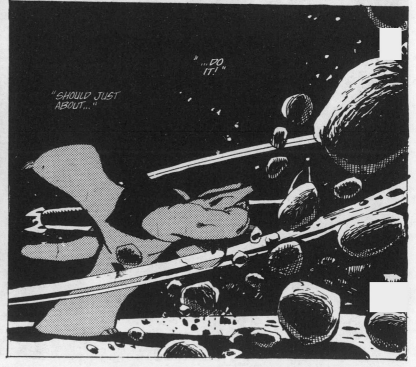

"SHOULD JUST ABOUT..."

"...DO IT!"

538

THE EARTH-PIG BLINKS SEVERAL TIMES AS HE RISES! IN THE DIM LIGHT, ONE OF THE LARGER FRAGMENTS APPEARS TO...

...*MOVE!*

SMAK

uh...

CEREBUS?

I HATE TO SEEM LIKE A PEST...

PEST? DON'T BE RIDICULOUS - THERE'S NOTHING CEREBUS LIKES **BETTER** THAN BASHING AWAY AT FLYING ROCKS...

TARIM.

CRAK

YOU KNOW WHAT *CEREBUS* THINKS?

NATURALLY, I AM GRATEFUL THAT YOU *PROTECTED* ME...

BUT TO BE PERFECTLY *HONEST*; NO... I *DON'T* KNOW WHAT YOU THINK...

NOR DO I *CARE* TO...

IF YOU'LL EXCUSE ME.

THIS IS WHERE I KEEP MY BEADWORK COLLECTION

AS SOON AS I LIGHT THIS TORCH...

...YOU CAN GET A BETTER LOOK AT IT...

IF YOU DON'T *MIND*, I THINK I'D LIKE TO SEE THE...uh...

..."TO SEE "FILBERT" *FIRST*...

OH, HEY..SURE!

HE'S UNDER THAT COVER OVER THERE

IT'LL TAKE ME A WHILE TO DIG OUT THE BOXES, SO HELP YOURSELF...

LOOK NOW, *PRECIOUS*, ON THE FACE OF THE GREATEST OF ALL THE BEASTS YET MANIFESTED...

LORD ROTH-SUMP'S...

CEREBUS HAS GOT TO GET GOING...

GOOD LUCK SCRAPING UP WHAT'S *LEFT* OF CLAREMONT

OH *WOW.*

HOW *INSENSITIVE* OF ME -- THAT GUY WAS YOUR *FRIEND!*

AND I'M ACTING LIKE HE WAS JUST A PIECE OF *REFERENCE MATERIAL*

I FEEL JUST *AWFUL*...

CAN I, LIKE, YOU KNOW... MAKE IT UP TO YOU... OR *SOMETHING*...

YOU CAN STAY HERE FOR A FEW DAYS -- I MIGHT EVEN BE ABLE TO FIND YOU A JOB!

DON'T LET IT WORRY YOU CLAREMONT WAS JUST ...

OR I COULD GIVE YOU SOME *MONEY!*

AS CEREBUS WAS ABOUT TO SAY, CLAREMONT WAS JUST ABOUT THE *BEST* FRIEND THAT AN AARDVARK EVER HAD!

OH, WOW. I HAD NO *IDEA!*

WOULD A POUCH OF GOLD HELP IN ANY WAY?

CEREBUS DOESN'T KNOW HOW HE'S GOING TO EXPLAIN THIS TO MRS. CLAREMONT AND THE SIX LITTLE CLAREMONTS ≡SIGH≡

EIGHT POUCHES OF GOLD! TAKE THEM...

PLEEEASE

I FEEL SO *GUILTY!!*

WELL·· AS LONG AS YOU *INSIST*...

THAT GOLD SERVING TRAY WOULD *CERTAINLY* CHEER UP THE WIDOW CLAREMONT...

TAKE IT!

...AND HOW MANY TIMES HAS LITTLE NELL SAID *"PLEASE UNCLE CEREBUS -- BRING ME HOME A FOOT-TALL JADE CARVING..."*

TAKE IT! TAKE IT!

AND THIS OVER HERE ...

About the author

Dave Sim was born in Hamilton, Ontario and moved to Kitchener at the age of two to rejoin his family. Since that time he has engaged in a number of unsavory practices including marriage and strip chess.